A GUIDE TO

Feeding Winter Birds in British Columbia

Bob Waldon

Whitecap Books
Vancouver / Toronto

Second Printing, 1993.

Edited by Timothy Dunn
Cover and interior design by Carolyn Deby
Cover and interior illustrations by Peter Sawatzky
Typeset by Vancouver Desktop Publishing
Printed and bound in Canada by D.W. Friesen and Sons Ltd.,
  Altona, Manitoba

Canadian Cataloguing in Publication Data
Waldon, Bob, 1932-
  Feeding winter birds in British Columbia

  Includes bibliographical references and index.
ISBN 1-55110-035-5

  1. Birds—British Columbia. 2. Birds—British Columbia—Food.
3. Bird feeders. 4. Birds—British Columbia—Wintering. I. Title.
QL685.5.B75W34 1992   598.29711   C92-091531-0

To Carole,

the most important part

of my life

Contents

Acknowledgements

Thanks are due to biologist and author R. Wayne Campbell of Victoria who took the time from a hectic schedule to review the manuscript and to pinpoint essential additions and corrections. He also offered helpful comment drawn from his wealth of personal and professional experience working with the bird life of British Columbia. It is a measure of his constructive spirit of generosity that he agreed to write the Foreword. His thoughtful encouragement was most appreciated.

A word of appreciation is also due biologist and author Neil Dawe of Qualicum Beach who checked part of the manuscript and who was likewise positive and helpful with suggestions drawn from his own unique work with birds in British Columbia. It is a matter of regret for me that a tangle of conflicting work schedules, and the pressure of publishing deadlines, prevented my gaining more input from both these knowledgeable and articulate professionals. I must point out that, notwithstanding the good counsel of these people, errors may have escaped notice, and some of the inconsistencies that routinely occur in my work may still be evident. For these everyone, save myself, must be held blameless.

Over the many years that I have known artist and wood carver Peter Sawatzky I have greatly enjoyed both his work and his friendship. Working with Peter is a pleasure not only because of the high level of his interpretive skill, but also because he brings to his profession a good business sense and an enthusiasm for developing new projects and for working in a partnership.

I would be remiss in not acknowledging the enthusiastic assistance of fellow bird feeders in this province who readily, and invariably on very short notice, offered my wife Carole and me instant hospitality, and the benefit of their own observations during our trips gathering firsthand material for the book. These include Margaret Barwis of Nelson, Loyd Groutage of Castlegar, Joan and Harold King of Osoyoos, Rory Paterson of Tofino, Doug Powell of Revelstoke, Madelon Schouton of Princeton, and Mildred White of Kimberley. And for being such knowledgeable companions and hosts during our stay at Qualicum Beach, I wish to thank Bob and Betty Drew-Brook.

For their particularly helpful responses to mailed enquiries I wish to thank Arnold Chaddock, Hilary Gordon, and Bert Lenny, all of Revelstoke, John and Bev McInerney of Bamfield, and Barbara Campbell of Tofino.

And last, but by no means least, Carole and I own much to June Hayward of Qualicum Beach, our cherished "Mrs. H," for her boundless hospitality and for being the person we could always—and frequently did—go to for help and all kinds of good counsel.

Foreword

Some forty years ago, as a young boy, I was introduced to the fascinating life of wild birds. It was Christmas time, when soccer fields were frozen, friends were visiting relatives, and the woods were too stark and cold to explore. It was going to be another holiday season of amusing myself indoors. One morning my grandfather, a retired game warden from Alberta, suggested I go outside and watch birds at the feeder. Anything, I thought, would be better than another day in the house! Thus, I bundled up and nestled my body in the newly fallen snow. The next hour was spent running in and out of the house with a million questions. What was that bird with the black head and pink bill? Why won't the robin eat seeds? Do birds like bread? Why do birds fight over their food? Can we build a house to keep the birds warm at night? My grandfather could see from my enthusiastic questions that birdwatching was soon to become a passion.

Today, as a professional ornithologist, I am still watching and feeding birds. Not surprisingly, about one-half of the three thousand or so questions I answer each year relate to feeding, attracting, and housing native birds. The interest is growing dramatically. About one-third of North Americans are now involved in these activities, and we know why. Feeding wild birds is simple. It requires little in the way of equipment, provides a sense of fulfilment in knowing we have helped fellow creatures during a stressful part of their lives, and encourages wildlife to visit us.

Bird feeding is also becoming big business. More than ever we must be sure we are spending our money wisely and that we are doing what is right for the birds—providing a safe, clean, disease-free environment along with nutritional foods. The appearance of Bob Waldon's book, then, is timely. In it he has collected and assimilated significant information on the natural history, ecology, behaviour, and feeding of wild birds in British Columbia. Furthermore, the book is especially valuable to B.C. birders because it takes into account the extreme biological and ecological diversity of this province.

Bob's writing reveals a lifelong enthusiasm for wild creatures and a dedication to their survival and understanding. He answers everyday questions we have about our winter birds and whets our appetite to learn more about their lives. Yet he is still able to discreetly suggest that there is much more to learn. Backyard research by bird lovers is the key. Pick a problem, develop a methodology to get the answer, and share the results with others. For instance, research by a Grade 6 student in Victoria has shown that bird kills from house cats can be reduced by as much as 75 percent if bells are attached during the winter season. Another student, who won a gold medal at the Canada-wide Science Fair, determined that Anna's Hummingbirds prefer a 75 percent sugar solution (three parts sugar to one part water) and that colour was not a major factor in selection of feeders by hummingbirds. These are the types of local research that have been incorporated into this book.

Bob Waldon has made a significant contribution to the literature on feeding birds. I know my grandfather would have been delighted to have this book in his library.

R. Wayne Campbell
Curator, Ornithology
Royal British Columbia Museum
Victoria, Canada

Introduction

 This book is intended for the information and enjoyment of the thousands of householders in British Columbia who feed birds in winter and whose bird watching is done mostly through a picture window.

My own feeding experience began in Manitoba. Some of it continues there, thanks to a rural cottage and a birding colleague who keeps the feeders stocked when we're not around. There—in winter conditions that imbue British Columbians with a feeling of deliverance—the birds and I adapted. If I was late arising, my morning coffee and the chickadees materialized at about the same time. Cradling the cup, I would watch them as frozen dawn seeped in from the east and the day's weather report reminded me that the wind chill of the moment would freeze exposed flesh in one minute, or less.

It was impossible for me to watch my birds without wondering how these tiny creatures could survive such conditions on the other side of that sheltering pane of glass. My own search for the answer led to the discovery of much that was fascinating in the world of birds and, in time, to the idea that other people would be interested in hearing what I had found out. There seemed to be a place for handy-sized references, each focussing on a discrete region, its particular winter birds, and the feeding of them.

Traditionally we associate fall with the departure of birds, and spring with their return. It may seem contradictory, therefore, to point out that in fact far more people spend far more time watching greater numbers of birds in winter than in the warm seasons. Although there are many more species around in summer, they are scattered throughout their habitat, busy with domestic chores amidst the concealing foliage. True seekers of birdlife must then arise before dawn and prowl amidst the dewy tangles and the mosquitoes. This is admirable beyond words, but exceeds the resolve of most of us. Besides, many of us are just as busy in summer as the birds are.

But winter, though it banishes most of the birds, also strips the concealing foliage from the deciduous trees and from much of the ground cover, clearing the view. Winter also changes the remaining birds' social habits. Many species gather into large flocks, roving widely in search of food. Most of these will congregate readily around feeders that can be placed near a convenient window where the birds can be continuously, closely, and comfortably observed. In effect, instead of having to seek out birds, winter birders can manipulate the birds into seeking out *them!*

Selecting what species of wintering birds to include in a book is a challenging task for a would-be author to contemplate. It is particularly complicated if his subject is British Columbia. There are many "British Columbias." In latitude they range from Victoria, where hummingbirds winter, to Fort St. John where ravens and Gray Jays winter and the Calliope Hummingbirds of summer are long vanished. If you lay over this a bewildering topographical jumble of rock, the picture gets very complicated indeed. Most other provinces, some with elevations that respectably rate the title "mountains," are nevertheless mainly two-dimensional. British Columbia is awesomely three-dimensional. Beginning in a valley that opens onto Georgia Strait you can drive or hike up adjacent slopes through a layer-cake of climatic zones until, at the top, you stand in a patch of Arctic tundra. From the permanent home of the White-tailed Ptarmigan you can look down upon balmy coastal groves where the Anna's Hummingbird winters.

Birders in southern British Columbia can tally twenty songbirds on a casual winter's outing. Their counterparts in Manitoba would consider this a highly respectable day's work with everything—owls, Rock Doves, grouse—included. Their British Columbia fellows, however, if they live near tidewater, can then set up their scopes on the beach and, on a decent day in a favoured location, run the total to sixty species.

Interesting though they are, gulls, scoters, shorebirds, and Bald Eagles don't qualify as "feeder" birds and rate at most only passing mention in a book like this.

The most accessible, reliable sources of information on birds that are realistic prospects as feeder visitors come from the annual Christmas Bird Count lists. The birds tallied in the "CBCs" fall into several categories. Each zone has its resident, nonmigratory regulars, like jays and chickadees. These might, or might not, be joined by flocks of nomadic northern finches whose numbers range, year to year, from abundant to absent. Then there are the rather hesitant migrants like juncos (which in British Columbia migrate up-down as much as north-south), and several species of sparrows. Parts of their population regularly forego the flight south, or go only part way, and end up wintering in the milder southern enclaves of British Columbia. "Holdovers" are that small percentage of a normally migratory population that stays behind. These include robins, some sparrows, flickers, blackbirds, and others.

In the minds of some, this list should also include stay-over waterfowl. In sheltered bays and rivermouths along the coast and in stretches of open river inland, flocks of mallards are joined by other species for as long as food holds out. In many urban areas—Vancouver's Stanley Park being the paramount example—ducks, gulls, swans, and squads of Canada Geese shake down the tourists for tidbits of fast food, and mob the regular benefactors who faithfully distribute corn, peanuts, and other non-junk foods by the bucketful. These accomplished mooches may be *fed* birds, but they're not *feeder* birds.

To complicate the problem of choosing what to include and what to leave out, there be the decidedly winter birds, like Horned Larks and Snow Buntings that rarely visit feeders, and shrikes, owls, hawks, and other predators that come with sinister motives. One would like to include them all, but sooner or later the limitations of space in a book assert themselves, and one is obliged to make cuts. In the end, at the risk of appearing inconsistent, and of offending some readers by leaving out their favourite bird, I mustered my biases and made arbitrary cuts.

As if cutting out hawks and buntings wasn't sufficient offence, I ran the risk of further angering the purists by using the space thus saved for a few mammals. "The walk-in trade" rarely gets respectful treatment in bird feeder books, even though some of these pedestrians play a major role in the activity around feeding stations. Their natural history is, to me, just as fascinating as that of the birds.

An obvious advantage of having a reference with only sixty-one bird species is that everything's easy to find; another is that the author has plenty of room for information that couldn't possibly be included in a continental guide that must cover over six hundred and fifty species. My species accounts are condensed and formally organized for quick reference, but the family writeups are informal and open-ended, each as long as is necessary to do justice to the natural history of the subject. My intention was to present the most interesting lore I could find, to the end that beyond mere identification my readers could look at each bird or mammal in a new light, with an enriched understanding of why each behaves the way it does, and how it survives and fits into the overall scheme of life.

This regional reference is intended to supplement the major North American field guides, one or more of which many readers will already have. To make cross-referencing easier, I have listed in each species account the page numbers where that bird can be found in the most recent editions (as of 1992) of the four most popular field guides, and in W. Earl Godfrey's *The Birds of Canada* (1986).

Writing this book has been a lot of fun, an admission one probably ought not to make. My research was essentially painless, consisting of foraging through the popular literature, constantly on the sniff for those neat bits of lore that we information junkies love to collect. Although these sources are readily available, not everyone has the determination to muster them, and the time to wade through the resulting piles of books and periodicals. In assuming the task, I have tried to assemble a truly absorbing collection of information and to present it from a fresh perspective.

There are few source references; most of my reading was from books and periodicals whose authors and writers themselves gave no sources. I therefore relied on my own judgement, and cross checking, to determine the reliability of the information I selected. Where material was obviously an author's own, or in rare cases where the statements bent credulity a little, I accorded in-text credit.

As well as bird lore, the content of this augmented guide includes practical information on the "how-to" aspects of winter feeding. There are things to do, and things not to do, that will help you maintain a feeding station with less effort, and enhance your viewing pleasure.

Regarding the capitalizing of the common names of species, I follow a widely used, but by no means universal, style. For the full, recognized common name, both words are capitalized; obsolete, regional, or partial names are not, and neither are the names of groups. Thus we have: "All our juncos, sometimes called "snowbirds," are members of the sparrow family and are variants of the Dark-eyed Junco." This also avoids confusion over name words and descriptive words: "Like the Blue Jay, Steller's Jay is also a blue jay."

A final word on style: I greatly wish there were a single, universally accepted word to use in place of "people who feed birds" or "feeding station operators." Trying to avoid tedious repetition of these cumbersome phrases is a constant vexation for a writer of a book like this. Coined words, such as "feedor" or "feedist," didn't work. In some frustration I decided to use "feeder" for the receptacle, "bird feeder" for the person, hoping that in context I could make the difference clear enough not to baffle my readers.

In conclusion, this is not the work of a scholar, nor even of a respectable birder. Rather, it is the offering of a writer with an abiding sense of excitement about nature and a shameless compulsion to infect others with it. I hope my fellow bird watchers enjoy reading this book as much as I enjoyed writing it.

CHAPTER ONE

Principles of Feeding

Why Feed Birds?

Sometimes it is a sense of curiosity, and nothing more, that prompts people to have a go at feeding birds. What *is* there about it that appeals to so many people? What'll happen when *I* hang up a feeder? Once begun, however, other incentives take over. Most of us readily sympathize with fellow creatures coping with the wet, the cold, and the snow, and feel good about helping them out. And it is a charity easily sustained; the gifts are small, and the response is immediate and obvious, sometimes overwhelmingly so.

Along with the instant gratification and all those positive vibes, the happy giver gets a ringside seat at an ongoing natural wonder—winter survival. When you develop a knowing relationship with birds, you can't help but marvel how such tiny, fragile creatures are able at all to live through the rigours of winter. We also cater to our own aesthetic sense by filling our environs with beautiful creatures that may be the major signs of life and colour in an otherwise drab, monochromatic landscape.

There can be intellectual stimulation as well. Even the most casual bird feeders develop a keener awareness of wildlife. And if we give our sense of curiosity at least half a chance, we'll find ourselves learning more about these engaging creatures and how they fit into their environment. I feel it my duty to warn those contemplating it that feeding birds has converted many an unsuspecting beginner into a lifelong student of nature.

Charity, aesthetics, and intellectual growth acknowledged, there is, as well, a gut-level element of self-esteem involved. A forlorn, unattended feeder stands for the expectant beginner as a symbol of rejection—a minor one, to be sure, but still perplexing. Doubts smoulder as time passes: Is there something wrong with my feeder? The seeds? Are the birds all over at the neighbour's? What is he doing better than I? But let the first chickadee alight on that brand new feeder and a spark of triumph ignites, and every doubt is forgotten. You've been accepted!

That feeling persists, with variations, for as long as you feed birds. Even those of us who consider ourselves hard-bitten and jaded relish the ego trip that goes with having a yardful of all the northern finches, every nonmigratory regular in the book, perhaps a holdover robin, a visiting pheasant, and maybe a Sharp-shinned Hawk or shrike that swoops in from time to time. The feeling of superiority is keenest if one's bird-feeding associates aren't quite so well blessed. Even the highest-minded charity isn't immune to the vanities of one-upmanship.

Before carrying the discussion further, it may be helpful to offer some definitions. A "feeder" is a device for holding bird feed, a "bird feeder" is the person who puts it up. A "bird watcher" is clearly descriptive, and applies to anyone who takes pleasure in looking at birds. Serious bird watchers nowadays insist on the title "birder," in part because the older "bird watcher" still has clinging to it the image of the eccentric spinster in pith helmet and tennis shoes. Birders include those highly motivated types referred to as "listers" who, as the term suggests, are preoccupied with accurately identifying and recording as many separate species as they can find.

Along with the pleasures of bird feeding, and the attendant watching, there is always the exciting prospect of inadvertent fame. Rory Paterson has fed birds during the fourteen years she's lived in Tofino on the west edge of Vancouver Island. Just as the northern leg of the cross-island highway stops here, so do a lot of birds. Tofino is on the end of a peninsula that roughly parallels the coast of the island. A peninsula, like the famous Point Pelee in Ontario, tends to attract birds flying toward it over open water, and concentrates at its tip those making their way up from its base. Tofino adds to the appeal with its mixed habitat of open spaces, ornamental shrubs, and deciduous trees—a more inviting stopover than the coniferous forest that dominates the landscape around it.

Tofino, in the parlance of birders, is a "hot spot." In the autumn of 1991 a Little Curlew appeared, a rarity even in its native Siberia. In November of 1990 Ms. Paterson casually noticed a "gull" nearby, did a double-take and then rushed to her camera just in time to get a slide of a Laysan Albatross gliding over the house. This open ocean bird is a highly unusual visitor to the coastal waters of British Columbia. The prize bird, however, a Rustic Bunting from Siberia, showed up at her feeder on December 7, 1990, and stayed until April 12, 1991. During those four months birders from as far away as Florida came specifically to see this rarity.

To a person of lesser hospitality, the succession of phone calls and visitors during that winter would have been a trial, but Rory Paterson welcomed everyone and kept the coffee pot simmering. Two hundred and eleven visitors viewed the bird from inside the house; uncounted others simply came to the yard, saw the bird, and left. The sometimes rapturous antics of the visitors who came, saw, and listed were a constant source of entertainment to Rory. The bird, for its part, remained steadfastly in or near her yard; no one who came to see it went away disappointed. In February of 1992 Rory received an award from The American Birding Association for "Gracious Hospitality and Service to the Birdwatching Community."

St. Francis isn't the only one to have been enchanted by the trust and closeness of birds.

Those of us who feed birds and like to think of ourselves as part of a long tradition could point to St. Francis of Assisi who lived in Italy from about 1181 to 1226. As well as founding the Franciscan Order, he is renowned for his love of wild birds and his mystical powers of attracting them; there are countless mediaeval paintings of "St. Francis and the Birds." His day is October 4, a fitting date for a bird-feeders' patron saint since it could serve as a last-date reminder to us that our stations should be readied for action.

A Touch of Analysis

At its basic level, feeding birds is blessedly uncomplicated and doesn't need a lot of fussing and advance planning to get started. However, if you temper that first flush of enthusiasm with a little forethought, subsequent experience is more likely to remain pleasurable and trouble-free.

Depending upon where you live, with whom, and who your neighbours are, their questions could challenge your seemingly innocent intentions: What about the mice and rats that spilled seeds will attract? What about weed seeds from your feeders that will infect our flowerbeds? What about the noise of the birds? What about sanitation—like droppings, and disease? Will we now have to put our cat into solitary confinement? What about the squirrels?

If you live in a small village, on an acreage, farm, or some other spacious setting where you have only your own household to answer to, most of these queries will be irrelevant. But on a street in a town or suburb, they should be addressed honestly. There *have* been cases where bird lovers in these locations have brought the hostility of their neighbours, and civic wrath, down upon themselves by going overboard with their enthusiasm. Some advice on how to head off difficulties, and how to deal with them if they occur, is offered in Chapter 5, "The Down-Side."

All things considered, however, problems are the rare exceptions; millions of urbanites happily feed birds winter after winter without a single hitch in neighbourly relations.

You can actually have a little fun doing a preaudit of your prospects, preferably on a summer's day long before the first winter chickadee has cracked a single sunflower seed. This assessment can proceed from the general to the specific—that is, from zone to habitat to site.

Zone assessment

It adds to your sense of anticipation if you know in advance the species present in your ecological zone of British Columbia. Latitude, altitude, and proximity to the sea combine to create a bewildering mosaic of habitats. In many of these, the chore of assessing the bird population has already been done and is published in the form of a local checklist or, in some cases, a regional bird-finding guide. This will list all of the regional species and rate their frequency. The category labels vary, but "abundant," "common" "uncommon," "rare," "occasional," "accidental," and "introduced" are the standbys. In some lists the occurrence of each species is given for each season, or even monthly.

If there is no checklist, check the range category in each species account in this book. This will give you some idea of what to expect for your zone. Bear in mind, of course, that in mountainous terrain, climate and vegetation, and hence animal life, are markedly affected by altitude. A valley town and an alpine resort, though they may be in sight of each other, will have very different mixes of birds. Human impact also plays a part. Clearcut logging, for example, obliterates large tracts of mature coniferous forest and replaces it with a totally different ecological mix.

Habitat assessment

Is your neighbourhood within a half kilometre (quarter mile) of a lake, river, marsh, the ocean, or a tract of undeveloped woodland? In such places, unless compulsive civic tidiness, heavy recreational impact, or overgrazing have denuded them, there should be ribbons or patches of good cover. Shoreside and/or floodland willow, scrubby gullies, or blocks of forest with an understorey of shrubbery are all good bird habitats, as is a large park with generous plantings of hedges and ornamental trees. The closer your house is to tangled tracts of the wild country that birds require, the better are your chances of attracting some of them to your yard.

Does your immediate neighbourhood have plenty of tall trees, thick hedges, an occasional vacant lot, and plenty of ornamental shrubbery? As subdivisions age, the trees get bigger, and hedges and ornamentals expand. If you live on a circular bay where all the backyards and, perhaps, a little park or playground combine to provide even a modest continuum of shrubby growth and reasonable tranquillity, your chances of getting some action are improved.

The less your neighbourhood resembles any of the foregoing, the poorer are your chances of attracting winter birds. Prepare yourself for modest returns if you live in a spanking-new subdivision where every square foot of natural growth has been landscaped out of existence, where the neat ornamentals are barely out of their root-ball diapers and the boulevard trees are spindly adolescents still in braces. If the wildest habitat around is the convenience store in the mall you may have to be content with a few pigeons and some starlings.

Site assessment

If your review of the area is encouraging, and other bird feeders in the vicinity report good results, your own property has potential.

It helps if you can look at the place from a small bird's point of view on a January morning when a howling gale is driving rain or snow through the thrashing branches. The main thing you'd want to do is find shelter from that bone-chilling wind as quickly as possible and stay there. If there were a cafeteria in that sheltered spot, you'd want a place to stand back and wait your turn, and a spot to sit down once you'd picked up your tray.

The best windbreak on most lots is the house itself, the best shelter in this latitude of prevailing westerlies its south or southeast side. An alcove formed by walls on the west and north is ideal. The waiting places, in the bird world, are simply trees or shrubs where they can perch, out of the worst of the wind and above the reach of cats. They might have to wait their turn in their own flock, as chickadees do, the "alpha" one first, the others in descending order of dominance. Or, they might have to bide their time while the big guys—jays, Evening Grosbeaks, or a squirrel—have finished pigging out.

There are easy ways of augmenting the bird-friendly features of your yard. Putting up a temporary thicket of dead trees or branches, making a brush pile, propping up discarded Christmas trees or tacking up a plywood baffle to cut the wind are all beneficial add-ons for birds. However, unless your yard is truly bleak, before rushing off to muster the raw materials it might be just as well to wait and let experience, that is, the birds themselves, suggest specific, short-term local improvements.

For long-term modifications such as fences, hedges, and plantings, the Reference section lists books that give yard plans and varieties of fruit trees and berry bushes that will attract birds.

There are people-friendly aspects to setting up your yard that bear keeping in mind. The naturalists in your area may conduct an annual Christmas Bird Count (CBC) which requires them to survey a large area as quickly and thoroughly as possible. Experienced bird feeders also familiar with the CBC will try to place feeders where people doing the count can see them from the road, and save a lot of time. For more on the Christmas Bird Count, see Chapter 9.

I have already discussed the possibility of your becoming the host to a truly rare bird. When you verify a rarity with the local birding experts, and they get on the "hot line," your yard could overnight become a destination for literally hundreds of people extremely anxious to add this bird to their lists. If you are a people-watcher the antics of the listers can be a source of amusement in themselves, and the chance to meet people from faraway places and to bask in the reflected status of "your" bird can be most gratifying.

A down-side to this is the aggravation of being interrupted by visitors at all hours, and of dealing with the occasional intrusive personality who, in the name of his quest (the zealots tend to be male), totally ignores your privacy, demands accountability if the bird isn't on hand, and in general operates under a self-declared moratorium on common courtesy. At such times, having your feeder out front, where the visitors can see it without having to truck through your yard, could save you a lot of hassle.

Basic Needs

Reduced to fundamentals, the basics are feed and something to serve it on. Both have been, and will continue to be, the subjects of lively discussion in bird feeding circles. They are dealt with in detail in the chapters "Seeds and Feeds" and "Feeders and Shelters."

To get started you can simply clump into the grocery or hardware store, buy a cheap little feeder, and pick up a bag of "wild bird seed." A better way, however, is to first find a local bird feeder and ask a few questions: "What feed are you using? How much do you go through in a winter? Where do you get it? What does it cost?" If there is a naturalist club around, or a nature columnist in a local paper, they will be your best source of advice. Moral support and practical counsel help you deal with the unexpected, such as a mob of northern finches descending on you and your tiny bag of seed, or having cat or squirrel problems. There is a list of naturalist groups and nature centres in the Appendix.

Storage is very important. Seeds must be kept dry and out of reach of rodents or raccoons. It is also nice to have them convenient to the feeder(s). The container that does this best for me is a new metal garbage can with a tight-fitting lid. For seeds on reserve, I stack extra bags in a rodent-proof metal shed.

This may seem to be a bit overcautious, except to someone who has caught a bad dose of mice or rats, or whose garage, back porch, workshop, or attic has been hit by break-and-enter squirrels. Once rodents discover a source of good food it is extremely difficult to keep them out of it. They can dig or gnaw their way into wooden sheds with ease and even bite access holes through plastic siding. Once in, they chew into bags or boxes and shred nesting materials from whatever valuables are stored there. With a reproductive capacity that is truly awesome, two mice can rapidly become a horde.

Birds and mammals are not the only animals that exploit the nutritious bounty of seeds; thousands of species of insects do so as well, some adapted to take special advantage of stored grain. Almost any sample of bulk seeds will have its share of these grain eaters, plus a few incidental ride-alongs. In a warm environment they can multiply at a rate that makes even mice seem chaste. Keeping your seeds outside in winter cools the reproductive capacity of these stowaways.

General neatness serves the ounce-of-prevention homily. Sweep up any spillage and put lids back on. I keep my trusty garbage can conveniently under my window-shelf feeder. Whatever spills is picked up by the birds or other foragers that stay where they belong . . . out!

I refer again to Chapter 5, "The Down-Side," for more suggestions on how to keep control of the situation and still be a generous host.

The Ethics of Feeding

Having dealt with the basics of feeding, touching upon subjects as far removed as saints and seeds, it is now appropriate to clear up questions of ethics that crop up often in discussions on bird feeding.

Will offering food to birds prompt some of them to delay migration so long they'll be stranded—lured to a wintry death by our generosity? This question may stem in part from cases where Canada Geese and ducks seem to be easily persuaded to stick around for the winter if feed, protection from hunting, and open water are provided.

In reply, I would point out that large waterfowl are one thing, small songbirds another. Canada geese and mallards can afford to be casual about migration. Even without the incentive of free feed many delay migration until after freezeup. If they do stay as guests of a city or park, the usual diet provided sustains a heavy layer of fat. The physics of size and energy expenditure allows them ample reserve to migrate in midwinter if they have to, a luxury small migratory birds can't afford.

Further, a large proportion of our summer songbirds are insectivorous and have to migrate once cool weather eliminates their food source. These birds don't eat seeds and wouldn't be tempted to stay no matter how plentiful the feeders. For those that *are* seed-eaters, migration isn't so pressing. Many simply follow advancing winter southward and stop whenever and wherever they find conditions acceptable. Other seed-eaters, like the northern finches, are more nomadic than migratory, flying east or west as well as south in search of plentiful fare. If birds from either of these groups stay behind to take advantage of your feeders, they are not in jeopardy since they have evolved to cope with cold weather.

In the final analysis, as much as we like to think how important our feeding stations are to the birds, we influence only a small percentage of the total populations of even the hesitantly migratory species. In some years great numbers of siskins or juncos, among others, will elect to winter in parts of their breeding range, well north of their usual winter haunts. It is an evolved behaviour, a response to natural conditions, not to the presence of our feeder tables. Once committed to stay, however, many lucky enough to find feeders will pull through a tough winter that would otherwise do them in.

Finally, holdovers of confirmed migrants such as Yellow-headed Blackbirds or White-throated Sparrows may have stayed behind because of some abnormal factor in either their behaviour or physiology. An unfit bird may not have the vitality to join the hustle and commotion of large premigratory flocks and will simply miss the boat when the rest of its fellows abruptly vanish on some frosty, moonlit autumn night. Most of these unfortunates die. A few, lucky enough to find good shelter and a plentiful source of food, will survive to greet the reduced ranks of their returning relatives the following spring. In this instance, a feeder can be the difference between life and death.

Another question is whether you are morally bound to keep feeding once you've started. If you stop, won't the birds that have come to rely on your food starve to death?

This is one of a number of givens that some authors have of late been keen to set up and then shoot down as outdated "folk myths." At the risk of falling out of step with a trend, my own counsel is that once you start, be prepared to stay the course. In the first place, birds wouldn't flock to your feeders in the numbers they do unless it gave them a better chance of survival. This bit of common sense is supported by the findings of Margaret Clark Brittingham of the University of Wisconsin who discovered that during severe winters the survival rate of Black-capped Chickadees with access to sunflower seeds was twice that of chickadees that obtained all their food from natural sources.

Secondly, for your own satisfaction, being consistent gets better results. You are less likely to attract and hold interesting birds with on-again-off-again feeding.

Ultimately, your decision as to whether you can stop feeding in midwinter with a clear conscience depends on circumstances of climate and location.

Canada's winter climate, with the possible exception of parts of southwestern British Columbia, tests even the hardiest song birds to the limit. In long periods of severe cold, they hang on from day to day on the slimmest margin between life and death. The ones dependent on feeders don't need the added uncertainty of an on-again-off-again food supply. If an "off" happens to coincide with a blizzard, an ice storm, or a spell of really deep cold, the delay and added stress birds suffer in relocating to another feeder or in switching back to natural food could be fatal.

This obligation is particularly pressing if your feeder is the only one for some distance around, as at a rural acreage or a back-country cottage. Here, you will probably attract a large number of birds, many of them a long way from their home territories, and hence more critically dependent on you than those from territories close by. In this situation, in a region of harsh winters, you really do have a moral obligation to see to it that your feeders are kept supplied once you've started.

However, the farther south you are, and the closer your bird-feeding neighbours are, the less binding is your obligation to be consistent. If you must stop feeding, perhaps for a midwinter holiday, do it during a mild spell well before you depart. That means you'll have to watch your expectant birds come to empty feeders until they give up and go elsewhere. You can avoid the forlorn gaze of your little friends by simply continuing to feed until you leave, and they'll run out when you're gone. But if you choose the skip-out method and it coincides with the worst blast of the winter, some of your trusting little dependants could be not only forlorn, but dead.

The Enemy—Aid and Comfort?

There is an upwelling of concern amongst the birding constituency that by feeding birds in winter we unwittingly give aid and comfort to the "enemy." If true, to what degree does this compromise our benevolence, or even make of it a liability to those whom we would help?

Who, or what, is the "enemy"? Well, to paraphrase Pogo's famous line, "One of 'em is us!" We lure the birds in, then turn loose upon them our cats. We cut down old trees, we drain and fill in boggy spots and "clean up" ditches and watercourses of unsightly brush and weeds, thus depriving our visitors of critical shelter. Squirrels, raccoons, skunks, rats, crows, jays, and magpies all prosper mightily on our garbage, gardens, and feeders. Between courses on our leftovers, all will prey on songbirds and/or, in summer, their nests. In parts of southwest British Columbia, add the opossum, a prolific scourge introduced by hunters seeking to set up for themselves a hunting thrill their brethren in the southern United States enjoy.

Not only do we support nest predators in unnaturally high numbers, we spray, mow, and trim our yards and parks to a fare-thee-well. This compulsive neatness restricts small birds to nesting and escape cover so limited and tightly ordered it is custom-designed for easy predator surveillance.

Just *how* easy was outlined in an article, "Why American Songbirds Are Vanishing" by John Terborgh in the May, 1992 *Scientific American.* Terborgh drew in part on work by American biologist David S. Wilcove of Princeton University. In a study ending in 1985, Wilcove stocked artificial nests with quail eggs and set them out in small, medium, and large forest tracts in both rural and suburban settings in the eastern United States where raccoons and opossums abound. Half the nests were placed on the ground, half at eye level. He distributed the same number of nests in a section of undisturbed forest in the Great Smoky Mountains National Park. Predation ranged from slightly under 25 percent for larger rural woodlots to close to 100 percent in some of the smaller woodlots, both rural and suburban. In the Smokies only one nest in fifty (2 percent), was raided.

The question must be asked: "Do our feeders lure birds into what amounts to a breeding 'black hole' from which no young emerge?"

Before you rush out to tear down your bird feeders, please note that Wilcove's disturbing statistics would be but little changed if there were no feeders in either suburbia or the semi-rural acreage. As far as backyard predators are concerned, uncontrolled garbage is the main villain. Wildlife biologists discovered long ago that raccoons, skunks, opossums, and squirrels not only thrive in urban environs in artificially high population densities, they also grow faster, get bigger, and have a higher birth rate than their backwoods relatives. So, direct your disenchanted eye to your garbage cans and make sure they cannot be tipped over, and the lids fit tightly. Get rid of scrap piles and other ground-level refuges where coons and rats can shelter.

Feeders, unlike loose garbage, afford a means of influencing who gets access to the goodies and who doesn't, especially when it comes to separating the birds from the mammals. Methods outlined elsewhere in this book tell how this can be done. You can also make your yard more bird-friendly and less predator-friendly in all seasons by planting appropriate shrubs and trees. Check the References in the Appendix for a list of books that deal with yard improvement.

The Cowbird—A Dilemma

There is one bird, the Brown-headed Cowbird, that presents a real dilemma to the bird feeder. This unobtrusive-looking nest parasite has expanded its range enormously since settlement times. It is becoming more and more familiar at feeders as it lingers ever farther north of its traditional winter range.

As we are all aware, songbird species are threatened by massive habitat loss in both their northern breeding range and their tropical rainforest wintering grounds. However, some of these losses can't be adequately explained solely by habitat destruction. Referring again to the *Scientific American* feature, there is another "pathology" at work. A credible body of opinion is accumulating that fingers the cowbird as the critical factor. The dilemma for us bird feeders is that the cowbirds we help through the winter may be the agent for wiping out clutches of songbirds around our yards the following summer. But how do you feed selectively to exclude this critter? It cheerfully eats most seeds. You cannot bar it from feeders on the basis of size, as you can, for example, crows or pigeons, since it is considerably trimmer than an Evening Grosbeak.

The cowbird is a further dilemma for me because I am highly mistrustful of the time-worn woodlore that in the past has made "good guys" and "bad guys" out of animals on grounds that often amounted to nothing more than blind prejudice or the selfish interests of human predators. I examine this problem in Chapter 7 in the discussion on the crow family. But because we are no longer dealing with a "natural" world, there is room, indeed at times a need, to attempt to reestablish some degree of balance between invasive species (including ourselves) and those they are crowding out. Our obligation is to make such manipulations as well-informed and as free of irrational emotion as we know how. To offer my own contribution to this end, I have included a lengthy discussion of the natural history of the cowbird, with some reference to the general subject of nest parasitism, in the section on blackbirds in Chapter 7.

Meanwhile, what is one to do? My own answer is nest surveillance around my own yard in spring and early summer. Any that I locate I simply check for cowbird eggs, and on finding one, throw it out. Checking is made quicker and easier with a mirror mounted on a long, light pole and held over high-up nests.

CHAPTER TWO

Seeds and Feeds

The "KISS" Principle

Although I am taken up with the idea and pleasures of feeding birds, there are other things in my life that have a justifiable claim on my time. Therefore, I have avoided getting too fussy about feeds, operating on the "KISS" principle: "Keep It Simple, Stupid." To those who take pleasure in melting suet twice, in cooking and mixing bird cakes, in rolling balls of suet and peanut butter in cornmeal and chopped almonds, I say, "go for it!"

To demonstrate my open-mindedness on the subject, I have provided a few tantalizing bird recipes in the Appendix, under the heading "The Non-KISS Gourmet." One of these is "bird stone," a classic that will test the greatness of those who really get off on unusual mixtures. It is attributed to one Baron von Berlepsch.

What to Feed?

The most primitive form of feeding is found in the householder who tosses a handful or two of breadcrumbs out the back door and lets the sparrows pick them off the snow. Offering breadcrumbs is sometimes a very good way of initially baiting birds in since the white fragments of bread are eyecatching. And although white bread is nutritionally impoverished, many winter birds do enjoy it, and there is usually no problem later in switching to seeds.

Baits and switches notwithstanding, the very best attractant to a feeder is a bird already busy at it. Chickadees, nuthatches, and Downy Woodpeckers commonly form loose foraging flocks. When one of these discovers your feeder the others are quick to get in on the action. Their activity, in turn, will attract other foragers like Steller's Jays and the finches. How long they stay with you, and in what numbers, depends on the attractiveness of the setting and the quality and quantity of the feed.

Exactly what you feed may depend on what is available locally at a reasonable price. "Reasonable" is a relative term; prices for various seeds vary greatly between locations and from one season to another. The key is to shop around. Buying name-brand seed in two-kg plastic bags at the grocery store is the costliest way to buy. Purchasing directly from a grower is usually the cheapest. In between, the best prices are to be found at seed and feed plants and farm feed stores. Pet stores and nature shops are the next best bet.

To provide some idea of relative costs, I checked prices charged by one major seed and feed retailer on south Vancouver Island as of the winter of 1992, and matched these with prices from an Alberta wholesaler. These are listed in the Appendix.

If you have a choice of seeds there are good reasons for making deliberate selections. Understandably, food preferences vary among species, so manipulating the kinds of feeds and where you offer them enables you, within limits, to control where various species will congregate around your yard. To help you with this I list the food preferences of each bird in the species accounts in Chapter 7.

Bird feeders are sometimes perplexed to discover that within species, preferences often vary markedly from region to region; what is a favourite in one locale may be totally ignored in another. Like young children, most seed-eating birds are very conservative in their food choices and refuse to try anything unfamiliar. I don't blame this on juvenile intransigence, but on the fact that they simply don't recognize strange seeds as food.

The nutritional worthiness of any given feed isn't something to worry about; the birds balance their diet themselves by supplementing your feed with a continuing menu of their natural foods. I routinely see chickadees interrupt a session of to-and-fro at my feeders to search nearby shrubs, presumably hunting for insect eggs or dormants.

On "Expert" Advice

There is a strong urge, particularly if one is writing a book, to play the sage and solemnly hand down pronouncements as if from the Mount. But almost certainly, if you begin to talk about animals in terms of absolutes, they will do something to make a fool of you in the eyes of your readers.

Take the subject of rapeseed. Some time ago in Canada we developed varieties that process more easily into edible oil and (perhaps just as well) changed the name from rape to "canola." All the books tell me that nothing, except for partridges scratching for it in a field, will eat it. Bird-feeding friends of long experience have hooted at the idea of offering birds canola. But this winter, the friend who looks after the feeders at our country place in Manitoba consistently placed canola in one of the big feeders, and I noticed on my last visit there that the redpolls were eating it. And the folks at the feed store near Parksville on Vancouver Island, where I've been picking up my sunflower seeds, millet, and hen scratch for my feeders here, tell me that rapeseed (as they still call it) is a steady seller.

One sunny day in early March a cat demonstrated convincingly that there is nothing to behold that doesn't have an exception to it. This beast clambered up over the wire around my window feeder and sat there for a good half hour eating sunflower seeds! I had plenty of time for pictures. Aside from an exploratory sniff and a half-hearted lick, the cat ignored a small block of rendered suet and a fragment of chicken fat.

If I were compiling statistics, that cat's strange tastes would produce some interesting pronouncements, such as: "17.3 percent of the cats observed during March of 1990 ate sunflower seeds." But since I'm not, I'm left musing on the cause. The cat was obviously not starved, being sleek and fit-looking. She might have been pregnant and responding to the sort of dill pickles-with-ice cream compulsion that besets some human ladies-in-waiting. I think not, however, for the sounds she made from time to time suggested that she was interested in *becoming* pregnant. Perhaps her state of hormonal excitement can explain her taste for sunflower seeds straight, rather than in bird form, which is the way her contemporaries have, thus far, unfailingly preferred them.

Seeds

The Noble Sunflower

Cultivated sunflower seeds come in several varieties, all of them arising from a Eurasian species *Helianthus annuus*. The familiar ones we munch are referred to in the grain and processing trades as "confectionary" sunflower seeds. Whole seeds are large—up to 1.5 cm (5/8 in.) long—and striped lengthwise in buff and dusty black. Roasted, salted or unsalted, they are sold as a confection everywhere, the infamous "spits" so hated by pool hall, bowling alley, and arcade operators across the land. In a quite different role, hulled, roasted, or raw, with or without salt, they are standard items in the bulk bins of organic food shops.

Large, striped "confectionary" sunflower seeds.

Confectionary seeds are universally relished at feeders, and until 1975 were the unchallenged choice of those who fed sunflower seed. But their size and thick hulls made them awkward for birds smaller than Purple Finches to husk, especially if they got damp and turned leathery. Hulled or cracked they are, of course, supremely palatable, but even at wholesale prices, very expensive as bird feed.

In 1975, a particularly heavy crop of the small, black oilseed sunflower pushed it onto the bird feed market as a much cheaper substitute for the confectionary seeds, and it quickly became the big seller. It was helped by the widely publicized findings of Dr. Aelred D. Geis of the U.S. Fish and Wildlife Service who scientifically assessed the food preferences of wild birds that visit feeders.

Among other things, Dr. Geis discovered that all birds tested except Tufted Titmice, Common Grackles, and Blue Jays selected oilseeds over confectionary when given a choice between the two. It is now accepted that oilseed sunflowers are eaten readily by nearly fifty species of birds, and are the first choice of many.

Small, black "oilseed" sunflower seeds.

Oilseeds are about half the size of the confectionary seeds and their much thinner hulls make them manageable by birds right down to siskin size. Unfortunately, they are not cultivated in British Columbia; supplies come from either Alberta or Washington. They are least expensive bought in

Whole sunflower seed heads can be very attractive to birds such as this Evening Grosbeak.

bulk from feed stores or seed plants, if you have one close at hand. It pays to shop around; in a busy winter my birds and squirrels will go through over five hundred pounds.

Not quite so economical are the sunflower "hearts" (or "harts") that are advertised for sale by some seed suppliers. Unlike peanut hearts, which are the germs of peanut seeds, sunflower "harts" are the damaged and undersized kernels culled during the preparation of confectionary sunflowers for human consumption. Hulls are discarded, but there is a small percentage of chaff and milling debris mixed in.

Not that the birds care. As an experiment I obtained a few kilos of hulled and cracked oilseeds, hulls still in the mixture, from a processing plant and tried them on my birds. My window feeder is separated down the middle by a low divider. I put crushed seeds on one half, whole on the other. That winter, siskins were abundant, and they virtually ignored the whole seeds in favour of the cracked. This is understandable; siskins are one of the smallest feeder birds, with small, lightly constructed bills. I would, however, expect all small to midsized birds to favour the easier pickings offered by cracked seeds.

This preference may create a seed wastage problem. In any sack of seeds there are always a few hulled seeds. Some individual birds learn that if they dig they'll find the easy, hulled seeds. On a table or shelf feeder this is no problem, but in a tube or bin feeder it means an incredible waste, since for every hulled seed the birds find, they dump several hundred others onto the ground below. I had a vexing problem with siskins in my tube feeders one winter and was able to solve the problem only by offering either cracked or hulled sunflower seeds. I haven't heard of this problem with other small species, but wouldn't be surprised if it occurred with them also.

I first noticed "harts" advertised by American seed suppliers, and a number of retailers offer them in British Columbia. Anyone fortunate enough to live within reach of a processing plant has the best chance of getting this premium feed at a reasonable price. Failing this, you might have seeds custom-ground, or do it yourself. I know of one ingenious bird feeder who cracks sunflower seeds with his power mower. He sets a couple of two-by-fours parallel on the concrete floor of his garage, spaced just wide enough to take the mower. Then he strews the seeds between them and "mows" them up into the grass catcher.

An advantage of hulled and cleaned (no hulls) seed, aside from waste control discussed above, is that there is no pile of husks under the feeder to contend with in spring. A disadvantage is that cracked sunflower seeds "weep" oil—the finer the crush, the faster the loss. That oil very quickly turns rancid in mild weather. I would think that cracked seeds, with the hulls left in the mixture, might keep a little better since the husks would tend to absorb the oil. With or without the hulls, however, broken sunflower seeds should not be stored over the summer, except in the freezer.

Throwing a few bags of seeds into the back of the car or camper the next time you're in Manitoba or some other sunflower-growing area is the most economical source. However, seeds right out of the combine often contain a high percentage of debris—broken stems, small chunks of the heads, and lots of chaff. This will clog up the ports of small feeders and create a layer of litter at the bottom of them that has to be frequently cleaned out.

I feel downright smug about feeding sunflower seeds to my birds (and squirrels). In that little black package is the closest to a universal feed that is commonly available. With over 40 percent oil content, plus a wholesome component of carbohydrate, protein, and minerals, they are richly nutritious. Their excellent palatability is supported not only by the scientific findings of Dr. Geis, but by users of mixed seed. They are known to complain that much of it is wasted by birds flicking through it to pick out the sunflowers, like party guests who eat all the cashews and filberts from the mixed nuts and leave the peanuts in the bowl.

Some authors claim, by the way, that sunflower husks are plant growth inhibitors. I find that the grass under my feeders thrives just fine whether I rake up or not.

Mixed Seed

This is variously marketed as "Wild Bird Seed," "Wild Bird Mix," "Finch Mix" and so on. Compositions vary, but millet (red and/or white) usually dominates, with cracked cereal grain (wheat, oats, barley), cracked corn, milo (sorghum), canary seed, and black sunflowers added in differing ratios. Finch mixes are generally limited to the smaller whole seeds; millet, canary, niger.

There are no regulations about any of these; seed houses and retailers mix their own, and they may or may not declare the contents, in percentages by weight, on the package. Buying the components separately and mixing them yourself is the only way of being absolutely sure of what you're scooping into your feeders. You will shortly discover, if you don't know it already, that mixtures containing sunflower seeds can be very wasteful because the birds flip away the other seeds in search of them.

On the subject of mixtures, acceptable bird fodder can be dished out in the form of "screenings," available if you happen to live near a feed manufacturer or seed cleaning plant. This is the weed seeds, damaged and undersized grain kernels, dust, and other debris winnowed out of grain when it's cleaned. It's usually very cheap, but you take your chances on what it contains. Not that the birds mind; weed seeds are part of the regular diet of many of our winter species. But many of the seeds are lightweight and blow far and wide in the winter wind, sowing the possibility of a bumper crop of objectionable weeds and neighbourhood resentment.

You can easily solve this problem at home; see "Sterilizing Seeds" at the end of this seeds section.

Millets

Common or proso millet, *Panicum miliaceum*, comes in white or red, and is the major constituent in commercial wild bird mixes. It is grown as human food in Asia and Europe, and as poultry and livestock feed here. Other varieties, more expensive than proso, include golden German, gold, and Siberian which are marketed more to the cage bird trade than to wild bird feeders. All millet seeds are small, round, fairly thin-hulled; in proso the white variety is slightly favoured over the red in selection tests. House Sparrows love millet, and it is highly acceptable to most finches, after the sunflowers are all gone.

Canary Seed

This is a European grass, *Phalaris canariensis*, now cultivated in Canada as a specialty crop. The seeds are flat, small, spindle-shaped, grey-buff with a polished, slippery coat, like flax. Free-flowing, it is excellent for tube feeders especially suited to smaller birds. Thus, while a feeding frenzy of House Finches or Evening Grosbeaks is devouring commoner fare by the pound at the main tray, the gold-finches and siskins will be extracting the high-priced canary seeds one at a time from the dainty little ports in the tube feeder. Or so the theory goes.

Grains—Hen and Chick Scratch

Oats, barley, rye, and feed wheat, particularly if you get them in bulk from a grower or processor, can be very cheap bird feed. Whole, they are acceptable to pheasants, quail, pigeons, Mourning Doves, crows, starlings, rodents of all kinds, and deer. Cracked or crushed they are acceptable to the foregoing, with added appeal to blackbirds, starlings, House Sparrows, several species of native sparrows, and to finches and buntings if no sunflowers or millet are offered. "Hen scratch" is a mixture of cracked corn and whole grains used as a feed supplement for poultry. "Chick scratch," the "baby food" version of hen scratch, is usually a mix of cracked wheat and crushed corn. Both are readily obtainable at feed stores.

Hen or chick scratch is great stuff to scatter on the ground for pheasants, quail, and pigeons. But its limited appeal to most songbirds makes it, in my view, most useful as cheap lure fodder for uninvited guests. It can be scattered on the ground, away from the feeders, to divert crows, starlings, and House Sparrows.

It is also useful if you find yourself host to some heavy eaters. For example, hard winters may drive deer into yards to browse on ornamentals or paw into compost heaps. They quickly learn to rear up to reach elevated bird feeders, and will bash at them with their front hooves to liberate more food. Hunger overcomes fear; frightened off, they return when vigilance lapses. Whether moved by sympathy or self-preservation to feed them, you'll find that once you begin, the word spreads and others arrive. Shovelling bird seed at them can get very expensive.

Some government game management agencies, and occasional sportsmen's clubs, supply free alfalfa pellet deer chow to people willing to dispense it. Otherwise, the cheapest whole grain you can get is the best alternative.

There are other hearty eaters you might wish, or be forced, to cater to. These include porcupines, and rabbits or hares, in which case a protective collar of wire or sheet metal around the bottoms of your favourite trees and shrubs is a wise precaution, even as you lay on the oats. In fall and early spring raccoons can become prime nuisances, cleaning you out of sunflower seeds and suet in one raid. Improved security measures for these goodies, combined with a diversionary offering of grain, could be the answer.

Canola (Rapeseed)

The little black seeds of *Brassica napus* look as if they *should* be good bird feed. Rich in oil, and otherwise nutritious, canola is abundant and low priced in parts of the Prairie Provinces, the chief growing area in Canada. But this region also produces the delectable black oilseed sunflower which has become the most-used feed. Thus, many birds are accustomed to sunflowers, have never seen canola, and offered the two together, ignore it. This dismal showing has been reflected in various controlled tests, to the end that most of the current books on feeding birds dismiss rapeseed as a feed fit only for pheasants, quail, and pigeons.

This may be about to change. Bird feeders, myself included, who have persisted in offering canola have discovered that even prairie species, conditioned on sunflower seeds to be finicky, will switch. Redpolls seem the most willing to give it a try, and once familiar with it, will feed on it even when the alternative is sunflowers.

The major reason for this transition may be that rapeseed itself has changed. The level of erucic acid in the old varieties of rape required extra refining to make the oil palatable for human use. Canada developed new, low-acid varieties and re-named rape "canola." Perhaps the milder-flavoured canola is also more palatable to the birds.

Corn

Zea mays can be offered on the dry cob, as whole kernels, or cracked and ground to various consistencies. Whole, it is attractive to birds like grouse, pheasants, crows, and pigeons, and it is reportedly acceptable to Steller's Jays and grackles. Cracked, it is much more widely accepted by the smaller species, including blackbirds, starlings, and House Sparrows. It is easily obtainable in most parts of British Columbia. However, in a damp climate, cracked corn cakes up and spoils quickly. Birds feeding on any musty grains inhale the spores of *Aspergillis* mould and contract aspergillosis, a lethal respiratory disease. An alternate, less risky use of crushed or cracked corn is as an addition to suet and/or peanut butter to make them more palatable.

Milo (Sorghum)

Sorghum vulgare originated in Africa and is a significant crop in parts of Canada for both fodder and grain for livestock. Most of our bird-seed sorghum comes from the United States. Two to three times the size of millet, the round, reddish seeds are tough-coated and can be handled readily by pigeons, grouse, and partridge, but otherwise are not popular at all at the feeder. In times when millet or other palatable seeds are high-priced, sorghum may find its way into commercial mixes as a filler. Watch for the telltale reddish hue to the mix; if it isn't small red proso millet seeds, skip it.

Peanuts

It would be surprising indeed if peanuts *weren't* high on the palatability list of birds and mammals, since we humans relish them so. *Arachis hypogaea* are tasty, rich, and as bird feed, damnably expensive. When you split a peanut, one half has

Surprisingly, even squirrels may take awhile to discover the delicious food inside these shells.

a little knuckle on one end. This is discarded during the manufacture of peanut butter and sold as "peanut hearts." One finds them advertised in bird magazines and in bins in pet and nature shops. At one time they were readily available for bird feed, even at reasonable prices. But now high cost relegates them to use in pinch-penny feeders for small species, as a treat, or to add to mixed concoctions.

Nowadays, most of us buy a few in the shell, string them on a wire or cord and hang them where the jays and chickadees can get at them. Once they've discovered what they are, and if the squirrels don't get there first, it's a diversion to watch the antics of the birds trying to shell them out.

Safflower

Safflowers are an oilseed crop grown here and there in British Columbia, but not extensively. They are in some locales referred to as "cardinal bait," in spite of the fact that cardinals now prefer sunflowers three-to-one. *Carthamus tinctorius* is also accepted by pigeons, House and Purple Finches, Evening Grosbeaks, and House Sparrows. Some station operators see as an advantage the fact that it is not readily eaten by Grey Squirrels.

Niger or "Thistle"

Guizotia abyssinica is a small tropical African sunflower called either "niger" or "thistle" seed, although it appears on some wholesalers' lists as "inga." It isn't related to our roadside thistles, although these produce seeds in abundance that are very important to small birds, notably goldfinches. Niger is a small, black seed that has long been a mainstay of cage birds, and is a highly desirable item with the smaller finches. It is usually considered too expensive to be served from large, generous hopper feeders or on tables. Most people use tube feeders; some designs are even called "thistle" feeders. You can also purchase a "thistle bag" with mesh tight enough to hold the seeds but large enough to permit their being pulled through by small, probing bills. Being an unrepentant sunflower advocate, I have never felt the need to own a thistle bag, but read they don't always work and can be leaky and wasteful. Niger seed is imported from Africa, which probably explains the price.

Sterilizing Seeds

Winter's innocent diversion can turn into summer's aggravation if spilled seeds fall on gardens and flower borders and do what they're designed to do—sprout. Lawns are no problem as a rule; the mower looks after any errant shoots. But prepared, fertile soil can be a different matter. Does this mean you have to choose between feeding birds and gardening? Does it mean you have to put the feeders where you don't really want them because the best place is the middle of the garden?

Prevention, as always, is the best alternative. Shop for, or build, feeders that minimize spillage. Small, slippery seeds, like millet, which is quick to germinate, easily get lost in snow or duff. The larger seeds, like sunflowers, which are slower to sprout, stay visible longer. Finches, jays, sparrows, starlings, and juncos are very happy foraging on the ground and will do a good job of gleaning the fallout. Mice and chipmunks perform a similar service. You can help them by raking away leaves and duff from beneath your feeders in the fall. And during winter, pack down each fresh layer of snow so that spilled seeds don't get mixed in with it.

To be really sure there's going to be no problem, heat-sterilize your seeds. Put a couple of inches in a roasting pan or foil tray and give it thirty minutes in the oven at just over 100°C (220°F). The idea is to heat the seeds, not roast them, so sniff and peek at the first batch to get the right timing and temperature for your particular stove. The microwave will do the same job in a matter of moments, depending on the amount you treat and the type of oven you have.

You can do a germination test by putting a few seeds between layers of damp paper towelling in the bottom of a plastic container. Put the lid on and check in a few days' time. If a week passes by with no sprouting, you've solved the problem. As a double-check set up a simultaneous "control" test with untreated seeds.

Feeds

If reasonably priced seeds are available to you without too much bother, and you're happy with the birds they attract, don't worry about extras. Birds happily live, day after day, week after week, on what to humans would be a deadly boring and deficient diet. It probably isn't as monotonous as their fixation on one type of seed would appear. Between sessions at your feeders birds forage for their natural foods which compensates for deficiencies in their one-item feeder menu.

Extra feeds, novelty items, and treats are useful for expanding your clientele to include a greater variety of species. I supplement my sunflower seeds (no reflection on them), with suet, partly because it may provide a critical extra boost of energy during especially cold periods, and partly because it is especially tempting to nuthatches and jays, and the main item for woodpeckers, including the magnificent Pileated.

In suburbia, bird-feeding neighbours often get into competitive excesses to attract the most birds. This demands the utmost of the contenders—the laying on of as many tempting goodies as they can buy or invent, dished up in a dazzling array of dispensers. Such "power feeding" is usually a harmless rivalry in which the real winners are the birds and the local bird feed retailers.

Peanut Butter

A jar of peanut butter that's been too long at the back of the fridge is my only source of it for feed or bait. Otherwise, I find it too expensive, especially when the squirrels catch on. However, others look for bargains and buy it for their birds. It is rich nourishment, and can be handled like suet, smeared into open pine cones and holes in suet logs. Some writers claim that it can be dangerous because it may clog up birds' mouths and throats and suffocate them. I doubt very much if a healthy bird would have much of a problem getting peanut butter "off the woof of its mouf." It *is* gooey, and accumulates around the base of the bill as the bird feeds. The oil might in time saturate the facial feathers and cause acute irritation and the loss of the feathers. You can cut the gooyness of peanut butter by mixing it with softened suet or cooking grease. Adding corn meal, oatmeal, or flour will absorb the oiliness.

Suet

Suet is the fat deposited around the kidneys and loin in the body cavity of cattle and sheep. It comes from the carcass as rounded white globs held together with light sheets of clear connective tissue. It doesn't freeze solid, so birds can feed on it without too much effort even at very low temperatures.

Many people have difficulty getting suet; it is usually trimmed off before it gets to the local meat counter. If they carry it at all, it is ground up and prepackaged for use in cooking, and is extremely expensive for bird feed. Many feed, pet food, and nature shops sell it in one form or another. If the local butcher can't (or won't) get you any, phone an abattoir or packing house. The price is usually very reasonable,

Slowly pouring melted suet on a tree branch and letting it harden is a "feeder" for birds like this chickadee.

and you can get all you need for the winter in one trip. It's a good idea to take your own containers.

Suet can be put out "as is." Pure, raw suet won't rot, although it will get rancid and very stale-smelling in warm weather. Any pieces of meat in the suet *will* rot, so it is a good idea to pull the globs apart while everything's still fresh and trim them out. Dispensing it is simple—plastic mesh onion bags, wire screen baskets, or similar dispensers give birds something to cling to while pecking through for small bits, but prevent their carting everything off wholesale.

"Suet logs" are made by boring holes into a stick of firewood with a one to two-cm (half to three-quarter-inch) bit, filling them with suet, and hanging it up. Making suet logs is a time-honoured way of giving youngsters, and their grandfathers, a way of occupying themselves constructively and, for the most part, harmlessly.

Some writers worry that birds' feet, eyes, or tongues will stick to the frozen metal of wire suet baskets. Having in childhood stuck my own tongue to the pump handle, I can sympathize. But I know of no direct account of this having happened to birds; their feet are dry, and their reflexes so quick I doubt very much if their eyes or tongues are at hazard. A panicked bird, or one that is ill, *might* be vulnerable. If it worries you, buy liquid latex and coat the wire or metal parts of your suet baskets, but be prepared for a price shock.

If you're not sufficiently fulfilled by hanging raw suet out in an onion bag, it can be refined by "rendering"—melting—it. Chop it into small pieces first. Rendering should be done with care since hot fat inflicts a severe burn if splattered on skin, and can burst into a very stubborn fire if mishandled. A double boiler is safe, but seems to take forever. A slow fry is my way, gently pressing the chunks to get all the oil out as the meltdown proceeds. Fished out, the crunchy brown "cracklings" are themselves a tasty bird treat. I just scatter a few on the feeder among the seeds every now and then, breaking them up so the jays can't immediately cart everything off in big chunks.

The oil is poured into moulds for cooling. These can be any container of convenient shape and size, preferably of destructible material. Used aluminum foil bowls, waxed paper cups, melon shells, and grapefruit rinds have all been pressed into service. For variety, peanut butter, corn meal, or dried fruit can be added and stirred in as the mixture cools.

In my own view, suet and seeds are best *not* mixed together because grease-soaked seed hulls are harder to husk. Also, birds not interested in suet will dig into it looking for seeds, with the increased likelihood of getting their facial and breast feathers saturated with grease, particularly if the mix is left out as spring weather warms. Softened and rancid, it more readily saturates facial feathers and may cause infected follicles and feather loss around the beak and eyes.

There are two advantages to rendering. One is that if suet is to be fed in warm weather, melting it down twice will make it harder when it's cooled the second time. The other is that liquefying the suet makes it easy to fish out nonfat fragments that would rot quickly at warm temperatures. For any bits that you miss, the heat of rendering has a sterilizing effect that slows down decay.

Suet will continue to be eaten by some species well after the arrival of warm weather. Since the high-energy feeds become less crucial in warm weather, and since natural foods like insects become available then, it is better to withdraw suet once spring has truly set in.

Not long ago I was solemnly assured by a butcher that suet should *not* be fed to birds at all because "the fat plugs their nostrils and they fly away and suffocate!" Aside from the fact that birds can breathe through their mouths as easily as we can, they can also snort or sneeze blockages out of their nostrils. This is more of the silly alarmism that "experts" let loose into popular lore, and which a little common sense easily exposes as the nonsense it is.

Suet is, of course, attractive to scavengers such as raccoons, weasels, coyotes, and, the worst nuisances of all, roaming dogs. Hanging it at least two metres (six feet) up will keep it out of easy reach of these pillagers.

One final word on this excellent bird food. If you buy a prepared ball of frozen, ready-to-serve suet mixed with what-have-you, keep an eye, and your nose, on it as weather warms. I once got one of these for Christmas, moulded into a cute bell, and parked it on the woodshed roof. Around about Mother's Day I discovered that it had transformed itself into a putrid blob.

Slab Fat

In the trimming process butchers slice slabs of fat off the outside surface of sides of beef. This is tougher, much stringier, and lacks the flakiness of suet. It can be rendered, or you can simply nail a chunk to a tree. Slabs of pork fat, with or without the rind, can be similarly used. "Slab" fat (my name) can be useful in keeping heavy users like crows or ravens diverted from the higher-quality stuff in the fragile onion bags where the chickadees feed.

"Cod" Fat

You might encounter this term when asking for fat from your butcher. This has nothing to do with fish, being instead fat trimmed from beef carcasses. What part, I've been unable to find out, and am left guessing if there's some connection with "cod" as in "codpiece."

Cooking Grease

Leftover cooking fat is as nutritious and palatable as suet, providing it isn't charged with particularly hot spices. The higher the percentage of pork fat and/or vegetable oils, the softer and greasier it will be. Soft fats should be offered only during really cold weather, and in wire cages or other rigid containers that the birds can cling to or approach without having to press directly against the fat, as they tend to when it's in a net bag. Grease-saturated breast feathers lose their insulating properties, which could inflict severe stress on a bird in particularly cold conditions. Mixing soft fats with suet stiffens the mixture, and absorbent fillers like bran, dry cereal, or corn meal cut down the greasiness.

Bones

The birds that take suet seem to be strongly attracted to large, raw bones; some prefer to hammer away at them for the tiny shreds and scraps their labours produce rather than take easier pickings from a nearby suet bag. Such scavenging probably evolved at predator kills. Hence nuthatches, woodpeckers, and chickadees may get atavistic satisfaction out of picking at bones that hanging on a plastic onion bag just doesn't afford. If I come by a fresh beef, horse, or deer hip, or large leg bone, I park it in the snow on top of the back shed. By the time it has turned from its original startling red to a sombre brown, the birds will have pulled all but the toughest shreds of sinew from it.

Meat/Carrion

If you live near the coast of British Columbia, the sight of a Bald Eagle isn't something to get excited about. But in less favoured settings, spotting one of these great birds is an event. Away from their oceanside haunts, Bald Eagles migrate. But some may now and then stay over at inland locations, especially near open water, living off crippled waterfowl left behind from the goose and duck hunting seasons, the plentiful supply of carrion in gut piles, and dead and dying animals from the deer, elk, and moose seasons.

Slab fat can simply be nailed to a tree trunk to attract chickadees, woodpeckers, and jays.

Unless you live well up in the mountains, a confirmed Golden Eagle sighting is worth a note in the diary. Goldens drift down from their nesting ramparts in the high country and the far north, cruising the southern forests and farmlands for snowshoe hares, cottontail rabbits, and game birds.

Several years ago, noting the presence of both these great raptors near my country place in southern Manitoba, I erected a stout shelf on a post, high enough off the ground so the coyotes couldn't reach a chunk of road-killed deer that I lashed onto the deck. Magpies were the most numerous visitors, until one morning a dark, hulking bird had banished them. It was a Golden Eagle, and it came only two or three times that winter.

On two succeeding winters I have attracted Bald Eagles, one adult and one immature. Between visits from these big raptors, my "eagle feeder" out in the meadow gives the magpies something to do besides ganging up at the suet feeders in the yard.

Another big bird has recently become the benefactor of a similar feeding effort in British Columbia. The main breeding grounds for the province's Turkey Vultures is the Gulf Islands. There, and on Vancouver Island in the vicinity of Duncan, farmers and others with an interest in these great scavengers have set up platforms and stock them regularly with road kills. This is a highly civilized approach to a bird that has often been persecuted in the past simply because it feeds on carrion.

Baked Goods

A restaurant, bakery, or doughnut shop can be an inexhaustible source of stale stock and leftovers. Doughnuts, cakes, and pastries are tasty-rich in carbohydrates and fats—just the ticket for winter calories. Unlike these, straight white bread, hotdog and burger buns, etc., have limited nutritional value. I can't recommend their use except as a filler for a recipe containing other, more nutritious, fare.

Take care not to be overwhelmed by the generosity of donors; some outlets create leftovers in awesome quantities and are only too happy to give them to anyone who'll cart them off.

Before you start strewing these goodies about the yard, and making regular runs to the garbage dump with the stuff the yard won't hold, go to the dump ahead of time and survey the clientele there. In the bird department we're talking starlings, House Sparrows, pigeons, crows, swarms of gulls, and ravens—lots of ravens if we're in their range. Amongst the ground crew are rats, mice, raccoons, errant mutts, and cats of no fixed address.

The point is that dispensing leftover baked goodies could turn your yard into a satellite garbage dump, unless it's done with discretion. Some of your regular clients will learn to relish this offering, if they haven't already developed the taste. Keep such fare well up off the ground; the local dogs will smell it out quickly and, if they can reach it, will become constant nuisances.

Fruit

Dried fruit, especially raisins because of their small size and easy availability, has been frequently used as a specialty or "treat" food. Waxwings, if they stick around long enough for you to get their attention, will take raisins with enthusiasm.

Wintering robins and their kindred Varied Thrushes are said to sustain themselves mainly on tree-dried berries. I have seen a backyard crabapple in early spring surrounded by dozens of robins gathered to feed on the fallen fruit. The interesting bit was that neighbouring crabs, having dropped just as abundantly, were totally ignored. If you discover such a tree, gather a basket or two of its fruit the next fall. Keep them frozen in case you happen to be host to a robin, flicker, or some waxwings that winter. If not, the returning robins will appreciate them, come spring.

The literature regularly mentions bananas, oranges, apples, strawberries, raspberries, and other fruits as being good for tempting birds that aren't interested in the traditional seeds or suet. A half orange, for example, impaled on a nail or stout twig in a tree, is said to be irresistible to orioles. If no birds show up to claim these goodies, you can recover your investment by eating the unused ones yourself.

In the gentler climes of coastal and southern British Columbia there is an abundance of natural and ornamental shrubbery, much of it berry-bearing and used by birds as winter feed. However, the farther inland, the higher up, and the farther north you get, the less of this bounty one finds. A provident bird feeder in these regions could watch for a good summer crop of wild fruit and gather a few buckets. Held in the freezer they would be ready for the appearance of a flock of waxwings or a nonmigrant robin.

Sweets

Sugar solutions and hummingbirds go together. But other birds are also attracted to sugar water once they discover it. Chickadees, House Sparrows, and Purple Finches are among these, but the real "sweet tooth" belongs to House Finches. This treat should not be dispensed in a bowl or bath where unsuspecting birds might bathe in it. Rather, it could be offered in the kind of hummingbird feeders that have a simple bent glass tube hanging down from the stopper on an inverted bottle or jug, placed where the nonhummingbirds can perch and feed from it. An alternative is a waterer for poultry chicks that is readily available at feed stores or rural hardwares.

For hummingbirds, popular wisdom advocates a solution of one part sugar to four parts water. However, as a result of research on hummingbirds wintering in cooler climates, a solution of 75 percent sugar is advocated for winter feeding. Honey, in spite of being a "natural" food, can harbour a mould that can be fatal to hummers, and is best avoided.

Frequently in the literature one reads of small woodpeckers, chickadees, creepers, hummingbirds, squirrels, and others feeding at the neat rows of holes sapsuckers drill in trees. They lap up the oozing sap and pick up the insects stuck in it. As a modification of the suet log, a "sugar log" could be made by drilling rows of small, shallow holes in a length of smooth-barked tree trunk and filling these with honey, thick syrup, jelly, jam, or any of these mixed with peanut butter. Such a lure might not only divert sapsuckers from your smooth-barked ornamentals in summer, it might bring otherwise reclusive creepers, possibly even kinglets, into view in winter.

Grit

Most birds require grit of some kind in their gizzards to grind up their food; it is particularly important to seed eaters. I've never supplied it for my birds, assuming the adjacent gravel roads to be a more-than-adequate source. So is the grit that washes out of the asphalt shingles on my roof.

However, if you live in what you believe to be a grit-deficient neighbourhood, you can do your part for avian digestion by putting a shovelful of gravel or coarse sand out where the birds can get it. Feed companies sell poultry grit in three or more sizes; "chick" grade would be most suitable for the small-calibre plumbing of most feeder species. Crushed oyster shell, even the "pullet" size, would likely be too coarse except for grouse, pheasants, and pigeons.

Salt

Crossbills are frequently seen picking at the ashes around barbecues and fire pits, presumably to satisfy a craving for the minerals they contain. Many crossbills, Evening Grosbeaks, siskins, and Common Redpolls are killed by traffic when they flock onto roads for the salt scattered there in winter. A small pan of coarse salt mixed with ashes, grit, or soil might prove to be a highly tempting treat to a flock of crossbills or grosbeaks. By offering it, you might save the lives of birds that would otherwise seek this attractive supplement in traffic.

Water

There is nothing, including feeders, that attracts birds in summer better than an inviting pool of water, particularly one where a trickle or spray splashes invitingly into it. This reflects the importance of water to the well-being of birds. In the winter they get it by eating snow. This is a long-established adaptation, so I don't agree with those authors who worry at length about the necessity of installing a heated watering pan for birds. In Winnipeg, where I fed birds for many years, water mains occasionally burst in midwinter, creating ponds and rivulets on the street. If the birds nearby craved water, they'd be flocking to it. But I have yet to see a single one come to drink at these breaks.

The combination of circumstances where they might be stressed would be during a protracted fall freeze-up when natural sources of open water would be iced over and no snow fell. In this situation, there might be a case for providing a bird bath, or pan of water, warmed. The heat source could be a light bulb, heat lamp, battery warmer, or submersible heating coil. Just be certain the water is kept *warm*, not scalding hot!

There is some evidence that having access to warmed water in extremely cold weather can be fatal to some birds. One of my references noted that starlings bathed in the warmed water he supplied, and then promptly froze to death! Other references suggest that wintering birds can bathe in water and suffer no overchill, but I suspect these observations come from places where winter isn't the bracing kind we enjoy in most of Canada.

CHAPTER 3

Feeders and Shelters

First Considerations

There are two beneficiaries to consider in setting up a feeding station: birds, and people, in that order. This basic priority suggests a sequence of things to ponder. Of primary importance are: (1) accessibility to the birds; (2) shelter from the wind, snow, and rain; (3) preventing or minimizing window strikes; and (4) safety from predators, especially cats.

Secondary considerations are: (1) ready visibility for people; (2) ease of filling and maintaining feeders; and (3) feeder capacity (which determines refill frequency).

Site (yard) assessment has already been discussed. This will suggest the kinds of feeders you should use: table, window shelf, post-mounted, hanging. If you have a big window facing into an alcove on the southeast side of the house, with ample shelter from the prevailing northwesterlies, there are no priorities to sort out, since this is a setup in which everybody wins.

The All-weather Yard

Suppose, however, that your best window faces west or north, and there is no shelter worth the name between it and Siberia. In this case, adjustments are in order.

My own option would be to put up two feeders, in effect one for me and one for the birds. For me, where the view is best, I'd fix a large shelf under the big exposed window, fitting raised sides on the windward edges so the seeds wouldn't be scattered with every passing gust. On calm days, or with the wind blowing from the opposite side of the house, the birds could feed comfortably at the big window, in full view. For the birds, I'd put up another feeder, a table or pole, in the place most sheltered from the prevailing westerlies; whether or not there was a window view of this alternate site would be a secondary consideration.

This combination, with perhaps a couple of hanging seed feeders and a suet bag at various selected spots, would make my yard an all-weather feeding haven, more likely to attract, and hold, birds there in all kinds of weather. My big window might be deserted on days when our continental westerlies whistled against it, but the feeders out back would keep everybody around until things calmed down.

Varieties of Feeders

From the Ground Up

The most basic feeder of all is the ground itself. Virtually all birds that use feeders, with the exception of hummingbirds, will feed there. Many, like House Sparrows, juncos, pigeons, grouse, starlings, and the blackbirds seem to favour the ground if given a choice. Redpolls, chickadees, goldfinches, Evening Grosbeaks, Purple Finches, and siskins also feed there but are just as happy, or more so, with something higher up.

The wire screen around this low table prevents cats from turning it into an ambush for these Evening Grosbeaks and Common Redpolls.

Throwing feed on the ground might not be as easy as it first appears. It can be wasteful. In rainy conditions seeds become one with the soggy ground or are washed away. They get mixed in with soft snow and disappear. Repeated snowfalls, or windblown snow, bury everything. In spots close to shrubbery or other hiding places, birds on the ground are most vulnerable to ambush by cats. From a high window, it may be awkward to see birds on the ground nearby. If I'm feeding on snow-covered ground, or wish to minimize wastage of seeds spilled from an overhead feeder, I pack the snow first by patting it down with a shovel or rolling it flat with a large plastic pail.

A sheet of plywood, an old door, even a piece of carpet, can be used as a modest improvement on bare ground or snow. It cuts wastage appreciably, and cleaning it off is merely a matter of upending it and giving it a kick, or flopping it over.

The Table—Next Step Up

If you take your plywood or old door and nail legs under the corners you have yourself a table feeder. Putting a low rim around the edges stiffens it and helps keep the seeds in place. You can make a neater job of sweeping it off if you leave gaps in the rim at the corners. A further modification is to give the table top a slight tilt by cutting two of the legs on a long side a bit shorter. This lets rain or meltwater drain off faster, through the gaps you've so cleverly left in the edging.

The height of the table is a matter of taste or convenience, as is its size—or both may be determined by the scrap lumber at hand. A general rule is that the bigger your feeder(s), the more birds you'll attract, particularly the sociable species like finches. A full 4 x 8 ft sheet of plywood can accommodate an awesome mob of siskins, redpolls, Purple Finches, and/or Evening Grosbeaks. But in years of real abundance, a modest feeder no more than 30 x 60 cm (1 x 2 ft) can attract an astonishing crowd of visitors.

At this point in the setting-up stage one might as well face the fact that in any location where there are neighbours there are going to be cats, sometimes a whole parade of them. It will be better for the birds, and your state of mind later on, to take preventive action now to minimize the cat problem. Recommended measures are to be found in Chapter 5, "The Down-Side," under the subhead, "Frustrating the Felines."

For now, I should point out that cats can turn a low table feeder into a deadly ambush. Seeds spilled from it bait the birds to the ground right in front of the lurking cats' noses. Cats also quickly master another lethal trick. They pinpoint the location of birds on the platform overhead from the sounds of their feet and, when one is near the edge, pounce over and grab it. My own experience is that the best way to prevent your table from becoming a cat-treats bar is to tack wire screen or wooden slats to the legs all the way around so they can't get underneath.

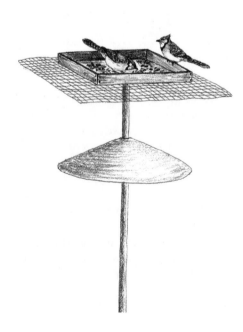

This simple pole feeder has both a cat and a squirrel guard.

Pole Feeders

One of the more pleasing arrangements, from both the birds' and their observers' points of view, is the pole feeder. This is basically a shelf-on-a-stick, with infinite variations. It can be made or bought.

Many manufactured feeders come with metal tubes that fit cleverly together in sections. The bottom end of the lowest section is crimped to a rough point, and to set the device up you simply tap it into the ground—*straight* into the ground, if possible. Don't beat on the top of the tube with a hammer or some other steel bludgeon; you'll crimp or bend the rim and it won't take the small end of the next section. Put a piece of soft wood on the top of the tube and thump on that.

The sectional rod idea is doubly convenient, since the feeders bolted to the top section are usually of the hopper variety and stretching up to fill them *in situ* can be awkward. You simply rotate and pull off the feeder, plus the attached top section of pipe, refill it at convenient working height, then replace it. To make sure that mine comes apart at the first section below the feeder, I apply a lubricant to that joint. If that doesn't work, I wrap a little electrician's tape around the other joints to hold them in place.

Increasingly, store-bought pole feeders come with squirrel baffles. If not, the merchant will happily sell you one as an add-on. The most widely used baffle is a cone- or frisbee-shaped metal disc loosely fixed to the pole just below the feeder. You can also get sheet metal "squirrel-proof" feeders with perches that close the feeding hole under a squirrel's weight, but not under a bird's weight. Some poles are fitted with a loose metal sleeve connected by a line over a pulley to a counter-weight in the main tube. A squirrel on its way up the pole gets a free ride back down as soon as it grabs the sleeve and hangs its weight on it. All this takes place, presumably, to the intense frustration of the squirrel and the huge amusement of the guy who bought the contraption. It no doubt works, at least once, or until the squirrel discovers that if it just

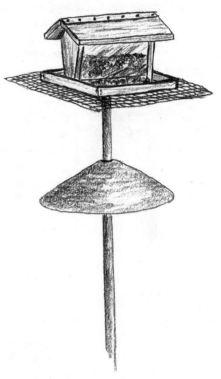

A hopper feeder suitable for a cold, dry winter without much rain.

keeps right on climbing the sleeve during the glide down it will reach the main pole again and, perhaps with no more than a couple of gentle bumps on the heels from the rising tube, gain its objective. This is called the frustration/entertainment reversal factor.

My largest feeder is mounted on a sawed-off telephone pole, two-plus metres (7 ft) above ground, clad top to bottom in sheet metal. The hopper on the platform at the top is made of a 76 cm (30 in) section of 46 cm (18 in) culvert. It looks like a small water tower designed by Paw Kettle, and has been uncharitably described as an eyesore. But it is out behind the cottage in the country where few, save myself, the critic, and the birds, can see it. I have to fill it from a stepladder, but since it holds upwards of 40 kg (88 lb) of seeds, this isn't too frequent a chore, and I can go away for a fortnight or more and not have to worry about my birds running short. Among its other sturdy virtues my tower is raccoon- and deer-proof, and squirrel-proof except for the flying squirrels and one big male Grey that does a magnificent Moscow Circus leap from a nearby maple.

Beer-box Craft

As I have already mentioned, the variations that can be worked into the basic pole-and-shelf pattern are infinite. The most primitive can be large berry-baskets, small wooden boxes, or even twelve-pack beer cartons nailed on their sides to the tops of fenceposts. For the carton, use a small scrap of plywood as a washer so the nail won't rip through the cardboard in the wind. It's crude, but the birds don't care, and the materials can be recycled out of any roadside ditch. At this level of technology you are not only benefiting the birds, but helping to keep British Columbia's roadscapes litter-free.

Opposite to crude can be a finely crafted, multi-storey platform with several hoppers, one or two sides made of plexiglass, little balconies for baked scraps and other treats, eye screws on little booms for suet bags and thistle feeders, all tucked under a trimly shingled roof. Such a feeder doesn't have to be very big to accommodate a large number of birds at once. With rustic natural finish, or tastefully selected paint, a station like this can be a quaint and attractive centrepiece to the yardscape. My only word of caution is that if you're just starting out, begin near the primitive end of the technology and let experience mellow and guide your decorative enthusiasm.

A recycled beer-box feeder.

How High?

We've already discussed some variations in squirrel-proofing as found in commercially made feeders. If you're making your own, your attitude to squirrels will dictate basic features of construction and placement.

The platform of any pole-mounted feeder must be high enough to prevent squirrels' jumping directly up to it. For Red and Douglas Squirrels, this means a *minimum* of 1.22 m (4 ft). Depending on snowfall in your area, allow extra height for snow pack under the feeder. It must also be set far enough away from trees or other launch points to prevent squirrels' jumping across to, or down onto it. Horizontally, that means a span of 1.8 m (6 ft), more from a launch point higher than the top of the feeder. For Grey Squirrels, vertical clearance should be a minimum of 1.5 m (5 ft), horizontal distances at least 2.4 m (8 ft).

The pole can be metal or polyvinyl chloride (PVC) pipe, a post, two-by-four or other dimension lumber, or a slender tree trunk—anything, as long as it's sturdy enough to hold whatever you intend to fix to the top. Squirrels cannot climb a pole made of smooth material, like metal or PVC, if it's too big for them to wrap their front legs around; four inches' (10 cm) diameter should stop a Red Squirrel, five (12.7 cm), a Grey.

Wood, and metal poles slender enough for them to climb, can be made squirrel-proof in several ways. One method is to wrap the top couple of feet of a wooden pole in sheet metal or substantial plastic film. Another is to slip a 45-cm (18 in) sleeve of metal or plastic pipe over the pole and hang it just under the feeder. It must be too big around for squirrels to shinny up it, and snug enough to keep them from squeezing under. A baffle made from garbage can lids, old LP records, or sheets of stiff plastic may do the trick. Put it high enough on the pole so squirrels can't jump past it from the ground, and attach it loosely so that it tilts easily when a squirrel grabs the edge.

For further discussion of squirrels see "A Gnawing Problem" in Chapter 5.

Low-rise Ladder

If a pole feeder is high enough to keep squirrels from jumping onto it, it means that top-loading hoppers will be awkward to fill for people of average height. If the pole is fitted with telescoping joints, as described previously, there is no problem, but for a solid pole one should have a sturdy wooden box or something broad-based to stand on. An old chair or stool is most untrustworthy on packed snow or boggy, rain-soaked ground. Just when you're teetering aloft a leg, or two, will suddenly poke through the unstable surface and dump you.

My own answer is a 1-m (3-ft) ladder. The sides are set very wide apart at the bottom, very close together at the top; it looks like an isosceles triangle with the odd side left off. The idea is that the close-set ends at the top rest loosely against the sides of the pole while the splayed bottom affords a very secure base. You can augment this simple design with an extension set at an angle to the top. With this resting against the pole you're set back more comfortably from your work. See the accompanying diagram.

My squatty ladder is very light and also comes in handy for filling or cleaning high window-shelf feeders, servicing bluebird houses, cleaning windows, and doing other odd jobs at modest elevations where a full-size ladder is awkward.

Light, solid, and handy—the three-step ladder.

Window Shelves

Shelter and serviceability permitting, a window shelf feeder offers the ultimate for closeup viewing and photography. I say "shelf," but several makes of commercial window feeders exploit windows to the ultimate in other ways.

Some commercial models mount directly onto the glass with suction cups. In very cold conditions some cups are unreliable fixtures, prone to pop off when you're filling the feeders or cleaning the glass. Proper installation helps: Heat the cups in hot water, dry them off, apply a little oily film by rubbing the inner surface with your fingers, and put them on the glass while they're still warm. If the cups hold, and the birds grow accustomed to being so close to you, the eye-to-eye proximity is captivating indeed.

Another idea, the ultimate attempt at cosy intimacy, is a plexiglass box that fits into a window frame, like an air conditioner, extending into the room. The outer side is open and the birds feed in what is an extension of the outdoors into your home. The room-side surface is coated with reflecting film to dim the birds' view of the occupants. A neat hinged door opens on the inside for easy servicing.

This alcove-in-a-window is the ultimate in intimacy, but where winters bring really cold temperatures I would recommend some heat-conserving accessories. I'd put an insulated door or lid on the outside and close it at nights. When I wasn't actually watching the birds, I'd cover the feeder with a foam box fitting over it from the inside. Without these modifications, our infamous Canadian wind chills would turn this novel feeder into a chronic heat haemorrhage. There might also be the problem of condensation and excessive frost accumulation, and dripping. The measures suggested in Chapter 4 under "Window Management" could be helpful.

Shelf Control

For most of us, attaching a simple shelf to the outside of the windowsill is quite sufficient. For a small shelf, bracing and bracketing can be simple and light, even flimsy, since seeds and birds don't weigh much. However, the bigger a shelf gets, the sturdier the supports will have to be. And any shelf should be anchored solidly

The window shelf, ideal for closeness, with cat guard.

enough to withstand vigorous action if you're going to have to scrape or chop away ice and crusted snow. Whatever the size, I leave 2.5 cm (1 in) of space between the glass and the inside of the shelf so that snow and seeds won't collect there and form an icy plug that will be messy-looking and awkward to chip away.

If the platform is close enough to the ground for cats to leap up to it, that is, 1.8 metres (6 ft) or less, staple a fringe of woven wire around the three outside edges before you install it. If stucco or chicken wire is aesthetically displeasing to you, buy the decorative wire border trim that garden shops sell.

The shelf should have a rim at least 2.5 cm (1 in) high around the three outside edges; otherwise the wind and the birds will waste most of the seeds. As already mentioned for tables, it will be much easier to sweep snow and seed leftovers off the shelf if you leave the outside corners open by 5 to 6 cm (2 in) or more. And when you make your plans, allow for a moderate slope to the outer edge so that rainwater and melting snow will run off through the corner openings.

Baffled

If the spot you really want for a feeder isn't adequately sheltered, you can set up baffles, separate from the feeder. In a previous home my south-facing office window, where I wanted my main feeder to be, also happened to be wind-scoured. I mounted a sheet of plywood on the wall of the house three feet to windward. A frame and braces fit onto cleats on the wall and it could be installed and taken down quickly with eight wood screws. It was painted to provide reflected backlight for enhanced bird photography—my idea—and to not deface the house—hers.

The feeder itself can be partially self-protecting with a higher side on the upwind edge. How high? The amount of downwind shelter afforded by a wall is proportional to its height. A 10-cm-(4-in) wall would provide sufficient shelter for a shelf 30 cm (1 ft) square, but be less than adequate for one 1.2 m (4 ft) square.

You want protection, but don't want to go overboard and create a deep, enclosed box. Birds feel trapped in constricted spaces where vision and escape are cut off. Leaving one or two sides with just a low rim helps dispel that claustrophobia. Even for a single side, the higher it is the more the birds will constantly startle each other as arrivals abruptly flutter onto it from the blind side. Your own sense of proportion, observation of the birds' behaviour, and the action of the wind will ultimately be your best guide.

The measurements of the shelf will be determined by your own taste, skill, and ambition, and the size of the window. Bear in mind that whisking snow off and chipping crusted ice away are chores directly proportional to the expanse of the feeder.

Finish and Colour

When all these heavy matters have been pondered through to a conclusion, and the sawing and nailing are done, you might want to paint your creation. I favour a finish rather than leaving the wood bare, even though this is less "natural." My choice is more practical than decorative; with a good quality paint the smoother surfaces are easier to clean, water runs off them more readily, and ice doesn't bond to a smooth paint finish nearly as tenaciously as to the exposed fibres of bare wood.

For the feeding surface of the shelf I pick light colours that absorb less of the sun's radiation, and hence are slower to melt accumulated snow into what will later freeze into a thick crust of ice. Also, from the point-of-view of the birds, most seeds show up better on a light base.

Photogenic Feeders

While you're thinking paint, you might consider what tones would complement colour photography, particularly if there are raised sides on the edges of your feeder. Bright ones will reflect light and have to be allowed for on your exposure meter readings. Depending on the angle of sunlight, they will provide fill-in lighting to soften the hard shadows. They will also enter into the composition of your photographs, adding or detracting from them with their shape, texture, and colour.

These are things you might not notice in the excitement of fiddling with your camera to get that super close-up of a beautiful bird before it takes off. But there is nothing more annoying, when you get your slides back, than discovering a scrappy-looking or off-colour slab of plywood sticking out like a sore thumb in every one of them.

Hanging Feeders

Hanging feeders can be as large as the strength of the support will allow. But I find that their best advantage is as satellites to larger, fixed feeders. Compact and self-enclosed, hanging feeders make it easy to diversify with special feeds, and to cater to smaller species. They can also be the cheapest and easiest to construct.

The commercial manufacture of hanging feeders lends itself to the whims of the plastic moulder's craft. They are extruded in globe, hemisphere, toadstool, space station, and animal shapes. Some are great, but many have been crafted to catch the eye of buyers who know nothing of feeding birds but recognize "cute" when they see it. Some of the resulting baubles are fit only to hang on Christmas trees.

Classic Javex

Consider the homemade end of tacky, the classic Javex bottle. Numberless backyard *improvisarios* have rescued them in the nick of time from the garbage, hacked holes in their sides, charged them with seeds, and hung them by the neck from a tree limb for the winter. Children cart them off to school science fairs as proud evidence of their ingenuity.

Of equal honour are empty cardboard milk cartons.

Deserving of their historic place as the Javex bottle and milk carton are, I have nevertheless abandoned both in favour of the larger and more conveniently squared-off shape of the four-litre windshield-washer jug. The accompanying diagram shows how to use the flap of plastic as a little roof over the cut-out hole. You attach the cord through a hole in the cap. The handle (not shown) is ever-so-convenient when you tilt the jug side-up to pour the seeds in through the holes.

Some writers recommend putting in little perches just below the holes. The birds will alight on the perches, but don't really need them because most go right inside. Viewers and photographers will appreciate perches because the birds, while on them, are in full view. If the holes are about 7 or 8 cm wide by 8 or 9 high (2.5 by

3 in), small birds have no difficulty getting in. I wasn't surprised to see that the acrobatic chickadees took only a pass or two to master the small hole and slippery plastic rim. With a bit more practice they could fly right in. What *did* surprise me was that Purple Finches, and nuthatches, redpolls, and goldfinches also quickly mastered the trick. You can afford them a better grip by sticking adhesive or hockey tape along the rim.

My squirrels, of course, quickly got into the act by sliding down the string. To satisfy their gnawing urge for improvements they enlarged my neat little doors to gaping, ragged holes, chewed away the clever little flaps and cut the string holding them up. Then somebody learned to cut the main cord and collect the seeds on the ground. When I substituted a length of wire, they cut the branch. A neighbour foiled the slide-down-the-string trick by putting an old twelve-inch LP on a stop knot a few inches above the cap of the bottle. I haven't applied this since replacement bottles are so cheap and easy to make, and I'm just not ready yet to hang my old Beatles classics out to warp.

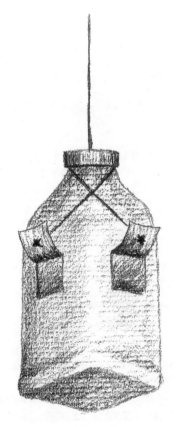

This square plastic jug holds plenty of seeds and is partially rainproof.

Thistle Feeders

There are a number of commercial hanging feeders that are basically a cylinder with a number of small feeding ports in the side. Inside baffles over each one allow the birds to pick out seeds but control flow. The birds don't go inside, and since the slippery plastic sides don't allow them to cling, there are little perches below each hole. The cap at the top functions as both a roof and filler hole. Some of them come in sets of tubes, like an oversized pan pipe, joined with three or four long wooden dowels that serve as perches. With a good crowd on hand there will often be a bird on every perch, a beguilingly busy sight indeed.

As a group, these are often referred to as "thistle" feeders because that's the feed they are often used for. Thistle, or "niger" seed is much prized by some birds but too expensive for the average station operator to shovel out in bulk on a come-one-come-all basis. Since the small, smooth seeds dispense well in tube feeders, and can be extracted only one or two at a time from each hole, feed and feeder are a nice combination for the person wanting to cater to the smaller birds on a somewhat selective basis. While the heavy eaters like Evening Grosbeaks, Steller's Jays, and

The pop-bottle feeder, a free-swinging favourite with smaller birds.

Purple Finches are elbowing each other over the low-budget fodder at the communal table or shelf, the siskins and goldfinches are on the perches, daintily extracting the costly imported seeds from their little portholes.

Canary seed and millet work equally well in these tube feeders. Depending on the length and diameter of the cylinder, they can hold quite a lot of seed and don't need constant filling. The top ports run out first, of course, but the feeder isn't empty until the lowest one is exhausted. Almost all the commercial varieties are clear plastic, so the level of seeds can be easily seen.

Keep in mind that squirrels, if they can reach hanging feeders (and in all but rare situations they can) won't be content with licking up little seeds one at a time through the dinky little holes. If the material is gnawable, and the ports aren't reinforced with metal, they'll chew holes in it to suit themselves and ruin a feeder that is expensive to buy or time-consuming to make. Retrofitting holes with metal is a fussy and awkward bit of frustration.

Laying on an easily accessible alternate supply of seeds is the simplest way of trying to beguile squirrels into leaving the hanging feeders alone. But if you have no faith in this ploy, make your thistle feeders out of galvanized drainpipes. In one important respect they are much easier to make, since the baffles and the holes can be made by cutting horizontal slits with a hacksaw in the side of the cylinder and pushing the top flaps inward.

If you're looking for the ultimate in quick and cheap thistle-style feeders, the plastic container comes to the rescue again. This time it's pop bottles; any size will suffice, but the 1-litre size is best. Make a one-port feeder by slicing a 5-cm (2-in) cut through the side of the bottle along the ridge just above the bottom. If you push in the wall of the bottle above the cut it will pop back out again. You can make it stay in by pinching the plastic between thumb and finger at each corner just above the cut, making permanent creases. The material is more workable if you warm it under the hot-water tap. Punch or burn a hole through the cap, run a piece of string through with a stop-knot, and . . . Voila!, a neat hanging feeder.

For birds new to this clever device, just fill it and set it on the ground or feeder shelf until they discover it, then hang it up. A strip of fabric tape stuck to the lip of the port gives the birds a bit better grip. I'm quite happy with the one-hole model, but you can make a multi-port feeder by slicing more holes, as in the accompanying diagram. Your fertile imagination has no doubt already conceived the idea of cutting off the top of another pop bottle to use as a custom-sized filler funnel.

This type of feeder is the ultimate in free-swinging, gyrating instability, even in a light breeze. It's enlightening to see how quickly the birds perfect an offhand precision at grabbing the moving lip. Many authors of bird-feeding books assure their readers that such an unstable feeder is not to the liking of House Sparrows. My sparrows might not *like* them, but they damn well enjoyed the challenge of getting their docking technique down pat, lining up to take turns! This is my only explanation, because the same black sunflower seed was more easily available at nearby pole and shelf feeders.

Suet Dispensers

Suet can be left in chunks on a table or shelf. The basic law of supply and demand may impose itself, however; if there are gulls, crows, ravens, or raccoons around, your place could become a bulk station supplying suet for miles around. In the interests of economy and of fair sharing, you're better to put your suet into a dispenser that limits withdrawals and is securely out of reach.

What could be handier and cheaper than the plastic net bags that onions or peanuts are sold in? The chunks of suet are tucked in, the neck tied to a hank of cord, and the lot looped onto a tree branch or a hook on some overhead structure where the birds, but not roving mutts, can reach it. The birds that love suet—all the woodpeckers, chickadees, nuthatches, and jays and their relatives—have no trouble clinging to the bag while they peck fragments of suet from between the strands of netting.

The netting is strong enough to prevent the jays from chopping off big chunks and carting it off wholesale, which they'll do if given the chance. As the suet is eaten, the bag collapses around it and the remnants remain available until there's nothing left but strands of stringy tissue.

Occasionally one hears people worry that birds can entangle their claws in the netting and die struggling to free themselves. None of my contacts, nor my own experience, backs this up, but there is a verified account of kinglets having become entangled in broken and frayed netting. Replacing bags before they become tattered would therefore minimize this problem.

One shortcoming of the onion bag is that there is a limit to the amount of bulk you can cram into it. Another is that if you have crows, ravens, or magpies to contend with, they'll rip it apart and clean you out in no time. In that case, the answer is wire mesh or coarse screen. As with most classes of feeders, you can buy

commercial suet cages, generally made of wire, often coated with latex.

If you wish to make your own, the material that I have found most useful is hardware cloth with either 6-mm (1/4-in) or 12-mm (1/2-in) mesh. Respectively, it's called "4 by 4″ and "2 by 2″ in the trade, which means four squares or two squares per inch. In spite of the name, the "cloth" is actually made of good stiff wire soldered together, rather than woven. It can be bought off a roll at some building or hardware supply retailers; you might have to phone around to find it.

Match Size to Demand

With a pair of tinsnips you can cut your hardware cloth to conform to an imaginative array of dispensers. Size depends on the anticipated use. In the city, I feed at most only 1 or 2 kg (2 to 4 lb) of suet during most winters, but in the country that amount would last only a few days.

This Red-breasted Nuthatch appreciates the simplest of suet feeders, a net onion bag.

In town, therefore, I have a neat little cage that measures about 15 cm (6 in) square by 8 cm (3 in) deep. It is "2 by 2″ mesh on four sides. Only the back, a solid 30-cm (1-ft) board 2.5 x 15 cm (1 x 6 in) and the lid are made of wood. It can be tacked to a wall, tree trunk, or post. Whether it's the solid feel of the cage, or the bigger mesh, the woodpeckers, nuthatches, and jays prefer the cage to the hanging onion bag. Chickadees don't seem to care.

In the country I have built a much larger feeder based on a one-metre (3-ft) slab of 5 x 15 cm (2 x 6 in) plank. The screen is cut to form a semicircular cage against the wood, large at the top, narrowing down to a very close fit at the bottom, like a very long, narrow funnel. This is to give the birds continued access to the suet. As they peck it away it tends to slide down into the constricted bottom of the cage where they can still reach it through the mesh.

A wire cage suet feeder keeps crows and ravens from taking everything.

This feeder holds about 4 kg (9 lb) of suet which is gone in two weeks thanks to the magpies, a family of Blue Jays, a large clan of chickadees, several Hairy and Downy Woodpeckers, and at least one pair of White-breasted Nuthatches. I can't use onion bags any more because the magpies tear them apart, a task that the Northwestern Crow would be pleased to

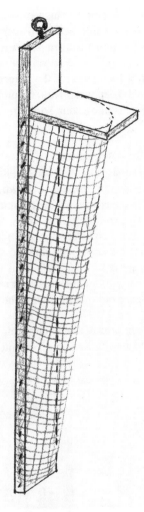

This metre-long suet holder ensures a supply over long periods of time.

This suet feeder is virtually crow-proof.

take over, I'm sure, along coastal British Columbia.

The next time the handyman urge comes over me, I plan a box or tube suet feeder with access through wire mesh only at the bottom. This will be no inconvenience to the woodpeckers, nuthatches, and chickadees, since they are just as happy clinging upside-down as rightside-up when they eat. But it will put a crimp in the Blue Jays' access, and (I hope) shut out the magpies entirely.

If you want to coat wire, I have already referred to liquid latex in the previous chapter under the "Suet" subhead. It comes in ordinary and aerosol cans, and makes snaggly wire, or any metal, more comfortable to handle in cold weather. But as a safety factor for birds it is unnecessary in my view. Northern birds have to deal with superchilled ice in various forms, which will also do an instant freeze-on if touched with something damp.

Hoppers

It is probably to our chicken-raising forebears that we owe the invention of the "self-feeder." This is merely a storage bin mounted over a trough, with a slot at the bottom constructed to let feed trickle out only as fast as it is eaten. The store of feed saves the tedious bother of having to attend the livestock every feeding time. The covered hopper protects the reserve of feed from the weather and from being wasted by the animals themselves. Clever, those ancestors!

The hopper does the same for wild bird feeding as for poultry husbandry, ensuring a continuing supply of feed until the hopper is empty. This handy feature guarantees the birds an unfailing supply of seeds if you can't feed them every day.

Most commercially built feeders, and the plans for homemade ones, incorporate a hopper of some kind. Most will give the capacity of the hopper in volume. Given a choice between two models with similar features, I tend to pick the bigger. In a rainy climate, look for roofs with a generous eave to keep water from seeping into the hopper bottom, plugging it and turning the contents into a sour, sprouting mess.

Buckets and Bottles

The simplest hopper, one that can be used in combination with a table or good-sized shelf, is merely a container filled with seeds and inverted. A bottle can be attached (tape, string, screws) firmly to a wooden upright, upside down, with the neck just clear enough of the feeder floor so the seeds will dribble out and then stop until some are cleared away. For a large bucket, arrange boards on the feeder floor in a circle the same size as the rim, but leave gaps between them as feeding ports. With practice you can learn to plop the full bucket upside down over the boards without spilling too much. Metal buckets are best if squirrels have access to the feeder. And it's a good idea to put a rock or weight on the container to hold it in place when the contents run low and no longer hold it firm against the wind or pushy raccoons.

The size of the container can vary according to the area of the feeder; a big table could take a 20-litre (4.4 gal) bucket, a small shelf a two-litre (1.75 quart) juice can or plastic pop bottle.

For filling bottles and other small-port receptacles you can buy funnels with a

A simple hopper made from a bottle keeps a continuous supply of seeds on this window shelf feeder.

gizmo that closes off the spout until you've stuck it into the hole. Whether you buy one, or improvise a funnel from a plastic jug, it is most important to avoid the curse of the itty-bitty filler hole when either buying or building feeders. Not all designers are aware of the joys of playing thread-the-needle with a can, a funnel, and an awkward filler hole in a whistling gale, with rain or snow, in the dark.

The Basic Bin

The standard hopper bin is a "V" shape, with the sides tapering in to the run-out slot at the bottom. This ensures that even the last of the seeds are within reach as the supply runs out. The roof, or part of it, comes off or is fitted with a hinge for filling. Whatever the arrangement, the roof must be waterproof and extend out far enough to provide shelter for the feeding tray at the bottom. If water or melting snow accumulates on the tray it will saturate the seeds in the slot, soaking upward into the bin. If the water itself doesn't block the flow of seeds, cold weather certainly will, turning the wet into a frozen mass. Mild weather promotes sprouting and mould, an even messier problem.

A bin like this can be retrofitted to an existing feeder. If you have a big table or shelf catering to a great many birds, a large hopper is a labour-saving feature that also keeps feed on the table if you have to be absent for a spell.

A final word about squirrels. If they're going to be feeding from any hopper, the edges of the run-out hole or slot should be tooth-proofed. In a homemade bin, you can floor the tray with sheet metal—a tin can will supply the necessary raw material if nothing else is at hand—and the upper lip of the slot should be similarly clad.

Roofs

I'm an advocate of roofs. In wet weather they give birds a place to dry off and feed. They save work and waste; clearing a shelf or table of snow means work, and seeds are wasted in the process. Furthermore, rain-soaked seeds are not as palatable as nice dry ones. A roof can also be a decorative addition; shingles, shakes, thatch, and other novel materials have been used to add that quaint touch.

Almost all small birds have problems dealing with even a couple of centimetres of snow over top of seeds; burrowing simply isn't part of their evolved behaviour patterns. If someone doesn't sweep the snow off and uncover the seeds, they will perch and peer in expectant befuddlement, not realizing that food is right beneath their feet. Jays are good at digging, redpolls poke little holes in the snow, and Song and Fox Sparrows scratch their way down. But the best burrowers are the squirrels. They'll dig in and scatter enough seeds around to see everyone else through until you can clear the deck properly. All this becomes academic, of course, with a good roof overhead.

Recalling that birds are rather claustrophobic creatures, don't set the roof too low. For adequate weather protection a high roof therefore needs lots of overhang.

Maintenance Kit

Some time ago I installed a permanent shade over my study window. It serves as a passive solar control in summer when the sun is high, and in winter keeps the snow off the feeder shelf—sort of. A gusty flurry will cover the shelf with a couple of inches of fluff, so I have to sweep it off. Being cheap, I hate to whisk the sunflower seeds onto the ground with the snow where they will probably spoil before even the resident chipmunk finds them first thing in spring. Therefore, as well as a stiff-bristled little hand brush for whisking off the feeder, and a putty knife for chipping away crusty snow, droppings, and occasional frozen squirrel urine (I quickly learned to keep my mouth closed as I hacked away), I have a screen sieve, the largest I could find.

All three hang in a neat row on the outside wall, beside the feeder. Come a snow problem, I mount my stubby ladder (remember it?), sweep the snow and the seeds off the feeder through the open corners (remember them?), and into the waiting sieve. With a bit of vigorous shaking and winnowing, the snow and smaller fragments are gone, and the seeds are replaced on the feeder. Voila!

I repeat the process until the snow is all sifted away and the seeds replaced on their clean shelf. Then I hang my tools back up in their neat row and retire, enormously satisfied that this little ritual would be the best-organized part of my daily routine, if I had one.

Feeders crowded with birds for months on end could be a source of communicable infection among them. This would be more likely in a mild climate with damp winters, much less likely in a severe climate where winter would keep everything, including any pathogens, deep-frozen.

Disinfecting feeder ports, shelves, perches, baths, and any surfaces that birds regularly come in contact with will help reduce the spread of disease. A tablespoon of chlorine bleach in a litre of water makes an effective, inexpensive disinfectant solution—the more thoroughly and regularly applied the better.

This is also a good solution for disinfecting hummingbird feeders. Yeasts and bacteria thrive mightily in the warm sugar solutions. Without a thorough cleaning between refills the residue from the old solution acts like a bread starter to get a new population of fermenters going in the new one.

Shelters

A shelter, as meant here, is basically a winter birdhouse, except that it isn't used for nesting. Many of our birds, notably chickadees, nuthatches, woodpeckers, House Sparrows, and starlings use cavities of one sort or another for both nesting and as nighttime roosts. These are so important that some tree-hole nesters that do not excavate their own remain paired over the winter in order to defend property rights to a territory that has the all-important, second-hand nesting/roosting hole.

Every winter I am told by puzzled bird feeders that they began putting out feed early, attracted a nice clientele of chickadees, nuthatches, and sparrows, but that with the first onset of cold weather or snow, the chickadees vanished. I have no pat answers, but I speculate that there might have been no suitable winter quarters close at hand, and the chickadees moved to another feeder that had a den tree close by.

If this notion is true, then it might be worthwhile to provide an artificial tree hole in the form of a box or a length of hollow tree trunk. Chickadees excavate their own holes, pecking the soft, punky wood from decayed branch sockets in dead or aging trees. Nuthatches may either do this or take over a vacated woodpecker hole. I have even had a Downy Woodpecker, a bird quite able to excavate a tree cavity, take up winter quarters in a bluebird house.

It is important that a shelter like this be on the side of the tree away from the prevailing winds.

If you already have bluebird houses at hand, shelters can be made quickly by taking the fronts off and tacking them on again with the holes at the bottom. This helps retain heat better. It would be helpful to put in several pegs or some twigs for roosts, and to plug all holes and cracks other than the entrance. They should then be set up in trees, preferably conifers, dense hedges, or in some other natural shelter from the wind.

Since chickadees really feel better about clearing out their own quarters, fill a birdhouse with wood chips or shavings (not sawdust) that they can empty out.

Lacking a store of birdhouses, you can of course go to work and construct custom-made shelters. I refer you to the Appendix for specifics.

CHAPTER FOUR

Enjoying Your Birds

Assuming you've set up your feeders, have a good stock of seeds and suet securely laid by, and the birds are starting to pay regular calls, there are a few things you can do to enhance your pleasure and increase your knowledge.

Field Guides and References

Obviously, it is very useful to have one of the major field guides at hand. The colour illustrations are a very helpful supplement to this book, and the six to seven hundred listings from all over North America will be most useful in identifying summer birds or unusual winter strays. With each species writeup in Chapter 7, I have listed the page in each of the four major field guides where that bird is found. All refer to the most recent editions, as of 1992.

In addition to the field guides I have included page references in Godfrey's *The Birds of Canada*, revised edition, (1986). It is, of course, not a field guide, being anything but compact with 595 pages, 22 cm by 30 cm (8.5 in x 11.75 in) in size, and it costs considerably more than a guide. But for most serious Canadian birders their "Godfrey" is *the* reference.

The Birds of British Columbia is an exhaustively detailed inventory of bird occurrence and breeding distribution throughout the province. The first two volumes, as of 1992, are out. And although the price for the full four-volume set (due for completion in 1994) will tend to weed out the triflers, this up-to-date work merits consideration by serious birders anywhere in western Canada, and demands space in the libraries of those in British Columbia. The large-format pages—22.5 cm x 30.5 (9 in x 12 in)—allow ample space for full-page distribution maps, black-and-white photographs, and graphs and charts, all adding detail and interest to this attractive set. Each species account is accorded at least two pages, some as many as six.

Beginning birders can learn much from this work, but should keep in mind that it is primarily an inventory of occurrence and observed breeding activity, and doesn't discuss birds' natural history and behaviour beyond those aspects necessary to clarify reasons for their occurrence, or in some cases, their disappearance. Of particular interest in each volume is the summary of all Christmas Bird Count results, listed species-by-species, over the twenty-eight years from 1957 to 1984 inclusive.

Birds of the Okanagan Valley (1987) is another excellent reference book for British Columbia birders, especially those living in, or planning a visit to, the

Okanagan. It is the product of the Cannings family's lifelong dedication to nature, written by three brothers—Robert, Richard, and Sydney. Graphs and tables augment text that is obviously crafted with scholarly care, but is lively enough to furnish nonscholars with an absorbing browse.

Software and Oldware

Computer-owning birders wishing to keep in step with the Space Age can shop around for a range of birding software that stores, cross-references, retrieves, and transmits their accumulated observations with dazzling speed. For some, the humble notebook and pencil are almost relics of the past, replaced by electronic "notebooks" in which data can be entered afield. In the right hands they are powerful tools for enriching one's knowledge base. In certain others the gadgetry takes over and the birding becomes a way of keeping a new toy in play.

The mindset that goes with computer technology and the information explosion fosters the attitude that any reference published before 1980 isn't worth space on the shelf. In my view such an assumption robs one of the opportunity to acquire knowledge, and along with it the chance to gain an historical perspective on the traditions of bird watching. Nature study, birding, and bird feeding have their own well-established body of literature, much of it written by talented amateurs whose dedication and scholarship have added enormously to our understanding of the life sciences.

The suggestion follows that the Compleat Birder should pop into a good used-book shop on the way to the computer centre. For example, P.A. Taverner's *Birds of Canada*, published in 1934, or the preceding books *Birds of Eastern Canada* (1919) and *Birds of Western Canada* (1926), are well worth having. Taverner, and others of his time, mixed scientific fact with lyric prose; some of them unashamedly rhapsodized. Today, however, even in popular publications, writers anxious to be taken seriously grind out copy purged of any taint of fervour. Dulled as we are by such dry fare, old-style writers seem at first to be grandiloquent, emotional, even pompous. But placed in the right perspective, the lyric style of the best of them is a refreshing antidote to the sterile research-paper prose of many of today's writers.

Binoculars

To casual observers, songbirds may be pleasant to the ear. But most of the singers themselves are too elusive, too small or too well concealed to be worth the bother of looking for.

But clap a set of binoculars on them, and suddenly they're at breathtaking arm's length. The diminutive warblers are a particular delight, each species with its distinctive colours and patterns, some of them tropically beautiful. The immediate response, particularly from children, is "Wow!" It's easy to get hooked.

The pleasure of having feeders in your yard can be enormously enhanced with binoculars. But what kind to buy? What's wrong with Grandpa's old set of World War II field glasses? The answer is, nothing—until you compare them with modern, lightweight models. Until after World War II, field glasses of the sort the average person could afford were bulky, heavy, and optically low-performance. Birders of

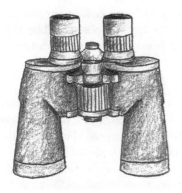

Large or small, good binoculars are very important for the thorough appreciation of birds.

earlier generations used opera glasses—handier, but from samples I have seen, of toy-shop optical quality.

Today's binoculars are sophisticated, lightweight, versatile optical instruments. Without them birding could not have grown to the level of popularity it enjoys today. They are as essential as the trusted field guide.

Power

The capacity of binoculars is indicated by a formula, "7 x 35" for example, in this case referred to as "seven-power." The "7" indicates the degree of magnification; an object will appear to be six to seven times closer than with the unaided eye. The "35" indicates the diameter in millimetres of the objective lenses, the big ones on the front end of the tubes.

At one time the 7 x 35 was the birder's standard. It is still very popular, and for most of us is the size with which others are compared; that is, the further you get from 7 x 35, the more you depart from "normal."

It's easy to depart from "normal" these days. The vast popularity of birding has turned the binocular market into a designers' free-for-all; the competitors woo customers with an array of choices that bedazzle the first-time buyer. There are lightweight, compact, armoured, and waterproof models, poro and roof prism designs, and a host of other features.

Magnification is of course important, but it isn't everything. Quality, and resulting clarity, must be considered; you will see far better with good seven-power binoculars than with poor ten-power. In binoculars, power range begins at 6x and ends at 10x—anything lower is rather unexciting, anything higher is extremely difficult to hold steadily enough to be useful. Even your heartbeat registers as a rhythmic shake with high-power, hand-held scopes. Prices range from $50.00 to well over $1,000.00.

In 1991 Carl Zeiss Optics abruptly rendered the foregoing obsolete for those to whom cost is no obstacle. In that year the company introduced to the European market 20 x 60 binoculars. A built-in stabilization system, activated with the touch of a button, eliminates most of the shakes. They are large—26 cm (10 in) long, 15 cm (6 in) wide, and weigh about 1.7 kg (3.5 lb). The "suggested retail" price of

$4,725 U.S.—about $5,481 Canadian plus GST—could be justified to some degree if owning a pair meant you wouldn't need to buy a spotting scope and tripod. As of 1992 these "super-binoculars" were available on the North American market.

Go for Quality

How to know good quality? Try them! Step out of the shop with a couple of sets. Focus down the street on signs and licence plates. You should be able to see at least as clearly through binoculars as you can without them in good light conditions. If you can't they're either poor quality or not focussed correctly. Is the image clear right to the edges? Are there streaks of stray light or flashes inside the image that are bothersome? Are elements of the image edged with borders of colour (the sign of really cheap optics)? How wide is the field of view?

It is important that binoculars *feel* right. How heavy are they? Do they fit your eyes comfortably? Is the focussing mechanism stiff, or is it so loose the binoculars will be turned off-focus with every nudge?

You may run into the term "exit pupil." This is a number obtained by dividing the objective lens diameter by the magnification. The larger the objective lens, the more light it gathers. Thus, you'll see better under dim light with 7 x 50s, exit pupil seven-plus, than with equal quality 7 x 35s, exit pupil five.

"Eye relief" is something you should pay attention to if you wear glasses. It describes the distance between the eyepiece (ocular) lens and your eyeball, the point where you get a full view. If you hold binoculars several inches away from your eyes, you see two tiny spots in the centre of each ocular lens. As you bring the glass closer, the spots increase until the image fills the lens, or the eyepieces bump your glasses and you're still looking through a peephole. Eye relief is a fixed function of the design of binoculars—it can't be adjusted. It ranges from 5 to 16 mm (1/4 to 5/8 in), with most falling between 10 and 14 mm (3/8 to 1/2 in). Some makes with relatively long eye relief have rubber eye cups that fold back, allowing you to use glasses.

In some very bright conditions—snow, sand, water—*not* having the eyepiece pushed close to your eyes lets a distracting amount of stray light into the space. A bit of practice at covering the gap between your eyebrows and the eyepieces may be necessary for comfortable use in bright sun.

The adjustment range of most binoculars compensates for quite a range of short- and long-sightedness. Since the focussing mechanism moves both barrels simultaneously, one eyepiece (usually the right) can be independently adjusted to allow for differences between your eyes. When you buy binoculars get the shop owner to show you how to "balance" them.

If it's too late for that and you must balance your binoculars yourself, go outdoors and select a distant object—a dead tree, power line tower, or high-rise building with good, sharp lines to focus on. Shut the right eye and, using the central focussing wheel, focus the left until you have the sharpest possible image of your distant object. Then shut the left eye, and focus the right on the same object using *only* the eyepiece focussing ring. Once you can see the distant object as clearly with the right as with the left, your binoculars are balanced and you will get equal sharpness at all distances.

When you've done your "balancing act," it's a good idea to note the position of the focussing ring on the "plus" and "minus" scale on the right eyepiece so that you can quickly reset it if it is nudged off-focus, or if a friend has a look and fiddles with the adjustments.

We associate binoculars with distance, hence "near focus" is usually ignored by beginning shoppers. But if you are buying binoculars in part at least for through-the-window viewing of feeders, a set that won't focus down to 3 metres (10 ft) will be useless some of the time. Try for the shortest focus you can get; 2 metres (6 ft) is great. These binoculars will come in handy for museums, art galleries, conservatories, and other exhibits where close-up study, or reading labels, may be otherwise impossible. As an item of interest, the near focus distance of the Zeiss 20-power binoculars discussed above is 15 metres.

A final word—on "zoom." Zoom is the ability to change magnification and is useful on cameras. On binoculars, cheap zoom is bad news. The question is whether the expense of good quality adds proportionally to operating usefulness. Zoom makes it easier for the beginner to pick up a difficult object, such as a flying bird, which you can then zoom in on. With practice you learn to pick up moving objects proficiently, and zoom becomes a little-used feature.

Spotting Scopes

In any well-used birding spot you'll see people with spotting scopes mounted on tripods. These are the trademark of the serious birder. They are essential for work on shorebirds, waterfowl, and hawks, where distant flocks or individuals can't be approached closely enough to be accurately identified with even the best of binoculars. The tripods are no affectation; at powers ranging from 20x to 60x, scopes can be used only on a very secure base. A good scope is a significant investment, one that should be made only after it has become evident that birding is, for you, a serious pastime.

Window Management

The charm of a window feeder—the closeness of the birds—can turn into its chief disadvantage under some circumstances. If there is a lot of activity inside the room, the birds may be constantly startled away. Some species are more flighty than others, and some individuals seem to quickly grow accustomed to the activity inside and ignore it altogether.

If there are drapes or venetian blinds on the window, leaving them closed, or partially so, for the first few days that a feeder is in use, and then gradually opening them, will enable the birds to get used to the sight of movement inside. It helps, as you move about or draw closer for a better look, if you are wearing neutral or dark clothing.

For my own feeder window in the city I installed a temporary curtain of dark netting across the lower half. White netting is difficult to see through, especially with the sun shining on it. Unless you enjoy the paramilitary association of camouflage netting, it is only slightly better than white. Black is best. It obstructs the birds' view of the room, which is relatively darker than the outdoors, and allows you a somewhat hazy view of them. For pictures from concealment, I have cut several strategically placed vertical slits in the netting big enough to poke the camera lens through.

Solar Films

A partially mirrored or tinted effect can be added to window glass with a thin sheet of reflective or tinting mylar film, the same stuff used for office building and vehicle windows. Accordingly, it is available from glass specialty dealers or auto accessory shops. In the event that you're willing to follow directions, it can be applied by the do-it-yourself method. It goes on the inside.

You should be aware that the silvered variety, which imparts a semimirrored effect, could precipitate window collisions in some locations. Try it, and if this is a problem, see the section on "Window Pain," Chapter 5. The only reaction from my birds that a newly installed film prompted was in a chickadee that challenged its own reflection a few times before dismissing it as no threat. Other than this minor reaction, there have been no complications, and I find that during full daylight, with my study lights on, I can move about on my side of the window without alarming those on the other side.

Both the tint and mirroring will cut down on the amount of light passing through the glass, and the tint will slightly affect the colour values of photos taken through it. There is also some loss of clarity, but this is not a critical handicap for the super-close-ups you can get with good telephoto lenses and the proximity of your subjects at window feeders.

Frost and Ice

In regions of British Columbia where winters are cold, frost on the inside of the glass can be a problem, particularly in kitchens or rooms close to the bathroom. Scraping at frost or wiping away vapour is a waste of time and frightens the birds.

One alternative is a fan. It can be quite small, and it needn't be a heater; all it has to do is move enough warm room air past the glass and the frost will disappear very rapidly. On severely cold days it will begin to re-form soon after you turn the fan off. At full speed the whirling blades are invisible to the birds, but if you turn the fan off so you won't stick your elbow into it while preoccupied with a camera, remember that in the last couple of revolutions the flash of the slowing blades will scare your subjects. My fan has pliable plastic blades that won't harm straying fingers—or elbows.

Photography

Taking pictures—prints, slides, or videos—of the birds at a feeder can be an absorbing way of recording their presence and behaviour and of sharing your interests with others. Behind your window, you can set your camera on a tripod, prefocus it on the feeder, and leave it there, ready for action. You enjoy shirt-sleeve comfort no matter how rough conditions are outside.

I won't go into detail over what to buy and how to use it since photography, although it can be a fascinating adjunct, is not one of bird watching's essentials.

The Notebook

If I were asked to recommend a gift of something essential to a young naturalist it would not be a camera, computer program, or set of binoculars. It would be a pencil and notepad.

Strange as it may seem, in this age when technology seems to need no justification other than to keep advancing, the most valuable aid to the nature watcher is the humble notebook. Keeping daily notes of weather, species, numbers, behaviour, and anything else of interest gives you an accurate and balanced record of your observations.

I say "balanced" because, if you trust to memory alone, you forget routine details and remember only the unusual or the dramatic. This explains why anecdotal evidence is treated with such scepticism by scientists, and why folklore is full of bizarre and misleading notions of animal behaviour. If everyone kept notes and glanced back through them from time to time, to restore the balance of recall between normal and unusual events, our natural history folklore would be much richer, better balanced, and more reliable.

As time goes by, the possessor of a growing pile of notebooks finds the ones on the bottom becoming increasingly valuable. They give you a look back into the history of your observations, and of your life. What was the weather like this time last year? Ten years ago? Was it in 1976 or 1977 that all those Varied Thrushes descended? When did they arrive, when did they depart?

Without notes, a lifetime of observations by even the most gifted observers is buried when they die. Those of the organized observer have a chance of making a permanent contribution to the body of knowledge that we call "science."

Next to sharp eyes and keen ears, the humble notebook is the naturalist's most important aid.

CHAPTER FIVE

The Down-Side

Idealism and harsh reality come face to face over our feeders. If the creatures that were expected to be cute and entertaining turn out to be inconvenient nuisances, idealism might not stand the test. When this happens, the erstwhile idealists may abruptly withdraw the charity the animals have come to rely on, or even turn on them as enemies. Either way the animals lose. The point of this is that anyone who deliberately elects to live close to wild animals owes it to them to know what to expect, and to prepare for it. Forewarned is forearmed.

"Animals," by the way, includes birds. When people refer to "birds and animals" they usually mean "birds and mammals."

This chapter deals with some of the obligations, and the precautions, and what to do if the safeguards fail. Some subjects are highly emotional. Cats, for example, are beloved pets, but are thoroughly hated by some folks because they eat birds and bury revolting things in the children's sandbox. And what should be done if you're faced with a sick or injured animal, or one that is plainly intolerable?

I'm not suggesting that "problem" animals are uniquely a bird feeders' headache. People who wouldn't dream of throwing a seed to a bird still have to confront raccoons, squirrels, rats, and cats. But those of us who feed birds adopt a special relationship to wildlife and in good conscience must deal with animal problems humanely and with the animals' interests in mind as well as our own. I therefore felt that readers would appreciate a discussion that emphasized prevention, but didn't mince words when it came to discussing cures.

No-limit Demands

One down-side of feeding arises from the fact that all animals, the desirable and the not-so-desirable, are programmed to survive by taking maximum advantage of resources whenever and wherever they find them. Therefore, they have no built-in limits to their demands on your hospitality, a trait we humans interpret as plain greed.

Not that this isn't an easily managed appetite. The demands of the vast majority of species can be met simply by ensuring that there is a continuing supply of the right kinds of feed, accessible in the right places. No matter how insatiable their appetites, a half dozen juncos, a sparrow or two, and a family of chickadees are not going to strain your patience or your budget. Their presence is not likely to be anything but a pleasure, their goings-on an amusing diversion.

That state of tranquil stability can change quickly if you are abruptly blessed with a big flock of Evening Grosbeaks, Purple Finches, Pine Siskins, or all of the above. These happy wanderers have big appetites and love to assault your feeders in noisy bunches. If you have one small feeder and elect to leave it at that, these cheerful birds will take their business to someone who has a bigger table. However, from time to time a few may drop in as they do the rounds of the neighbourhood.

But if you want to keep these avian gourmands for yourself, you had better be ready to serve up a lot of seeds. And be prepared to diversify as you expand; along with the new big table and shelves, you should put up several hanging feeders to give your faithful little chickadees and juncos a chance if they are crowded off the main feeder by the jostling finches.

What you'll have is more of everything; more feeders to fill and keep clear of snow and droppings, more window washing if you have a window shelf, more cats, and more seed husks to clean up in spring. None of this is a problem if you feel you're still in control and that the rewards of having more birds to entertain you more than offset the extra effort.

Bird Problems

Window Pain

A problem that leaves many bird lovers heartsore is birds colliding with their windows. Their concern is amply justified. In the 1989-1990 feeding season, Project FeederWatch asked its participants to tally window kills at their feeders. Nine hundred and forty-five deaths were recorded by those who responded. From this very small, preliminary sampling, an estimate of 95 million annual bird fatalities in North America was made.

This distressing figure is backed up by the studies of Daniel Klem of Muhlenberg College in Pennsylvania. Alarmed at both the extent of the carnage, and the indifference of the birding establishment to the problem, he began in the mid-1970s to conduct surveys and tests to quantify the damage and to make window kills a public conservation issue. Klem's current (1991) estimate of 98 million kills per year is based on the number of housing units, commercial complexes, and public institutions in the United States and Canada, assuming an average kill of one bird per year per unit. However, since this is based on only one building per company or school, when in fact most consist of more than one, and many office buildings are sheathed in glass, he suggests that his estimate may be ten times too low. This pushes the total per year to a possible 980 million kills.

There are several factors that cause window collisions.

If birds can see through the house, as they will if a corner has large, adjacent windows, they may attempt to fly through. Closing one set of drapes will correct this situation. But the main cause of collisions is due to mirror effect; birds see their world reflected in the glass and attempt to fly into it. The more birds there are and the closer the feed source is to the window, the more strikes there are likely to be. An exception to this is small feeders that actually attach to the glass; they accommodate very small numbers of birds at any one time, and the feeder itself breaks the reflecting surface. The most violent hits occur when birds are startled, or are fleeing a predator, a larger feeder bird, or an aggressor of their own kind.

Some windows, even large ones, rarely cause collisions. Others, even small ones, are real killers. If you have one of these, and feed birds, you are conscience-bound to do immediately what you can to minimize the casualties. The hastiest fix is to cut the reflecting effect of the glass by smearing or spraying the outside of it with something, such as soap, to create a visible film. This may look messy, but can be quickly hosed off when you've devised something more satisfactory.

Paper Hawks

Among the touted correctives are silhouettes or cutouts of birds of prey that can be mounted on the glass. I have never tried these; some who have say they work, others say they are useless. Remember that if you put a black silhouette of a hawk on a window with a darkened room behind it, the "hawk" will be almost invisible. Try a white one. I have also heard that sticking a round piece of bright red paper in the middle of the window will work. If one doesn't, maybe a scattering of them will. Whatever you do, apply these warnings or deterrents to the *outside* surface; anything on the inside will lose most of its effect.

This falcon silhouette might help prevent window hits.

The only sure method is to put some kind of obstruction between the birds and the glass. Nylon or twine fish net, or the kind gardeners use to cover fruit trees, stretched over the outside will do; beware of nets so small-meshed and fine that birds might entangle themselves. A friend made a variation of this by attaching boards along the bottom and top of a problem window. In each, spaced about 5 cm (2 in) apart, were small nails. She strung grocery string back and forth between the boards, creating vertical lines, like the strings of a harp, over the entire window. This stopped the birds and was only a minor intrusion on her view.

Rescue and Recovery

Contrary to the prevailing assumption, birds that kill themselves against windows do not die of broken necks. Severe concussion, of the sort humans sustain in vehicle crashes, is the cause of death. Birds that stun themselves against a window should be picked up right away; cats are very quick to connect the thump of a bird on glass with an easy grab. Put the bird into a small box or paper bag, closed but with provision for air. Put it in a quiet place, outdoors if it isn't too cold, indoors in a cool spot if it is. Don't be hasty to pronounce a victim dead; some will revive after several hours in trauma. If you hear it scrabbling about, leave the box closed, take it outside, and give the convalescent a chance to fly. If nightfall comes while the bird is recovering, leave it alone until morning, then liberate it.

If you do end up with a dead bird on your hands, don't just chuck it into the garbage. Museums, universities, provincial and federal wildlife agencies, wildlife artists, and some serious birders maintain collections and appreciate getting specimens. Wrap the bird in a plastic bag and put it into the freezer, labelled with the date of death, the location, and your name. If you don't have a connection start checking around for someone who accepts animal specimens.

Injured birds unable to fly after a decent period of recovery might be nursed back to health if they can be persuaded to eat. Fruit- and seed-eaters are easy to provide for; a generous cage, food, water, and patience could have the desired effect.

Woodpeckers

Now and then woodpeckers drill holes in a building or hammer on parts of it at dawn, for reasons that may baffle and annoy the owner. The most frequent drummers are Downy and Hairy Woodpeckers and Northern Flickers.

This Downy Woodpecker is drilling for insects in small spaces in the wood.

The drumming is a super-fast rapping on surfaces that resonate well. It is a courting ritual, the preliminaries beginning in late winter. Denying the drummer access to his instrument can be done by draping it loosely with netting or some heavy fabric. Or you might muffle it with scraps of carpet. Putting up hardware cloth with spacers to keep it a couple of centimetres (an inch) clear of the surface may be sufficient foil. These deterrents can be tacked temporarily in place until the birds find other drums, or the silly season ends.

Sufferers who have simply persisted in scaring off the birds when they begin their drumming report that this works. As a diversion, one might put up a piece of thin plywood some distance from the house and hope that this will give the birds an alternative.

Another form of damage is drilling—in some cases a full-sized hole obviously intended as a nest. In a shed or outbuilding this may be acceptable, but it is not usually considered tolerable when done on a house. Again, scaring off the birds or covering the hole with metal or screen will eventually discourage them.

What they really need is a nest tree—a dead-hearted or hollow trunk, still fairly sound on the surface, 3 to 5 m (10 to 15 ft) long and 15 cm (6 in) in diameter at the top. Here, you might repeat an experiment conducted by Lawrence Kilham, medical scientist and amateur ornithologist of note. One autumn when work prevented his getting to the woods to study Downy Woodpeckers, he collected a number of fallen tree trunks of various degrees of unsoundness and wired them upright to the posts in his backyard. To his delight, four Downies soon called and began tapping up and down and around the new snags. All eventually made roost holes.

It was apparently important that Dr. Kilham gave the Downies a choice, so if you decide to repeat the experiment, don't be stingy with the imported "trees." And don't trim the branches off closely; some woodpeckers show a definite preference for locating holes under good-sized limbs.

Frequently, woodpecker drilling has nothing to do with either sex or nesting, but consists of rows of punctures in plywood, cedar, or other wood siding. The birds are insect-hunting, probing into natural cavities or preexisting insect tunnels in boards, or into gaps between the inner layers of plywood that resemble tunnels. They may actually be digging out flies, wasps, or tunnelling insects that get in through the edges of the plywood and shelter or nest in the gaps.

In some cases a good coat of paint abruptly stops the damage. If this doesn't fit in with the decorative scheme, however, a filler material of an unobtrusive colour can be applied to any exposed ends of board or ply siding. This will block both the insects' access points and the woodpeckers' reasons for poking holes.

A Gnawing Problem

Rats and Mice

Rodents of all kinds are enthusiastic about seeds, as any squirrel will be glad to demonstrate. But inadvertently attracting rats and mice is another matter, hence, prevention, *strict* prevention, is necessary.

In the chapter on seeds I have stressed the importance of vermin-proof storage. Anything made of plastic can easily be chewed into by a determined rodent. The best vessels for me are metal garbage cans with tight-fitting lids that are also raccoon-and rain-proof and can be left outside.

In advance of each winter I do a patrol of the premises to check for burrows and gnawings. Be particularly careful to examine the compost heap. Tunnels under ground-level footings or slabs I doctor with a few mothballs and then fill with coarse crushed rock. I close off above-ground breaks or holes with sheet metal, heavy wire screen, or even a flattened tin can if the patch is out of sight. I'm not proud.

Having taken all reasonable measures to keep rodents from getting in where they don't belong, I set out small containers of rodent poison in crawl spaces and attics where it is securely out of reach of anything except a rodent that has dug or chewed its way in. I realize that this might include something cute, like a chipmunk, but I repeat that these lethal baits are set out *behind* my main perimeter of defences; I have done all I can to keep the baits away from animals willing to stay on their side of the wall.

Before discussing this subject further, I should say that my system of preventive maintenance works; it has been several seasons since I have had problems with squirrels, and longer ago than I can easily recall since a mouse breached security and lived long enough to make its presence felt, or to reproduce.

British Columbia's Own Rats

The most recent exception occurred as a result of my living during the winter of 1991-1992 along coastal British Columbia. The Fraser River delta, southern Vancouver Island, and the Queen Charlotte islands share the distinction of being the only areas in Canada still blessed with populations of the Roof Rat, *Rattus rattus*, also called the black rat. These jumped ship wherever European sailing vessels tied up, which meant the harbours and ports of southern coastal British Columbia likely got theirs in the early nineteenth century. Historically, both here and in Europe, the Roof Rat was displaced whenever the larger and more aggressive Norway Rat, *Rattus norvegicus*, moved in. However, the Roof Rat has managed to do well in its limited range in the province, including the compost pile in my yard.

I first noticed one of these animals at dusk, sitting on the top rail of the picket fence near a hanging feeder that dangled amidst the stems of a mock orange growing against the kitchen wall. The rat, a rounded ball of soft black fur with beady little eyes, big ears, and a long tail, looked like a giant mouse, cute in a way. It, and others, quickly demonstrated their climbing ability by whisking up and down the thin stems as nimbly as any squirrel to grab seeds from the feeder. I noticed that they came in two colours, the other being more your basic rat grey.

We might still be living in commensal harmony except that the colony promptly opened up a branch office under the foundations of the house, a move I was sure the landlord wouldn't appreciate. With some reluctance I purchased a rat trap, and a package each of the usual anticoagulant poison, first marketed as "Warfarin," a slow-acting agent, plus a much more potent version of the same product said to be fatal after one feeding. I laid my baits out in condensed milk cans, opened only enough for a rat-sized animal to get in. Before too long the after-hours scrabbling at the window ceased and the compost heap was vacant. When the holes under the foundation were no longer cleared out after I had filled them in, I concluded the poison had done its sinister work, and removed the baits. I didn't, at this time, use the trap at all.

Even with the rats, unsavoury reputation and all, I would have preferred exclusion rather than "control." The episode simply demonstrated for me, again, that when prevention fails, or cannot be applied adequately, the animals come out second best.

Squirrels

It takes a dose of personal experience to appreciate the damage large rodents can do to a house from the inside, and how difficult it is to evict them once they've established themselves. Squirrels are no exception; they can be highly destructive, and there is also the nagging fear of their chewing through electrical wiring and starting a fire.

Sheeting over or boarding up entrance holes, or stuffing them with steel wool laced with mothballs will simply result in more damage when the squirrel chews its way around them. Sooner or later most people come to the grim conclusion that there are only two possible solutions, death or deportation.

Poison may seem very severe. I am certainly not promoting its use, but if it's going to be considered as a means of ridding yourself of an unwelcome animal when other measures fail, then it should be handled knowingly.

The only "rodenticide" available nowadays off the shelf is the aforementioned anticoagulant. I have found that although it is effective on rats and mice, it is of doubtful impact on squirrels. Firstly, they won't eat it readily, their preferred foods being nuts and fruits, which are often abundant, plus the seeds you're laying on so generously. Secondly, if they do take it, they appear to have to eat a great deal more of it than a similar-sized rat does to get a lethal dose.

Some brands are sold as small pellets, others incorporate the lethal agent into whole grain, usually wheat. In this case peanut butter can be stirred in with it as an appetizer. Peanut butter-flavoured poison must, of course, be kept strictly out of the way of pets and small children.

Cage Traps

But enough about deadly potions. Long ago I equipped myself with two cage traps, one squirrel-sized, one cat- and raccoon-sized. If you bait a cage trap with everything the squirrels seem to be eating, plus some peanut butter, and place it where they do most of their scurrying, you might make a catch. Be sure, of course, to check the trap at least a couple of times a day.

Now what? If you've caught a squirrel, particularly a Red, it'll be battling frantically to get out. You owe it to the animal to take prompt action. Whatever your plans, first check the animal from underneath through the wire bottom of the cage, particularly any time between March and the end of July. If it has a double row of swollen nipples, it is a nursing mother and you had better either apologize and turn her loose, or search out the nest and deal with the whole family. My own conscience would bid me turn her loose to finish her maternal duties rather than destroy a nestful of squirrel pups or be the agent of their death by starvation.

There is one slim hope of early solution to this particular dilemma. One spring some years ago I had a Red Squirrel nesting in a new workshop, and resolved to tolerate it until I was sure there were no innocent dependants involved. One afternoon, in the interests of improvement, I hammered something into the wall of the shop near the nest. Within a half hour the mother squirrel was busy moving her brood. Gripping each pup by the skin of its belly, its body curled around her neck like a pink shrimp, she carried them to a hole in a nearby maple. I boarded up the hole behind her and she didn't come back for the rest of the summer.

The lesson in this anecdote is that mothering squirrels may be very sensitive to unfamiliar disturbances, and the right kind of threatening din could cause them to relocate their litters to a quieter nursery.

Meanwhile, back in the cage. If you're not going to liberate your captive, cover the trap, or put it into a box or dark garbage bag (leave the opening loose for air). This calms the prisoner down.

"Nonreturnables"

If exile is an option, it should be timed with sensitivity. Assuming no maternal complications, the least stressful release time is between spring break-up and the end of September. This allows the deportee some chance of establishing itself and laying in a store of winter food. Later than this, its chances greatly diminish; dumping a squirrel into strange territory in winter is almost certainly condemning it to death by starvation and stress.

To ensure that your exile is "nonreturnable," drive it well out into the country and liberate it near an extensive patch of likely looking treed habitat. Taking squirrels a few blocks away, or even a couple of kilometres, probably means they will be back in your yard in a few hours.

If the time of year precludes conscionable relocation, and no alternative is possible, the animal will have to be destroyed. In earlier years this was frequently accomplished by rigging a hose from the exhaust pipe of a car to a box with the animal in it and letting the car run for ten minutes or so. But the emission controls of today's cars render the exhaust gases less lethal and unconsciousness and death take an inhumanely long time.

Most people, given access to a veterinary clinic, or a Humane Society centre, prefer to leave the "euthanizing" to the professionals. There is a fee, usually less if you take the carcass back and dispose of it.

However, if you must handle the unpleasant task yourself, my suggestion is to place the cage in a garbage bag with no punctures in it and spray in ether. This is easily available from automotive supply stores, in an aerosol can used for starting diesel motors in cold weather. Once the inside of the bag is thoroughly charged with the vapour (three or four long bursts), seal it quickly with a twist tie. The animal loses consciousness in a couple of minutes, sometimes almost immediately. Once it is down, repeat the process and then leave the bag sealed for a couple of hours.

Under no circumstances do this indoors. Ether is highly volatile and explosive, much more so than gasoline.

Once rid of a problem squirrel, promptly remove any nests and food caches you can find, and close off all access holes to the building. Sheeting or screening them over is better than simply plugging them. To mask the scent of the previous squirrel put moth balls into the holes before closing them, and spray or wipe the area around the holes, and the patch, with something strong-smelling, or apply a fresh coat of paint. Whatever you do, don't delay; replacements are quick to move into newly vacated premises.

Rat Traps

The standard "snap" trap is available in an oversized version for rats. When a mouse or rat is caught in a snap trap, it is usually held there, stunned instantly, and killed by the blow of the rigid wire jaw. Theoretically, a rat trap should be big enough to kill Red Squirrels, since they are about the same size and conformation as rats.

However, they often don't work; one finds the trap sprung. The reason is that Red Squirrels, given enough manoeuvring room, are too quick for the trap. They may get smashed on the head or the nose, but at the instant of contact are already recoiling and escape with an injury. For this reason, rat traps should not be used in an effort to trap Red Squirrels. As for the much larger Greys, I suspect a rat trap wouldn't kill one unless it caught it right behind the ears, or the animal was very young.

An incident with Roof Rats has aroused further reservations about the snap trap. After my session with the poisons, and the apparent end to rat incursions recounted previously, I discovered what appeared to be a bachelor rat living along the edge of the grove of trees, vines, shrubbery, escaped garden flowers, and assorted rubble on an uncleared road allowance bordering the yard. I first spotted the animal as it hopped out to feed on the hen scratch scattered on the ground nearby for the quail and pheasants. My attitude of "live-and-let-live" prevailed as long as it stayed where it was. However, in early summer I discovered at least one hole reopened under the kitchen foundation, so I baited the rat trap with sunflower seeds and peanut butter, and set it in a cubby to keep the birds off.

The set lay undisturbed for over two weeks. Then, one morning, I found the trap sprung and the rat, my bachelor male I assume, not in the trap, but lying dead next to it. There was no gross external sign of injury, but I've no doubt the animal was killed by a blow to the head or the neck. I suspect that the inherent quick reflexes of this nimble climbing species caused a train of events similar to those occurring when a squirrel and a snap trap meet. I therefore cannot recommend the use of this type of trap against Roof Rats.

Cats

Every autumn I get one or two stray cats around the house in the city, and at our country place, end-of-summer refugees from a nearby cottage tract show up, hunting birds around my feeders.

In a severe climate, stray cats cannot survive the winter entirely on their own. After the snow has been on the ground for a month, a stray's behaviour and appearance are giveaways. It can be seen on miserable days, rough-coated and humped-up in the cold, when house pets are comfortably indoors. A real stray will also tear into garbage bags and strew the contents around. It will pull down larger game, like rabbits. If you observe it carefully, you will discover it may be living under, or in, a shed, a brush pile, or a heap of scrap lumber.

If you don't want to adopt it, or feed it outdoors, ignoring it may be difficult. Aside from its preying on your birds, its deteriorating condition might be a sorry sight to watch. You may decide that a cage trap, and either the vet clinic or the ether are the most humane alternatives.

Capturing such a cat is usually very easy; a paper towel dabbed into a bit of smelly food grease or fish oil will do for bait. Put the trap up off the ground, out of reach of skunks and the neighbour's beagle. A chagrined dog, or raccoon, can be released with no problems, but a skunk is another matter. They den up in the dead of winter, but in autumn or early spring they are aprowl.

Some parts of lower mainland British Columbia and southern Vancouver Island have populations of feral cats. "Feral" animals are domestics that have reverted to the wild. In the case of these cats, they breed as wild animals and have become a considerable wildlife management problem.

Frustrating the Felines

In the vast majority of backyard cat-vs-bird cases, we're not talking half-wild strays, but well-fed pets hunting for sport and indulging a taste for fresh blood. And since they are neighbours' cherished pets, there is a definite limit to the counter-measures you can take. Nevertheless, ignoring the problem, or turning a diplomatic blind eye aren't conscionable alternatives. If you refer to the cat section of Chapter 8, and the damage they do, you may be convinced that it is worth taking some time to cut down on cat predation around your feeders.

Bill Merilees of Nanaimo, in his entertaining and informative book *Attracting Backyard Wildlife*, rates cats as "public enemy no. 1" to backyard wildlife. Obviously not a man of half measures, he recommends putting up a chain-link fence at least 1.8 m (6 ft) high around the yard. I know of one very dedicated bird lover in Winnipeg who lives with his birds behind an eight-foot high perimeter of chain-link topped with several strands of barbed wire.

Since most cats are lazy, disinclined to strenuous effort if it can be avoided, his high fence works almost all the time. But cats can be impressively agile when the need arises, so I'm not surprised to learn that once in awhile a determined one scrambles over even the Winnipeg bird lover's barrier. Looked at from another angle, would a chain-link fence keep a cat *in* its yard if it really wanted out?

Whose Problem?

On sober reflection, trying to make your premises cat-proof has an element of absurdity about it. For owners of all other types of livestock the onus is on them to keep their animals in, not on everyone else to keep them out. Tradition, however, exempts cats from confinement on the grounds that limiting their freedom is cruel. This is rubbish, as cats by the millions prove every winter by not only tolerating confinement indoors, but insisting on it. The owners of show cats who must keep their valuable bluebloods inside all their lives scorn the notion that doing so is inhumane.

The point is obviously not one of basic feline liberty, but of pet management. Whose problem is it, mine or the folks who conveniently absolve themselves of responsibility for their cat by letting it out the door?

The first thing the liberated cat does, of course, is head straight for your bird feeder. Unless frightened off, it will become an evasive but habitual hangabout.

Much as outraged bird lovers might fantasize about cat-bashing, setting booby traps of the Sylvester-and-Tweety-Pie variety, or otherwise taking revenge, such plots succeed only in the imagination. Dashing outside, yelling "scat!", throwing things, or brandishing the garden hose spread only temporary alarm. The cats quickly learn contempt for such futile spluttering, and add insult to injury by leaving little piles of bloodied feathers and wing-ends for you to find.

Even such intense provocation doesn't justify escalating the conflict with leghold traps and firearms. They are not only antisocial, but dangerous and potentially inhumane. Their use is also expressly forbidden under the statutes of most towns and cities.

Ownership of a spirited dog is one way of keeping the environs cat-free. However, a dog doesn't fit in with everyone's lifestyle, mine included. At one time I enlisted the help of a friend's dog, an explosively energetic terrier that responded with impressive zeal when the word "cats!" was spoken. We brought "Zip" in for visits from time to time. Once she had put several persistent cats up a tree, they got the message and avoided the yard.

Some well-meaning owners put a bell on their cat in the belief it will warn birds. Some creditable observations indicate this works, but in other instances the bird is still caught. The only really effective bell, as a friend wryly observed, would be one weighing about forty pounds.

Bells, dogs, and fences aside, my own strategy centres on doing what I can to help my birds avoid getting caught by making it difficult for cats to ambush them.

Think Like a Cat

The first step is reconnoitring the territory, getting the lay of the land from the point-of-view of a skulking cat. As a cat, your objective would be to get as close as possible to a preoccupied bird, undetected, and to strike from cover. Waiting in ambush would be much easier if there was a bush, scrap pile, or piece of yard furniture close to a feeder where birds, pursuing spilled seeds, habitually fed on the ground. In front of the hiding place there would have to be a clear space for an unobstructed rush.

If a cat can get into such a setting under cover it has only to wait. Eventually, pinpointing a target that is close-by, preoccupied with feeding, and has its back turned, the cat springs, claws clutching. Everything explodes as the birds burst away—all except one.

This yard has really been wired for cats.

My own answer could be called "passive obstruction." It is non-violent, calls for a minimum of time and cash, and needs no tending. Done with sufficient ingenuity it can create a safe haven for birds in which all but the suicidally foolhardy can happily feed and flaunt themselves before the cats.

First of all, get rid of any obvious ambush points that can be conveniently cleared away. For those that can't, the trick is to barricade them with a judicious placement of wire screen, using the same principle that governs the use of barbed wire entanglements by the military, which is to impede movement at key points. This simply means putting a low fence around places of concealment. Let the cat lash its tail and drool under the junipers all it wants; a low perimeter of stucco wire or poultry screen (chicken wire) around the bush robs it of a clear rush. The birds can, of course, clearly see through the screen, and if the cat has to break cover first by jumping over the wire at the start of its rush, they will have that split-second of warning they need to get away.

Construction requirements are simple. The wire barrier need be only 45 to 60 cm (18 to 24 in) high, and it can be tacked or stapled at the ends to a couple of stakes driven into the ground or packed snow. Curving the wire around the hideout gives it more stability and minimizes the need for props.

Similarly, if you have a feeding shelf close to a hideaway that you can't eliminate for some reason, (like not wanting to dynamite the garage), you can frustrate the grab-over-the-edge trick by installing a fringe of wire that sticks out horizontally around the sides of the shelf for 20 to 25 cm (8 to 10 in).

The most suitable and least expensive screen for my purposes has proven to be stucco wire. It comes in 1.2 and 1.4 m (4 and 4.5 ft) widths, with a 5-cm (2-in)-square mesh, and you can buy it off the roll from building supply retailers. It can be snipped to the desired shape with wire cutters or sturdy tinsnips. It stands up more stiffly than poultry screen, and thus doesn't need to be put in a frame or propped up except at the ends. It is also much neater; deployed around the ornamentals at the front of your house it tends less to give the place the look of an unfinished rabbit hutch.

A further advantage of stucco wire is that small birds can flit through it easily, larger ones like Steller's Jays and doves can squeeze through it, but crows and pigeons are excluded.

The level of feline frustration the wire treatment must generate should satisfy any reasonable thirst for vengeance, and give harmless rein to the streak of diabolical genius that cats arouse in even the most benign of bird feeders.

This little scene says it all.

CHAPTER SIX

Those Fascinating Creatures

Free, powered flight is the ultimate liberation. On a cushion of air you are free of earth's daunting barriers, of the rough, entangling path, the pounding impact of gravity. For aeons before we invented our imitation wings, birds were spanning hemispheres, crossing vast oceans, and soaring over forbidding mountain ranges.

Aside from the obvious fact that birds can fly, and we can't, they are endowed with many other physical capabilities that go beyond the capacities of most other mammals of our acquaintance. Those of us who feed birds where winter is a no-nonsense deep freeze see these tiny creatures feeding and fluttering about on their side of the window where it's -40°C—and in bare feet, even! We hear of pilots spotting geese, vultures, and other large birds migrating or soaring at heights three times beyond the altitude where humans require supplementary oxygen.

And yet, when you pick up a bird or hit one with the windshield of your car, it seems vulnerably delicate, light, and fragile. Obviously, this is a very special kind of body. And, since we're dealing with its ability to withstand our winters, it is appropriate to do a brief review of how it accomplishes this.

Physiology

There are, unavoidably, trade-offs. If you wish to fly, the laws of physics limit your weight to around 20 kg (44 lb), a maximum found in the Great Bustard of Europe and Asia. On this continent the flying heavyweight is the Trumpeter Swan with weights up to 15 kg (33 lb) not unusual. Audubon reported a Trumpeter at 17.2 kg (37 lb 2 oz). Much heavier than this and, like an ostrich, you walk. Flying is also extremely expensive of energy, which in turn requires a high relative intake of both food and oxygen.

To minimize the penalties of flight, birds evolved aeons ago for a combination of strength and lightness, beginning with the skeleton. The bird airframe must house the enormous flight muscles and be braced solidly enough not to crack under their power. To affect this, the backbone is fused along most of its length into one member, the ribs are braced against each other, and the sternum is a huge keel set in a supporting hull of thin bone. The wing and leg bones are light and hollow, but braced from within by a latticework of reinforcing struts. They are also part of the respiratory system. In some large, heavily plumaged birds the feathers actually weigh more than the skeleton does.

Supercharger Lungs

A bird's lungs are small, relative to those of comparably sized mammals. But they have phenomenal throughput, being connected to a system of air sacs and the hollow limb bones that permit a flow of air that is largely one-way. When a bird breathes under effort, each puff clears almost all the stale air out of the lungs. When a mammal gasps for breath, a certain percentage of each exhalation is left behind. In terms of performance, this means that birds can exert the considerable effort of flight and maintain it for long periods, even at high altitudes, as they have evolved to do in migration.

Birds of Britain and Europe cites an experiment that vividly demonstrates the relative respiratory ability of mammals and birds. Sparrows and mice were placed in a chamber where the air pressure was equivalent to that atop Mount Everest. The birds showed no stress and went on with their normal activities. The mice, severely distressed, could only stagger about.

To complement the capacity of the lungs, birds' hearts are much larger than those of mammals of similar size. And they operate at high-performance levels; even at rest a chickadee's heart beats four hundred times a minute, double that when it is active.

High Temperature

Metabolic processes work faster at higher temperatures. Not surprisingly, birds have higher normal body temperatures than mammals. As a farm lad, when farms were still a menagerie of various animals, I observed that hens could survive deep wounds that would have killed other animals from infection. The reason was that mammal-adapted bacteria can't survive in the birds' high body temperature which hovers around $40°C$ ($104°F$) at rest. This is very close to the critical upper limit; a couple of degrees above this and protein enzymes become unstable, begin to break down, and essential body functions go awry.

Very obviously, feathers are critical to the maintenance of stable body temperatures in our wintering birds. They are a double defence; the smooth, slick contour feathers, arranged shingle-fashion, are an efficient wind barrier. Beneath them lies a layer of insulating down, one of nature's most efficient ways of enclosing a small body in an envelope of warm air.

Fuel

Gathering the food to fuel this high-temperature, high-speed body is made possible by the very equipment that burns most of it, the wings. Birds have access to insects, their eggs, and their pupae in places few mammals can reach. This includes the outermost extremities of trees as well as their woody hearts; chickadees forage among the smallest twigs and branches of trees, and woodpeckers drill beneath the bark. In the chickadees' case the pressure to be productive is intense; it is estimated that to survive severe winter conditions they must find a food item on the average of every two or three seconds during their waking hours.

Winter Survival

A few winters ago I was watching a White-throated Sparrow on my window feeder in Winnipeg. He appeared to be dizzy; whenever he attempted to lift one foot into the warmth of his belly feathers he teetered sideways drunkenly. It would have been a mildly comical performance, except on that cold mid-February day he was in the last throes of starvation. Too weak to feed, he finally fluttered away. I never saw him again.

Every winter a few individuals from species that normally migrate are either forced, or choose, to stick around. With luck—a combination of a mild winter, very good shelter, and an unusual source of plentiful food—holdovers might survive. But considering the behavioural and physiological adaptations required for non-migrants to live through the rigours of (in this instance) a prairie winter, my unfortunate whitethroat was undoubtedly more the rule than the exception.

Cold Tolerance

Low temperature itself is a secondary problem, since birds are already equipped to fly about in frigid air, as they must do for extended stretches at high altitudes during migration. When at rest, and not generating heat through exercise, they fluff up their body plumage and stay out of the wind.

To test just how well-adapted birds are, winter-acclimatized goldfinches, Pine Siskins, and Purple Finches were experimentally subjected to sustained temperatures of -70°C (-94°F). They went on with their usual activities, apparently little stressed by the numbing cold. They maintained normal temperature and mobility as long as they had sufficient food to maintain a critical level of body fat.

Feathers explain how the body can stay warm, but all of us who feed birds have no doubt marvelled at why the wire-thin little legs and toes, unlike human fingers which become uselessly numb when chilled, are able to function no matter how cold it gets. It helps that the oily tissues of the fleshless feet and lower legs retain little residual moisture and resist freezing. Behaviour also plays a part; in severe conditions birds often pull one leg up into their belly feathers for warmth. Ground feeders like juncos and redpolls crouch low, from time to time squatting down to cover their legs and feet.

There is a further adaption in the circulatory system feeding the lower legs. In the upper, feathered leg, the arteries and veins pass close to each other in a heat-exchange network of capillaries where venous blood returning to the heart is warmed by the outgoing arterial blood, which is in turn cooled. Blood flow to the legs and feet can thus be controlled in response to the need to conserve or radiate heat.

For most birds the supply of winter food and, even more crucially, the amount of daylight in which to search for it, are severely restricted compared to summer conditions. To use an extreme example, in subarctic Whitehorse, midwinter daylight can be as short as three and a half hours, and temperatures during the long nights regularly drop to -40°C or lower. Yet Boreal Chickadees survive these conditions, with or without the help of Whitehorse bird feeders.

Hoarding

At feeding stations many wintering birds will store surplus food. Once they have stoked up, chickadees and nuthatches will spend much of every short winter day diligently stashing sunflower seeds, peanuts, or other food items to the end that, by springtime, each probably has enough hidden away to feed twenty of its kind. Complementing the hoarding impulse is a good memory; chickadees have shown an accurate recall interval of up to eight months.

Crows and their kin, which includes the jays, are also compulsive hoarders. Given unrestricted access to suet, they usually start hauling away chunks of it, in great haste, before eating. They will keep at it until the supply is exhausted, a habit that has taught bird benefactors to offer suet in protective cages that limit the take to peck-sized pieces.

Cuddling Up

Further behavioural adaptations help solve the problem of the long, cold, foodless nights. Woodpeckers roost in tree holes excavated for the purpose. Chickadees habitually sleep together in tree holes. Twenty-nine White-breasted Nuthatches have been found in one tree cavity, twenty or more Brown Creepers in close huddles beneath slabs of loose bark. Redpolls may avail themselves of mouse holes in the snow, or dig their own.

Among House Sparrows, the more fortunate get into buildings, signs, and light fixtures with a built-in source of heat. The less privileged wedge themselves into holes and crannies, perhaps utilizing last summer's nest for additional insulation. Ravens, sometimes in large numbers, roost in dense conifers. Chickadees conserve energy by becoming partially torpid in their winter roost holes. Their temperature drops by seven Celsius degrees (thirteen Fahrenheit degrees), and their respiration falls from ninety-five to sixty-five breaths per minute.

Big is Best

The smaller a creature is, the greater is its surface area relative to body mass, and the greater its problem of retaining heat. We demonstrate this ourselves when slim appendages like ears and fingers chill, even freeze, when the rest of the body is comfortably warm. Within warm-blooded species, northern animals tend to be larger-bodied and have smaller appendages than their southern counterparts. The Hairy Woodpeckers of the Yukon weigh over 120 grams (4.2 oz), those of the subtropics, 40 grams (1.4 oz).

Over a minimum body size, and given adequate reserves of fat, sitting still may be more efficient than foraging. When a domestic hen simply stands up from resting, its energy consumption increases by 40 to 50 percent. In his *Watching Birds*, Roger Pasquier relates perhaps the most marked manifestation of the sit-and-save strategy short of outright hibernation: in Finland, Ring-necked Pheasants are reported to roost in trees, immobile and insensitive to disturbance, for forty or more days at a stretch. This isn't as far-fetched as it may at first appear; captive Golden Pheasants routinely brood their eggs for twenty-two days, taking no food or water, and moving very little.

These examples make it less surprising that chickadees, too, opt for a similar strategy. They sit out storms and extreme cold in their roosts, maintaining their state of semi-torpor rather than fighting a losing battle in which the energy costs of foraging exceed the returns.

All-important Fat

The key to cutting losses in this manner, and indeed to overall winter well-being, is an all-important reserve of body fat. The high-performance metabolism of birds enables them to alternately lay on, and burn off, significant percentages of their body weight in fat with each twenty-four-hour cycle. A House Sparrow going to roost may weigh 25 grams (.9 oz), two of these being fat which it can metabolize overnight to maintain itself.

Chickadees will raise their daily fat deposits by from 4 to 7 percent of their body weight of 10 to 12 grams (.35 to .42 oz) on a natural diet of dormant insects and weed seeds, and up to 11.8 percent on black sunflower seeds. Under severe winter conditions most of this store of fat will be depleted by morning, and the birds must quickly begin replenishing it in order to survive. This accounts for the flurry of intense dawn feeding familiar to station proprietors. There is a similar last-minute stoking-up at dusk.

The Midnight Snack

Our seed-eating winter finches have an oesophageal diverticulum, a storage pouch part way down their gullet similar to a chicken's crop. Redpolls often feed by hastily collecting a load of seeds, husks and all, and then retiring to a sheltered hideaway to regurgitate and husk the seeds. During the long night they can arouse themselves from time to time to snack on what amounts to a packed lunch.

Midwinter Nests

A book on wintering birds may seem a strange place to find mention of nests at all. Actually, for those interested in birds in general, winter is the best time to study nest structure and to learn how different species apply this critical adaptive skill. Nest-hunting is easiest; bare stems and branches reveal nests otherwise concealed by foliage in summer. The nests themselves often carry tell-tale caps of snow that show up against the backdrop of frozen vegetation like scoops of ice cream.

Although one might clip and collect these abandoned lodgings with a clear conscience on the grounds that the builders have no further use for them, the law has other ideas. Almost all birds, and their nests, are protected, the migratory species by federal, the nonmigratory by provincial, law. The only exceptions are "nuisance" species such as the common pigeon, House Sparrow, and starling. You can obtain a salvage permit to collect nests by contacting Canadian Wildlife Service and provincial Ministry of the Environment offices. See the Appendix for addresses and phone numbers.

Studying nests used as winter roosts can also enrich one's appreciation for the adaptability of wintering species. Tracking chickadees, nuthatches, and woodpeckers to their nighttime bivouacs could be an entirely defensible way of postponing some tedious domestic chore in favour of the pursuit of enlightenment. One of the more unusual adaptations to winter as it relates to nests is found amongst owls.

Great Horned, Boreal, and Saw-whet Owls are known to thaw out frozen prey by incubating it in their roost nests as they would a clutch of eggs.

A marvel of the winter bird world is the ability of crossbills, ravens, and Gray Jays to nest in the harshest conditions. Crossbills have been found nesting every month of the year, the determinant being a supply of conifer seeds. Their winter nests are noticeably more bulky and well-insulated than those of summer, the chinks between the fibres of the lining filled with punky powdered wood. Thus, the temperature under a brooding female can be as much as sixty Celsius degrees (100 Fahrenheit degrees) warmer than the air temperature. For the first week the female broods the young, the male feeding both her and the nestlings a creamy soup of regurgitated seeds. Thereafter, both parents feed. When exposed to the cold the young chill and grow torpid, but revive quickly when the female resumes brooding.

This Gray Jay could be incubating at -20° C or lower.

Gray Jays commence nesting in late February or early March. Preparations begin early; the tidbits jays cadge from campers in summer are set aside for the next winter. They "scatter hoard," hiding each bit in the twigs at the tips of conifer branches, under holes in bark—anywhere that is high enough to not get buried in snow the following winter. They're aided in this by a set of oversized salivary glands that produce copious quantities of sticky saliva with which food is formed into a wad and globbed into its niche. An essential property of the saliva is that it glazes into a water-resistant skin, but doesn't freeze into solid ice. Not the least of the birds' skills is remembering where most of the hundreds and hundreds of snacks are concealed.

The nest is invariably in a dense conifer of middling size located in a site exposed to the south and east. Most nests are precisely oriented in the tree itself where the strongest rays of the late winter sun will strike them.

I was reminded, in a personal communication from C. Stuart Houston of Saskatoon, of a memorable photo in an early edition of the *Canadian Field-Naturalist* that gave "double brooding" a double meaning. This picture showed a male

Gray Jay sitting on top of his mate in their nest, presumably to help her keep warm in a spell of extremely low temperature.

By the time other birds have begun nesting, juvenile Gray Jays will be on the wing, following their parents and learning the art of snitching morsels from wolf kills and panhandling from cottagers and back-country picnickers.

A Meal of Ticks

An unusual source of winter food for Gray Jays was noted by Bill Walley of Dauphin, Manitoba, while doing work on these birds in Riding Mountain National Park. He observed several of them intently pursuing a moose, picking blood-gorged ticks from it, particularly around the tail.

These moose, or winter, ticks (not the "wood" ticks of picnic and hike infamy) can number over one hundred thousand on a severely infested animal. Every tick takes at least three blood meals, each time perforating the animal's skin to the blood level. The torment can be judged by the fact that some moose scratch and rub themselves so much that most of their hair is worn off by late winter. Small wonder many die from a combination of direct blood loss, stress, and exposure. Blood-engorged ticks would be a rich source of food for birds, and one might wonder if ravens, crows, and others could be among those also taking advantage of the poor moose's misery.

Knowing Your Visitors

This chapter describes the species of birds and mammals likely to visit British Columbia feeders in winter, and the families they belong to. Understanding how science classifies and names birds will clarify the organization of this chapter and help make the material more enjoyable.

Taxonomy

The science of classifying living things is called taxonomy. Within it all life is arranged into two huge family trees, one for the plant kingdom, one for the animal. All relationships in each "tree" are determined on the basis of recognizable differences and similarities in structure, physiology, and sometimes behaviour.

All plants and animals have folk names. The confusion inherent in this is typified by the name "gopher." In North America it can be a ground squirrel, a turtle, or a snake, depending on where you live. To bring order out of such chaos it was necessary first to devise a system of giving every living thing its own, exclusive

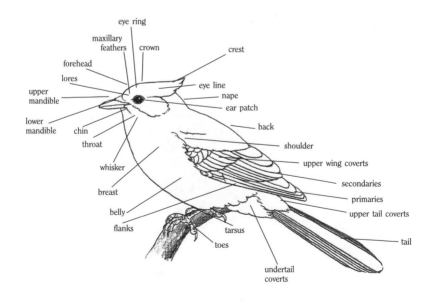

name, and second, to gain acceptance of that system among the world's scientists.

A Swedish botanist, Karl von Linné, developed a naming system using words and roots from Latin and classical Greek, neither of which is any longer a national language. Thus, in one stroke, he avoided putting anyone's linguistic nose out of joint, and he tapped into two rich vocabularies. Linne himself is now universally known by the Latinized version of his name, Linnaeus.

Thanks to him, all known plants and animals now have a scientific name of at least two words. As well as being a universal label, the names try, but don't always succeed, at being descriptive. Nor are they free of error, or the temptations of whimsy, favouritism, or sycophancy that even taxonomists seem prey to. According to Edward S. Gruson in his book *Words for Birds*, a "madly mixed bag of British admirals, U.S. Army doctors, fur traders, wives of friends of ornithologists (and at least one Italian paleobotanist) live on in the names of common (North) American birds."

Confusianus ignoramus

The use of scientific names is often viewed by ordinary folk as applied academic snobbery. Technical jargon can indeed be a frustrating enemy of understanding, as new owners of computers can attest. However, there is economy and clarity to be gained through the use of descriptive terms coined for a specific discipline where everyday words would be clumsy. Applied judiciously, as I tried to do in this nontechnical book, they needn't constitute a barrier if, in context or with definitions, their meanings are clear.

It is no accident that the bird families in almost all field guides are presented in more or less the same order, beginning with what is regarded as the earliest evolved (loons), and ending with the most recently evolved, usually finches. The order in this book follows the taxonomic lead of Earl Godfrey's *The Birds of Canada*.

Family Accounts

There turned out to be much more of interest about most birds and mammals than could be encompassed in the confining structure of the individual species

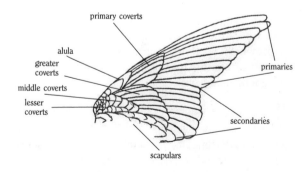

accounts. Therefore, I have incorporated the most interesting of the leftover bits into family write-ups. Where the subject and available material warranted it, I also wrote on subgroups, such as the crossbills, and even about individual species, like the redpolls.

Species Accounts

In this chapter each species is discussed under a standard set of subheads that cover its names, appearance, behaviour, range, food, and nest. The wording is spare, since the purpose is to provide a brief sketch. The "Comment" subhead allows me some space to fill out that sketch with interesting detail.

What's in a Name?

Each species account begins with a thumbnail summary of the sources of both the common and the scientific names.

British author R.D. Macleod separated common names into "popular" and "book" names. "Popular" names are those that develop with a language, like "hawk," "sparrow," "finch." "Book" names are more specific labels bestowed by biologists—or committees of them—like "Red-tailed Hawk," "Song Sparrow," and "Purple Finch."

As already pointed out, I don't approach scientific names as a necessary evil, but as an opportunity to learn something. Occasionally one can even have a little fun with them. For both purposes I have drawn on Ernest A. Choate's *The Dictionary of American Bird Names*, revised edition, 1985, and on Edward S. Gruson's *Words for Birds*, 1972, with some help from *Webster's New World Dictionary*.

Descriptions

For each species account where a comparison to another familiar bird could readily be made, I have given relative sizes. The surface anatomy, or "topography," of birds has long since been mapped in detail. The appendages, and each contour and pattern of the body and flight feathers, have been accorded names. The accompanying diagrams identify the major parts of a typical bird. Knowing these will aid in the enjoyment of this, and other, reference books and will also sharpen your ability to spot key field marks on birds at your feeders.

Range

In this book about winter birds of British Columbia it is entirely logical, and informative, to give provincial wintering ranges. However, since we share most of these birds with the rest of North America, it seemed equally logical to outline breeding ranges on a continental basis.

Nests and Roosts

In Chapter 6, "These Fascinating Creatures," I discussed nests, and their significance as objects of wintertime study. Therefore, each account features a brief description of that species' nest and preferred location. For those birds that actually nest in winter, I describe the eggs.

References

Each species account concludes with a line of page references in the four major North American field guides, plus Godfrey's *The Birds of Canada*. All are the latest editions available, as of mid-1992. The colour illustrations (photos in the Audubon guide) will provide a complementary reference to Peter Sawatzky's black-and-white interpretations in this book. In the Audubon guide the species accounts are separate from the pictures; the reference numbers here are for the write-ups.

Following is the key to the reference abbreviations:

A(W) *The Audubon Society Field Guide to North American Birds*, Western Region

BC *The Birds of Canada* (Godfrey)

GO Golden Guide *Birds of North America*

NG National Geographic *Field Guide to the Birds of North America*

P(W) Peterson: *A Field Guide to Western Birds*

Grouse, Patridges, Pheasants

Family *Phasianidae*

This family is a member of the larger Order, the *Galliformes*, which includes the chicken-like, scratching, ground-living birds found the world over. Collectively, they are often referred to as "game" birds due to their being regarded primarily as objects of sport hunting, or "upland game" birds as distinct from hunted waterfowl. *Galliformes* is from the Latin *gallina*, "a hen," and *Phasianidae* is from the Greek *phasianos*, "a pheasant."

Some five thousand years ago the Red Jungle Fowl of India was domesticated and became the farmyard chicken in its many varieties. The qualities that made it valuable were its high reproductive rate, flocking habit, and the tastiness of its meat. It was also easy to keep, scratching through manure and litter for waste grain, plucking shoots and leaves, and chasing insects around the dooryard. It was, conveniently, nonmigratory.

The high reproductive rate meant large clutches of eggs, a trait that could be exploited with a little management. If you systematically stole the hen's eggs as she laid them, preventing her from accumulating a clutch large enough to trigger her brooding mode, the confused bird just kept on producing. Wild Gray Partridges will fill nests occasionally with over twenty eggs, and if captives are subjected to nestbox larceny, will overproduce heroically. If you know where to shop you can buy tins of diminutive quail eggs.

Would Rather Walk

Given a choice, most members of this group prefer to keep their feet on the ground. Their wings have, in fact, been described as getaway devices held in reserve to escape predators that can't be hidden from or outrun. Our native grouse, however, do routinely use their wings as feeding aids when they flap a few feet up to browse on tree buds.

The grouse-type wing is short, broad, and rounded, and has to be flailed at a high speed to achieve flight. Liftoff, particularly for heavier species like turkeys and pheasants, is straight up in a burst of thrashing wings that gets the bird from zero to flat-out in a couple of seconds. The buffeting of this blastoff is often augmented by a simultaneous cackling or other vocal racket. The object is to startle the unsuspecting, to get out of reach, fast, before a predator can collect its shattered composure and pounce—or shoot.

Once airborne and at cruising speed, the bird sets its wings stiffly and glides, usually settling a short distance away.

The huge breast muscles that power this explosive burst of energy are the "white meat" of the dinner table. Powerful as they are, they can be exerted for only short periods because they contain fewer blood vessels and less oxygen-storing myoglobin than "dark" meat, and are made up of coarser fibre bundles. The breast muscles of migratory birds give evidence of different priorities. Compelled to work hard over long periods they are richly supplied with blood vessels and myoglobin, and are made of finer fibres. You can see, from the contrasting colour of the muscle groups, where evolution has put the emphasis: on a duck it's the breast meat that's "dark," on a chicken or grouse, it's the leg.

I have read that if you were able to pursue a pheasant or grouse closely enough to force it to fly repeatedly, after four or five takeoffs the bird's flight muscles would be exhausted and you could simply pick it up. But these birds have other evasive skills designed to keep them out of the frying pan. Pheasants have been clocked at thirty kilometres per hour on foot. They, and grouse, invariably do their best footwork in the most tangled cover they can find.

Snowshoe or Shovel?

A clue to the adaptive background of some members of this family can be seen in their footwear. Grouse have furlike leggings down to their toes, and in winter the toes grow combs of stiff bristles along each side. Neither pheasants nor quail have these accessories.

The toe bristles are assumed to be an adaptive "snowshoe" giving the wearers better "float" on soft snow. It has also been observed that the toenails grow longer, probably for the same reason. This is no doubt true. But there is another possibility that I would suggest, and that is increased digging facility in soft snow.

As most readers of nature lore know, grouse and ptarmigan sleep in winter under the snow, often plunging in from flight. They burrow along horizontally for thirty centimetres (one foot) or more, plugging the entrance as they dig. Their snow den is a snug, insulated pocket, with added safety from predators. In the morning they usually burst through the roof into flight.

How they actually dig through the soft, yielding snow is an interesting question. It is probably with a combination of beak and footwork. But scooping the loose stuff back behind them would have to be done with the feet. For this, those toe fringes would help a lot since, without them, moving loose snow would be a bit like trying to shovel sand with a fork.

An important factor in some native grouse's winter survival is their ability to switch to tree buds as food. Seton, in his *The Birds of Manitoba* mentions Sharp-tailed Grouse he shot toward the end of the winter having a large gap in their beaks behind the tip where both mandibles had been worn away, presumably from "budding"—plucking aspen and willow buds.

The Spruce Grouse has adapted to survive in winter on what constitutes most of the scenery in its vast range—evergreen needles! To handle such tough, dry fare its digestive tract increases markedly in size with the onset of winter. The constant ingestion of aromatic spruce, fir, and pine needles imparts to the flesh of the bird a distinct flavour of turpentine.

The Spruce Grouse's plumage pattern blends so well with the dead leaves and duff of the forest floor that to vanish from view it may merely have to sit stock still. But it frequently does the same thing when sitting in plain view in a tree, a behavioural error that makes the poor "fool hen" the first and easiest target for trigger-happy plinkers. Its superb camouflage, plus the fact that both plinking and bird surveying are done near roads and settlements, may in part account for the fact that the bird is routinely classed as rare or scarce, even where there is plenty of apparently suitable habitat.

Although this grouse is widespread throughout British Columbia east of the Coast Range, where to many it is still the "Franklin's Grouse," it is a very rare visitor to feeders so has not been included in the species accounts.

The Imports

Trying to do a quick fix on nature by introducing foreign species has fallen into rightful disrepute. That matched set of environmental calamities, the starling and House Sparrow, and the nuisance pigeon, are constant reminders of previous folly.

Thankfully, relatively few introduced birds have been successful in North America. Among those that became established are three that were brought in to provide sporting targets in place of native species either shot out or crowded aside by a combination of the axe, the cow, and the plough. These are the Ring-necked Pheasant, the Gray Partridge, and the Chukar. Some introductions were wildly successful; Gray Partridges stocked in southern Alberta around 1908 multiplied abundantly, inspiring similar efforts everywhere on the continent, including British Columbia. After a few years of heady success, however, all the population explosions fizzled out, some to oblivion, others to small but stable present-day levels. Whatever the impact of these birds upon the environment, and upon our attitudes to wildlife, it is difficult now to find fault with these hardy and beautiful imports.

Three other game birds—the California Quail, Mountain Quail, and Wild Turkey—are introduced, but their presence should be considered assisted range extensions, since all are native to North America. Of these the California Quail is doing best, the turkey is hanging on, and the Mountain Quail is barely staying in the records on the southern tip of Vancouver Island.

Assuming they are hardy enough to brave climatic change, the ability of introduced game birds to survive is directly related to land-use practices. Earlier introductees often started out well; older style farming, with brushy gullies, and weedy fence rows dividing the stubble fields and pastures, suited them. The ringneck, especially, relied heavily on strawstacks where the waste grain and weed seeds of an entire field were concentrated by the threshing machine. But the post-World War II combine did in the old threshing machine, and with it the life-sustaining strawstack. The bulldozer erased the gully and fence row, the sprayer took care of what was left of the nurturing weed seeds and insects.

✳ ✳ ✳

Gray Partridge

Perdix perdix

Pheasant family. Also "Hungarian partridge" or "Hun"; "partridge," says Webster, arises from Middle English *partriche*, a direct descendant of the Greek *perdix*, which in turn is probably akin to *perdesthai*, "to break wind" (whence "fart,") from whirring sound made as birds burst into flight; term incorrectly but widely applied also to Ruffed Grouse; *perdix* is from Latin and Greek, "a partridge."

Description

Chunky, squat, short-tailed, smaller than native grouse; grey chest and neck, flanks barred in rusty brown; males have a dark brown, rough U-shaped patch on belly; cheeks, throat, and outer tail feathers plain rust-brown; upper parts pattern of grey and browns, with light feather edgings and fine lines.

Behaviour

Social; feeds, flushes, and flies in close flock; strictly a ground bird of open country; family "covey" sleeps huddled in a circle, tails inward, presumably for a fast getaway if alarmed; they dig open craters through snow in fields, ditches, and weed patches to scratch for seeds and green bits, and apparently also sleep in these; call a harsh, rasping "krrrr-ik," heard particularly in spring; also cackle when they flush.

P. SAWATZKY ©
1990

Range

Nonmigratory; has been released widely, now limited to north Okanagan, and Thompson Valley in the vicinity of Kamloops; does best in grain and forage croplands.

Food

Seeds, green leaves, shoots, rose hips; growing chicks insectivorous, and may be starved out if agricultural insecticides are widely used; attracted (rarely) to feeding stations by spilled seeds and by scratch feed on the ground.

Nest

Very well hidden cup scratched in ground, lined with grasses; in crops, fencerows, tall grass, and edges of low shrubbery.

Comment

According to *The Birds of British Columbia* the first release of these hardy little game birds here was in 1904, near Vancouver. Others followed in the Fraser Valley, on Vancouver Island, and the Gulf Islands. However, the most successful "introduction" was by the birds themselves when migrants from the Okanagan Valley in Washington State came north, beginning around 1913. By the early 1920s they were abundant, but in 1926-1927 the population collapsed, recovering only well enough to rate the Gray Partridge at best as fairly common in its current limited range in the southern interior.

Winter is hard on them, especially when it brings ice storms. But they make up for losses with huge clutches, the largest in the bird world with an average of fifteen to sixteen eggs. In early summer the dominant pair from the covey you fed the previous winter might reappear in the vicinity of the feeder with a retinue of tiny, scuttling chicks. The attentive male will be bringing up the rear of his numerous brood, ready to fight, or to feign a broken wing to lead a predator away.

REF: A(W) - 577; BC - 153; GO - 92; NG - 220; P(W) - 164

Chukar

Alectoris chukar

Partridge and pheasant subfamily. Pronounced "ch-car'," possibly rooted in Indo-European echoic root *kau*, "to scream," (whence "howl"); *alectoris* from Greek *alektor*, "cock"; until recently considered a subspecies of the Rock Partridge, the "Grecian hen," hence listed as *A. graeca* in older references.

Description

Similar in size to Gray Partridge; throat and face light buff outlined in black; upper body brownish-grey, flanks boldly striped in vertical black and white; bill, eye-ring, and legs red.

Behaviour

Social; ground feeder; covey roosts on ground in a circle, tails in; normally very elusive, may evade hunters by scurrying upslope, flying back down when flushed; call described as a low, harsh cackling "chuck chuck" or "chuck-arr."

Range

Introduced and established in drier mountainous or hilly regions of American west and southwest; first successful plant in Canada in 1950 in vicinity of Kamloops; now present in British Columbia in Thompson-Nicola Valley and in southern Okanagan; described as "rock-loving," preferring grassy, arid, rocky slopes, canyons, and benchland.

- P. Sawatzky -

Food

Grass seeds, especially that of cheat grass, *Bromus tectorum*, with which it seems to have a close ecological relationship; grass, clover leaves, grasshoppers; *Birds of the Okanagan Valley* notes it is keen on the berries of the introduced Russian Olive; migrates to lowland during some winters at which times it may flock to haystacks and feed lots.

Nest

A shallow scrape with meagre lining of nearby straws, grass, leaves; one of few species to "double clutch," female leaving male to incubate and raise first brood while she starts a second in a new nest.

Comment

There is a good argument for *not* including the chukar in a book on feeder birds, shy and of limited distribution that it is. However, for those who share sagebrush uplands with this bird, getting it to come to the yard with a generous deployment of chaff and chicken scratch is a challenge well worth taking on.

REF: A(W) - 595; BC - 154; GO - 92; NG - 220; P(W) - 164

Ring-necked Pheasant

Phasianus colchicus

Pheasant family. Sometimes "Chinese" pheasant; "pheasant" is from Greek *phaisianos*, "a pheasant," referring to the river Phasis flowing into the Black Sea in the ancient country of Colchis which is now part of Georgia, and at the mouth of which these birds were especially numerous; *colchicus*, Latinized "of Colchis"; taxonomy has thus given us a double locality name.

Description

Chicken-sized; males resplendent in brilliant copper-maroon and gold with parts of body bearing beautifully contrasting base colours and varying patterns of spots, teardrops, bars, and checks; head iridescent green with small "ear" tufts; eyes set in red face patches; may have white ring around neck; long pointed tail; spurs on lower legs; females smaller, in subdued brown camouflage pattern, tails proportionately shorter.

Behaviour

Social; females and grown young may be escorted by territorial male; ranges in grainland, ditches, irrigated fields, and pastures; a swift runner; when flushed bursts straight up on thrashing wings, cackling; scratches through snow cover for seeds and green pickings in winter, may scrounge in farmyards and feedlots, sometimes in considerable numbers; male's call in spring a raucous two-note crow followed by rapid flurry of wingbeats.

Range

On coastal plain on southeast Vancouver Island north to Campbell River; along Fraser River lowlands; most plentiful in Okanagan where population centres in Vernon area; along South Thompson in small, scattered numbers; some in

Williams Lake area; a few on Queen Charlotte islands; totally absent or very scarce in many locations within this general area; favours agricultural lowlands, especially where grain is grown adjacent to brushy cover.

Food

Omnivorous; seeds, grain, green leaves, shoots, and buds; insects, small vertebrates; will feed on carrion in times of scarcity; at feeders will pick up spilled seeds of all kinds and can be attracted with scratch feed, corn, whole grain, and baked goods.

Nest

Depression in the ground lined with leaves or grass, in tall ground cover, fencerows, under bushes, and along woodlot edges.

Comment

Pheasants were brought to Britain by the Normans not long after 1066 where they rapidly became a favourite of the sportsman and the gourmet. Tufts, in *Birds of Nova Scotia*, notes that the legislature of Nova Scotia passed a statute in 1856 "for the preservation of pheasants." But this and many other attempted introductions didn't take in North America until 1881 when thirty birds from China were released in Oregon. First introduction here, as noted in *The Birds of British Columbia*, was at Victoria in 1882. Those twenty all died, but twenty-five released at Esquimalt the following year apparently did well and probably are the foundation stock for the Vancouver Island population.

In *A Birder's Guide to Vancouver Island*, 1990, K. Taylor notes that the "Green Pheasant," a Japanese form of the ringneck, was introduced in the vicinity of Alberni and is fairly common there.

REF: A(W) - 576; BC - 155; GO - 92; NG - 222; P(W) - 158

Ruffed Grouse
Bonasa umbellus

Grouse family. Also known as "bush" or "birch" "partridge"; "Ruffed" from dark ruff of erectile feathers on sides of neck; "Grouse" from French *griais*, "grey," descriptive of several kinds of partridges; *bonasa* from Latin *bonasum*, "aurocks" (wild ox), or "drumming," as voice of male European grouse suggested bellowing bull; *umbellus* from Latin for "sunshade" (umbrella), referring to shape of ruffs when erect.

Description

Larger, longer-legged than pigeon; large tail banded in black with especially obvious subterminal band, tips light tan; hackles on crown may be raised into ragged crest; dark or coppery ruff on sides of neck, raised if bird is excited; camouflage plumage a complicated pattern of flecks, bars, and edging in black, dark brown, rust-red; two colour phases present in all populations, some birds being an overall rusty brown, some greyish; legs feathered; female slightly smaller than male, tail shorter with two central feathers lacking the black subterminal band, neck ruffs are less prominent; buff line through eye; winter bird has fringe of stiff bristles on sides of toes.

Behaviour

Relies on concealment and camouflage to avoid detection; if disturbed but not flushed, first giveaway is urgent peeping and slight rustling of leaves as it high-steps cautiously away; alternately, it might await your close approach, then burst almost from underfoot, sailing swiftly away to re-alight a short distance off; male drums from low vantage points in cover, starting with hesitant, muffled "whups" that accelerate rapidly to a whir, then abruptly stop; drumming heaviest in spring, with secondary busy time in fall; outside of leafy seasons often seen scrambling and flapping about in bushes and trees nipping buds and catkins; roosts in tunnels under snow, locations of these revealed in spring by small piles of pale, macaroni-shaped droppings.

Range

Nonmigratory; throughout parklands and boreal forest to near tree line right across Canada; common through most of British Columbia, especially in lower mainland, Vancouver Island, Okanagan, and Kootenays; prefers open woods, favouring aspen, birch.

Food

Adult is vegetarian, taking shoots, leaves, buds, petals, berries, and seeds; young insectivorous; at feeder takes sunflower seeds, screenings, and cracked or whole grain.

Nest

Bowl scraped at foot of tree or stump, near log or clump; lined with leaves and some feathers; departs as soon as last-hatched young are up and active.

Comment

"I don't think that thing'll fly even if he does get it started!" Thus, my friend

and fellow naturalist Lawrence Stuckey aptly compared a grouse's amorous drumbeat to the starting putt-putt of a reluctant motor.

In her charming book, *The Wonder of Canadian Birds*, Candace Savage says that if you walk softly into the woods early in a spring morning and thump your hands rapidly on the ground, you'll get a reply from the nearest male grouse.

Like the lemming and Snowshoe Hare, Ruffed Grouse suffer drastic population changes. During highs in the roughly ten-year cycle they seem to be everywhere; at lows, scarcely a one can be found. In "high" autumns the young of the year act as if beset by a dispersal frenzy, and many dash themselves against utility wires, fences, windows, and vehicles.

REF: A(W) - 635; BC - 160; GO - 86; NG - 210; P(W) - 160

Sharp-tailed Grouse
Tympanuchus phasianellus

Grouse family. Also called "prairie chicken," a name shared with Greater and Lesser Prairie-Chicken; *Tympanuchus* is from Greek *tympanon*, "a drum," and *nucha*, "neck," from inflatable neck pouches of males; *phasianellus* is from Greek *phasianos*, "a pheasant," plus Latin *ellus* for "little"; in older guides generic name is *Pedioecetes* from Greek *pedion*, "a plain" and *oiketes*, "inhabiting."

Description

Plump, compact, chickenlike bird with short, pointed tail; no obvious field marks at a distance, but underparts beautifully "scaled" with V-marks; central quills of tail are brown with black bars, short outer feathers are white; in flight belly, underwings, and tail coverts noticeably pale; courting male displays small, purplish neck pouches and yellow eyebrow combs; legs feathered; toes in winter edged with stiff fringes.

Behaviour

Very sociable, rarely seen as single; more tendency to fly than most grouse, using short bursts of rapid wing beats with body rocking somewhat erratically from side to side, alternating with long glides on down-curved wings; bird often emits a low, guttural "kuk-kuk-kuk-kuk" on takeoff, and with each subsequent spurt, more or less in time with wingbeats; in spring, courting males gather into groups to display to females; in winter, roosts in plunge holes in snow, and may be seen, morning and evening, scrambling about in trees, plucking buds.

Range

At times erratically migratory; scattered irregularly through western Canada north to tree line wherever grassland, open deciduous woodlands, and openings in burns and boglands occur; in British Columbia absent west of Coast Range, much reduced or extirpated in former range in interior uplands where it favours crop or grassland adjacent to brush or open woods.

P. Sawatzky ©
1990

Food

Leaves, buds, flowers, berries, rose hips, waste grain in summer, and tree buds, especially aspen, in winter; may take screenings, grain, or hen scratch from ground at feeders if it overcomes wariness of human dwellings.

Nest

Cup on ground lined with grasses, in concealing grass, weeds, or low shrubbery.

Comment

In *Birds of the Okanagan Valley*, H. J. Parham, an early naturalist of the Okanagan, is quoted: "In 1900, when I first came to the southern Okanagan, they were very plentiful throughout what is now the Oliver-Osoyoos district . . .

but now they have been practically wiped out in this district; more's the pity, for there are no other grouse to take their place . . . ." Sharptails have indeed vanished from the Okanagan. For whatever consolation there is in it, their place has been taken by three Eurasian transplants, the pheasant, chukar, and Gray Partridge.

For the nature photographer willing to seek it out, a "lek," or group, of courting male sharptails is the ideal subject. A blind can be set up ahead of time a discreet distance from the court and moved a little closer each day as the birds become accustomed to it. It is worth the effort to be in place about an hour before dawn, to witness the ancient ritual performed and perfected as the sun rises upon it. You will see the orange light and the primitive intensity of their dance transform these plain birds into creatures of beauty and mystery.

REF: A(W) - 531; BC - 163; GO - 86; NG - 214; P(W) - 160

California Quail

Callipepla californica

Quail subfamily. "Quail" from Middle Dutch *quacken*, "to croak" (whence "quack") and *quackel*, "a quail"; entered Latin as *quaquila*, "a quail," evolving to Old French *quaille* which made it intact into Middle English; *callipepla* is from Greek *kallos*, "a beauty," and *peplos*, "a robe," hence "beautifully dressed"; former generic name *lophortyx* is from Greek *lophos*, "crest" and *ortyx*, "quail."

Description

Short-tailed, plump, chickenlike bird, smaller than street pigeon; male's comma-shaped black plume curves forward from crown; jet black throat and face bordered with bright white line, white headband above eye, forehead yellow; breast slate-blue, belly beautifully scaled in gold; flanks flecked with white streaks; female much more subdued pattern of browns overall, head plume smaller.

Behaviour

Social; covey scoots along in "follow-the-leader" fashion; nervous, alert, fast runner; feeds after dawn and before dusk, preferring to stick close to brush or other cover; unlike other quail, night roost in tree or thick bush; foraging call a soft clucking "ut ut"; assembly call is loud, three-note, usually short-long-short, usually with emphasis on long, having something of Pileated Woodpecker twang to it; "ku-kwa-kup," "shut-Jack-up," "cut-that-up," etc.

Range

Nonmigratory; originally southwest United States, small part of western Nevada, California, south Oregon; now more widely planted, including in British Columbia on the southeast lowlands of Vancouver Island, south of Vernon in the Okanagan, around Creston; was formerly found in Fraser Valley near Vancouver, now likely gone; favours lower-lying croplands adjacent to blackberry or broom cover, orchards, pastures, golf courses, gardens.

—P.Sawatzky—

Food

Weed seeds, especially clovers, waste grain, acorns, scratched for in leaf litter; leaves, tender grass shoots; at feeder almost any seeds, much preferring them scattered on the ground; very attracted to ground-level water during dry spells.

Nest

Shallow depression scratched out and lined with leaves, grass, rootlets, needles; concealed in ground cover, usually near log, post, tree, rock.

Comment

Quail love a good dust bath, a habit clever bird feeders can cater to by providing a suitable spot that stays dry in wet weather.

In my own limited experience with these delightful birds, I have found it takes patience, and a good supply of hen scratch, to lure them to the vicinity of a feeder. In dry weather a trickling fountain or birdbath would turn the trick much faster.

According to Starker Leopold in *The California Quail*, the early days of settlement in California saw "valley quail" shot and trapped by the hundreds of thousands to cater to the city taste for quail on toast. Hunters blocked off springs with brush, then lured the parched birds with pans of water under set nets. Since in dry times birds might have to fly many miles between springs, the takes were huge. "Ground sluicing" was shotgunning birds packed around springs; forty to sixty could be killed with one shot. The hunter got from 75c to $1.75 a dozen; in one good year during the height of the slaughter some shipped up to ten thousand birds.

In 1931 California officially made this quail its state bird.

REF: A(W) - 594; BC - 167; GO - 90; NG - 218; P(W) - 166

Pigeons

Family *Columbidae*

Three species of pigeons occur in Canada: the Mourning Dove, Band-tailed Pigeon, and the Rock Dove, or street pigeon. All of them are found in British Columbia. The difference between "doves" and "pigeons" is only one of semantics; the smaller tend to be called doves, the larger, pigeons.

We should coin a more accurate name for street pigeons; hearing birders refer to these mixed-breed ferals as "Rock Doves" has always struck me as a bit precious. In Canada they are quite removed in their habits, and usually in their appearance, from their ancestral stock. Are they any more Rock Doves than a stray mongrel dog is a wolf?

The wild Rock Dove still nests on cliffs from the Atlantic coasts of Europe south to North Africa and east to China. Around 4500 B.C. stock from the gorges and sea cliffs around the Mediterranean were domesticated. Since then over three hundred breeds have been developed, some for meat, some to satisfy a fancy for the exotic or bizarre, some for racing. Our street pigeons are the free-lance descendants of a mixture of these that were either liberated or flew the coop. They would in time revert to the ancestral type except for an ongoing recruitment of domestics that keeps the gene pool stirred up. In my view these would be more appropriately called "common" pigeons.

Pigeon "Milk"

Many birds regurgitate to feed their young; but pigeons, flamingos, and Emperor Penguins produce a special "milk." In pigeons, a few days before their two eggs hatch, the linings of both parents' crops swell and form thick folds, tripling in bulk. The surface layer of cells sloughs off continuously to form a thick semifluid like cottage cheese. Hatchlings are fed exclusively on this until they are about half grown; then it is increasingly supplemented with regurgitated seeds.

They thrive mightily on this ration; a day-old nestling is twice its hatching weight, and for several days thereafter gains 38 percent every twenty-four hours. In about a month it reaches adult weight. Pure "milk" is about 15 percent protein, 8 percent fat, 1 to 2 percent mineral, with several vitamins. Poultry chicks fed a ration supplemented with it were over 30 percent heavier at the end of the test than comparables on regular feed.

Pigeons make up for two-egg clutches by more or less nonstop nesting. Under optimum conditions they may begin a new clutch before the previous hatch has fledged.

The flying ability and "homing" instinct of pigeons have long been exploited by mankind for practical purposes and for sport. They have been used to carry messages in times of emergency and war. According to Taylor in *Wings Along the Winnipeg*, carrier pigeons played an important role in forest-fire fighting during the 1930s in Manitoba, displaced only by the advent of two-way radios.

In the sporting world, thousands of carefully bred birds are pampered and trained for racing every year. Champions' flight muscles constitute over 30 percent of their weight, compared to 20 percent for most other strong-flying birds. In July of 1992 a male racer from Holland was sold for two hundred thousand dollars to a British breeder. In three races from Barcelona to his home loft in Holland the bird had flown 1,156 km (720 miles), averaging 64 kph (40 mph). He lived up to his name, "Invincible Spirit," by flying straight over the Pyrenees where lesser birds veered off-course to seek easier flight paths. He was batted by high mountain winds, baked by the sun, and flew nonstop through the night.

Pigeons are said to be the favoured prey of Peregrine Falcons, particularly for those that have taken to nesting in cities where little other good-sized prey is available. Notwithstanding the dazzling speed a peregrine achieves in a hunting dive, considered opinion is that it would be hard-pressed to overtake and capture a healthy pigeon in level pursuit. Invincible Spirit's top speed is 96 kph (60 mph).

Supersenses

Explanations for the astonishing ability of pigeons to find their way home over long distances begin with the fact that the cliffs where ancestral birds nested, often along ocean coasts, could be far from inland fields and prairies where they foraged for seeds. A commuting lifestyle was thus demanded of the birds, which in turn developed the ability to fly accurately over long distances in all kinds of weather.

Several senses combine to affect an unusual navigating skill. They can recognize home territory by scent. An awesome hearing range allows them to detect infra-sounds as low as 0.05 Hz—about one cycle every ten seconds. These are sounds made by storms, winds flowing over mountains, and surf. Ultralow frequency sounds travel through the atmosphere for hundreds of kilometres, giving the birds a sound fix on geographic features far beyond visual limits. They have extraordinary visual memory; in experiments using several hundred colour slides of landscapes, they could recall months later which ones to respond to for a food reward. They can see ultraviolet light. As a light metre does, they can sense small differences in intensity. These together enable them to pinpoint the sun's location on overcast days. They are highly sensitive to changes in atmospheric pressure and are attuned to ground-borne vibrations.

These exquisite sensory gifts are shared in varying degrees by other birds. But what a rich world of signals and sensations our humble street nuisance lives in, a world far beyond the dull senses of its human critics.

✳ ✳ ✳

Rock Dove

Columba livia

Most commonly "pigeon"; "rock" is from wild stock's nesting on cliffs; "pigeon" from Old French *pijon*, "a young bird," derived from Latin *pipio*, "to peep" or "squab"; Latin *columba*, "a dove," *livia* from Latin *lividus*, "bluish."

Description

Smaller than crow; plump, with small, high-crowned head; short, pinkish legs;

varicoloured, but tending to grey body, wings, and tail, with darker iridescent head and neck; tail usually has dark bar at end.

Behaviour

Social; ground feeding in flocks, often on roads; gait a hurried walk, head bobbing in time; steady, strong wingbeats, glides with wings raised to high angle; wings clap sharply together over body on takeoff; courting males bow, coo, strut, and turn animatedly around female; coo is a soft, throaty, chortling "bucket-a-gooo."

Range

Nonmigratory; found throughout British Columbia where humans, deliberately or otherwise, provide food and nest sites.

Food

Seeds; buds, leaves, and shoots in season; garbage; at feeder takes grain, peanuts, baked scraps, popcorn.

Nest

Shallow saucer of straw and/or twigs on ledge in or on building, under bridge; casually colonial where facilities permit; two or three nestings per year, may even attempt winter nesting if shelter adequate.

P.SAWATZKY ©
1990

Comment

For many urban bird feeders, pigeons are greedy, messy usurpers, and there is a minor growth industry based on devising "pigeon-proof" feeders. However, for an apartment balcony station well above reach of other birds, street pigeons might be welcomed as the only clients.

In several sites in the Okanagan, geology and climate have allowed common pigeons to revert somewhat to the ancestral Rock Dove lifestyle. Colonies of them nest on the rock bluffs around Vaseux and Osoyoos Lakes, and in the silt cliffs over Okanagan Lake north of Penticton. According to *Birds of the Okanagan Valley*, they've been at it since at least the mid-1950s. Favourite locales along the coast are harbours which provide abundant nest sites amid the pilings and beams under wharfs. There is a particularly large colony on the ferry jetty at Tsawwassen.

REF: A(W) - 584; BC - 298; GO - 166; NG - 224; P(W) - 210

Band-tailed Pigeon
Columba fasciata

"Band-tailed" from field mark; *columba* Latin for "a dove," *fasciata* Latin for "a band," referring to tail markings.

Description

Darker, but closely resembles slightly smaller street pigeon; end of tail paler, separated from upper tail by dark band; feet yellow, bill yellow with dark end; narrow white line around back of neck; in flight doesn't show white rump as street pigeon does.

Behaviour

Social; feeds either on ground or in trees; more likely to perch well up in trees than street pigeon; voice a deep, owl-like "hoo-woo" or "woo-hoo-woo."

Range

Migratory; down west coast of continent to Nicaragua; once only a summer visitor to extreme southwest mainland, Gulf Islands, and vicinity of Victoria, now nests in these areas and is expanding eastward and northward; winters on southeastern Vancouver Island and in Vancouver and vicinity.

Food

Nuts, especially acorns; berries; fruit of manzanita, arbutus, holly, and ornamentals; visits urban yards for berries, and seeds at feeders.

Nest

Typical pigeon "nest," a flimsy lattice of twigs at widely variable heights but usually from 2 to 6 m (6 to 20 ft) up, often overhanging steep slope or cliff.

Comment

This bird shares some of the nomadic tendencies of the mourned Passenger Pigeon, roving widely in search of food, and on finding it, nesting. The pair broods only one egg, two nestings per year. The population seems to be on a continuing rebound from near-extinction due to hunting, and as a parallel adaptation is turning into an urban bird in cities of the American northwest.

REF: A(W) - 699; BC - 299; GO - 166; NG - 224; P(W) - 208

Mourning Dove

Zenaida macroura

"Mourning" from sad-sounding call; "dove" assumed to be from Anglo Saxon *dufon*, "to dive," from bird's swift flight; *zenaida* after wife of Prince Charles Bonaparte who, after uncle Napoleon's setback at Waterloo, moved to United States, where he is credited as establishing systematic ornithology there; *macroura* from Greek *macros*, "long" and *oura*, "tail."

Description

Trim pigeon shape; noticeably larger than robin; short-legged; slight iridescence to neck feathers; central tail feathers long and pointed, marginal tail feathers flared in flight to show white ends; overall, shades of soft beige, tan, and light smoky brown with hint of blush on breast; dark "ear spot" on sides of head, black flecks on wings.

Behaviour

Obviously a pigeon; often perches on utility wires; feeds on ground; in pairs during breeding season, but in small flocks at other times; wings whistle in flight, especially on takeoff; flight straight and swift on steady wingbeats; voice a measured series of ventriloquistic, hollow "coos," the first ending in a short rise in tone, the other two or three a monotone.

Range

Migratory; breeds across southern Canada to southern edge of boreal forest; in British Columbia doesn't breed west of coastal mountains except for Fraser River lowlands and southern end of Vancouver Island, where some winter; some winter in Okanagan, centred in Vernon area, a few in south Kootenays.

Food

Seeds; at feeder, or on ground beneath it, most seeds, cracked corn and grain; all pigeons drink by submerging bill in water and sucking it up rather than dabbling bill and raising head to let water run down as other birds do.

Nest

A flat, flimsy, sometimes see-through arrangement of twigs, up to 15 m (50 ft) up, but usually between 3 to 7.5 m (10 to 25 ft); may use abandoned nest of robin, catbird, or grackle; in southern Okanagan a large number nest on ground, steep slopes preferred.

Comment

Doves are symbols of peace and love, the expression "billing and cooing" arising from the courting and grooming activities of pairs. In fact, doves are very aggressive birds; mating-season fights between males are fierce, drawn-out, sometimes bloody, conflicts.

Almost every commentator has a go at doves' slovenly housing standards, wondering out loud how the flimsy basket that passes for a nest can hold eggs and young long enough for brooding. Candace Savage, as she often does, says it best in *The Wonder of Canadian Birds*: "The birds often turn lovey-dovey during nest-building . . . since every straw that the male brings to his mate may stimulate a new round of endearments. The finished nest is what you'd expect from a pair of love-blurred minds. . . ."

Sneers of critics to the contrary, the nests work very well judging from the high reproductive rate the birds sustain. Doves are diligent, all-season parents, in the milder parts of Canada bringing off as many as four clutches. Like pigeons, they feed their broods, usually a pair, on rich "pigeon milk." A game bird in much of the United States, and in parts of southern British Columbia, the annual kill runs around fifty million, the highest by far among all game birds.

REF: A(W) - 544; BC - 300; GO - 166; NG - 226; P(W) - 208

Hummingbirds

Family *Trochilidae*

Hummingbirds are strictly a New World avian phenomenon, and one of its most successful with 319 species thus far identified. Most of them live in the zone of tropical forest between ten degrees south and ten degrees north of the equator. One can say "thus far" because several known species are each found only in one very small pocket of habitat. It is reasonable to predict that in this vast region as yet undiscovered species exist in other pockets where the questing biologist has still to set foot. Unhappily, the biologist may lose the race to the chain saw and bulldozer.

Hidden in museum collections there are unsettling reminders, as if any more were needed, that exploitation has a way of outrunning biologists. Fashion decreed, in the late 1800s, that women's hats be adorned with stuffed hummingbirds. To answer the demand, dealers in tropical America paid natives for skins, shipping well over one million a year to London, Paris, and New York. Museums added to their collections by buying specimens from the importers. Among the collections there are six species known only by these trade skins. Were the birds wiped out for fashion, did they vanish when their habitat was obliterated, or do they still whir and dart among the orchids in places only the Indian huntsmen knew?

Tropical as they are, only thirteen species breed north of the Mexican border. Of these, four nest in British Columbia: The Black-chinned, Rufous, Calliope, and Anna's. The Rufous is listed as a summer resident and nester all the way up to Anchorage on the south coast of Alaska.

Avian helicopter

Hummingbirds are unique for their small size, but it is their whirring flight with its amazing speed and exquisite control that distinguishes them from all other birds. From a standing start they can zoom into full flight almost instantly, and "de-zoom" just as abruptly to hang, motionless except for the blurred wings, in front of a flower or feeder. They can fly backwards, even upside down, thanks to wing design and musculature that give them equal power on the up and the down stroke.

Like the human hand, the hummer wing can be turned "palm up" or "knuckles down" through a 180-degree rotation, except that the wing rotates at the shoulder socket, not in the forearm and wrist. On hover, the body hangs down from the shoulders. On the change from forward stroke to back, the wing rotates a full half-circle so that its front edge still leads; on the backstroke the top surface of the flight feathers is underneath. All this goes on at a rate of from twenty-two to eighty beats per second. In a real hurry, some hummers can accelerate this to two hundred per second. Small wonder they hum.

Hummingbirds and swifts are related, and both share the ability to go into a torpid state to conserve energy. The souped-up metabolism of the hummingbird needs copious quantities of fuel; deprived of food for even a couple of hours at the wrong time a hummer will starve. A hummer "low on gas," and unable to refill, has the option of going into torpor to save fuel. Sitting still gets it through a mild night. But if this doesn't cut heat loss sufficiently, the torpor mechanism takes over and drops the bird's temperature from 41°C (105°F) to within several degrees of the surrounding air. The heart rate slows to forty beats per minute, a drastic cutback from a rate of five hundred per minute on idle, twelve hundred at full throttle during flight. In the morning the system revs up again, but apparently doesn't achieve full recovery until the bird can take flight.

Going torpid isn't an option for brooding females because they must maintain their eggs at normal body temperature all night. This they can do thanks to their deep, snug-fitting nests.

A flurry of controversy has arisen recently over whether hummer feeders should have perches in front of the feeding holes. Hummers have been seen falling off perches and expiring on the ground below. A tempting explanation was that the birds were taking their first feed of the day and hadn't reached full operating temperature. It followed that if they had continued hovering, instead of perching, they would have maintained sufficient body temperature to withstand the chill of taking on a large draught of cold syrup at the feeder. Expert opinion greeted this explanation with much scepticism, to the end that for the time being at least I'm leaving the perches on my feeders.

In the Amazonian tropics many species of flowers have evolved in exclusive harmony with hummingbirds, to the exclusion of bees and other insect pollinators. Many blossoms have long, tubelike corollas with narrow openings and no landing pads for bees. Flowers are positioned well free of leaves and tendrils that would interfere with hovering hummers. They are red or orange, colours that the birds can distinguish but insects can't. They produce copious quantities of nectar that isn't as concentrated as that of the insect-pollinated blossoms, since bees are more efficient at collecting small quantities of concentrated nectar. In their turn, some hummingbird species have evolved bills specialized to probe or pierce flowers inaccessible to rival pollinators, including, in some cases, all other hummingbirds

❊ ❊ ❊

Anna's Hummingbird
Calypte anna

If there ever was any association between *calypte* and the Greek proper name *kalypte*, it has been lost; *anna* is from Anna, Duchess of Rivoli, whose beauty and grace, having caught the eye of Audubon, were memorialized by one of his associates, the French naturalist Lesson, who prudently also named another bird, *L. clemenciae* (the Blue-throated Hummingbird), after his own wife.

Description

The largest of British Columbia's hummers, 9 to 10.2 cm (3.5 to 4 in) long; in sunlight adult male flashes purplish-red iridescence on crown, throat patch, and sides of neck—areas that may appear black in duller light; upper body and sides greenish; female similar, paler, lacking iridescent patches.

P. Sawatzky
1992 ©

Behaviour

Visits feeders, flower beds, and blossoming shrubs; like all hummers very pugnacious in defending territory and feeders; courting male power-dives from height, zooms back up, giving an explosive "pop" at bottom of each dive; song a pattern of scratchy squeaks lasting several seconds; call a sharp "chip" or a series of rapid "chee-chee-chee-chees."

Range

Coastal, breeding from Baja California to Vancouver Island; nests on southern Vancouver Island, and in Fraser River Lowlands; winters in these areas and, rarely, in the Okanagan; associated exclusively thus far with yards, gardens, and feeders.

Food

Nectar and small insects extracted, while hovering, from a wide variety of flowers; readily visits feeders for sugar-water which, in winter, should be increased in strength to 60 percent sugar content from the 20 to 25 percent customarily used in hot weather.

Nest

Relatively large compared to other hummingbird nests; made of fine stems, plant down, fibres bound together with spider webbing, lined with plant down and feathers; often finished on outside with flakes of lichen; saddled to slim, horizontal support in a variety of locations.

Comment

Even in the benign climate of Victoria and environs it is astonishing that a hummingbird regularly winters there successfully, albeit with help from feeders in most cases. Although this hardy little mite is expanding from its population centre in California, it isn't an entirely recent phenomenon on our west coast. *The Birds of British Columbia* quotes a published letter from J.O. Clay of Victoria, in January of 1953, stating that "a hummingbird was observed here for three winters since 1944 until January 13, 1947, and this season at intervals until January 12."

The normal diet of hummingbirds includes small insects and spiders as well as nectar, and possibly pollen. Joan and Harold King of Osoyoos had an Anna's come to their feeder on October 17, 1991. At that date there were still flowers in bloom. On one occasion fellow birder Steve Cannings observed it fly-catching on the wing near the feeder. As winter proceeded the feeder even froze several times, but the bird persisted. The insects vanished, and Joan considered replacing the missing protein with beef blood or homemade beef stock in the sugar water, fearful that egg albumen, the usual protein additive, could pass a poultry-borne bird disease to the hummer. But before she could apply the idea the bird vanished, last seen on the morning of December 10 when it took twenty-three drinks at the feeder and departed.

REF: A(W) - 597; BC -338; GO - 186; NG - 258; P(W) - 216

Woodpeckers

Family *Picidae*

Worldwide there are 210 species, twenty breeding in North America, eleven in British Columbia. They are a highly successful group, having evolved to exploit, virtually unchallenged, the rich food buried in the bark and wood of the earth's abundant forest habitat.

Others have made creditable attempts to imitate woodpeckers, not surprisingly two of them members of the limitlessly ingenious finch family. The Maui Parrotbill chews into branches with its stout lower mandible, seeking insects. The Akiapolaau, another Hawaiian, chips into soft wood with its heavy lower mandible while holding out of the way the curved upper one which it brings into play as a probe for the insects its gouging exposes. But none of these has mastered the wood-chipper's trade as thoroughly as the woodpecker.

A number of specialized adaptations combine in woodpeckers to enable them to excavate efficiently into hard wood. It isn't enough to have a straight, hard, chisel-shaped bill and strong neck muscles. In a day's work a busy bird might peck eight to ten thousand times, whacking a hard surface with sufficient energy to generate 10 G's of force on the rebound from each blow. Under such a merciless hammering a normal skull would disintegrate and the brains turn to bloody slop. But the woodpecker skull is strong, heavily reinforced, and bound about with unusually heavy muscles. The mountings of the bill are set with components that slide enough to absorb and dissipate impact shock; the brain is packed snugly into its bony housing and protected with both air- and fluid-filled cushions. The delicate eyes are similarly shielded.

This chopping implement is mounted on a body supported solidly on a tripod arrangement—two sturdy clamps, the feet, and a brace, the stiff tail quills. Thus bracketed, the woodpecker maintains a secure but relaxed stance. This is obviously an important consideration; anyone who has watched a woodpecker at work notices that its torso bobs slightly back and forth in time with its head, adding speed and force to each stroke of the bill.

A Versatile Tongue

The capabilities of the chiselling beak are admirably complemented by a highly extensible, probing tongue. It is mounted on a remarkable apparatus, a stiff but flexible probe of bone, muscle, and cartilage. This divides at the back of the mouth and, supported by the forked hyoid bone, lies in a sheath that curls around the back of each side of the skull, over the top of the head, and is anchored near the nostrils. In most woodpeckers this elongated organ enables the tongue to be stuck out from three to five times the length of the bill. Extended, it resembles the tongue of a garter snake, whiplike and quick. The tip is fitted with a horny point carrying rows of backward-pointing barbs—a miniature harpoon. As tongues tend to be, it is richly supplied with nerves and the ability to taste. Oversized salivary glands on the floor of the mouth coat the tongue with sticky saliva that entraps small insects.

Together, the chiselling beak and the gooey, highly flexible, probing tongue give the woodpecker access to a menu few other insect-eaters can reach. The fact that many of our woodpeckers have no need to migrate is evidence of their year-round ability to exploit a nourishing and abundant food source.

The spectacular Pileated Woodpecker uses its bill to hatchet gaping holes through the outer walls of carpenter ants' tree-trunk fortresses and into their inner galleries. Alarmed by the breach, the ants swarm to their colony's defence, unwittingly playing into the invader's scheme. They are lapped up by the hundreds on the darting, gummy tongue. The size of the Pileated—as big as a crow—is testimony to its ability to exploit the nourishing abundance of carpenter ants in the mature forests it inhabits.

A Big Investment

Chopping into wood to obtain food is hard work. Not surprisingly, woodpeckers are known to have prodigious appetites. The stomach of a Pileated Woodpecker was found by an enquiring investigator to contain 2500 ants. Nest preparation also demands a heavy investment in time and energy. Most woodpeckers seek out punky-cored trees or dead snags, drilling through solid outer sapwood into the softened heartwood where they excavate a spacious cavity. The larger birds must chop out and dump some ten thousand chips; depending on the species, nest building can occupy from ten to twenty-eight days. The reward for all this effort is a secure home, well off the ground, where the young are protected from most predators and from the elements.

There is a further benefit. Unlike small birds in exposed open nests whose strategy is to rush their young through the hazardous nestling period, cavity nesters can afford more time to raise their securely sheltered broods. From hatching to nest-leaving a young Downy Woodpecker takes three weeks, a Hairy a leisurely four. Young robins are off and crash-landing on the lawn in two weeks, most warblers are out in eight to ten days. Such fast-tracking puts a limit on the number of young—the more mouths there are to feed, the longer the process takes.

One serious down-side to living in a hole with no back exit is that when a predator attacks, it's much more difficult for a brooding parent to escape. Observations of titmice showed that 20 percent of brooding females get caught by nest predators.

Woodpeckers may or may not reuse last year's nest hole; most in fact do not, preferring to chip out a new one. Wintering Downy and Hairy Woodpeckers also excavate separate roosting holes. The result is a good number of used tree cavities that, with minimum renovations, can be used by all manner of tenants. Depending on the size of the original builders, swallows, bluebirds, chickadees, squirrels, small owls, Wood Ducks, and others are the most frequent beneficiaries. Most of the above, in fact, cannot breed unless they have access to suitable tree cavities.

There are subtleties that go beyond the obvious tree woodpecker relationship. Woodpeckers evolved to the demands and opportunities presented by natural forests, which means a mixture of tree species in all stages of growth and decay. To many birds, young, or healthy mature trees are of little value. It is the old, the decaying, the dead that furnish the key element to survival. Trees in decline become insect nurseries, their punky innards and rotted knotholes prime cavity nesting sites. To many woodpeckers a forest without a supply of dead snags is just not suitable habitat.

A case in point could be the Lewis's Woodpecker. According to *The Birds of British Columbia*, this species was abundant from 1920 to 1940 around Vancouver and southeast Vancouver Island. Here, fires and the logging practices of the time had left an abundance of tall snags and standing trunks of giant Douglas-fir, Western Redcedar and Western Hemlock. This mix ideally suited the Lewis's unusual foraging behaviour. It feeds on fruit, acorns,

and berries, but its main food is flying insects which it pursues like a flycatcher. The isolated snags and tall trees provided ideal lookouts from which to launch pursuit of winged prey.

Unfortunately, from the woodpecker's point-of-view, after 1940 the cutting of snags for firewood and as a safety requirement by the Forest Service wiped out its livelihood. On southeast Vancouver Island the destruction of Garry Oak stands removed a crucial component there. The extent of the change can be judged by the fact that the last sighting of this once-abundant bird in the Vancouver area was in 1963. Its centre of population in British Columbia is now the Okanagan.

The Drummer

Singing is a proclamation of a bird's being, a claim to territory, an invitation to mate, a threat to a rival. Lacking the voice for it, at least for the kind of noises we humans arbitrarily declare to be "song," woodpeckers advertise themselves and their intentions by drumming. Hammering on a resonating hollow trunk, dead limb, sheet of plywood, or a piece of sheet metal is a song in the generic sense of the word, although it is anything but melodious, particularly if played on your metal chimney at daybreak, morning after morning.

Signs of this tympanic exuberance begin showing up in early February if you happen to be neighbour to a pair of courting Downy or Hairy Woodpeckers. Later, when they begin house-hunting, they will drum at each other in debate over potential locations. Whatever the reason, their staccato bursts enliven the frosty silence of a late winter's day, or most emphatically punctuate the chorus of bird song of an echoing spring sunrise

❄ ❄ ❄

Downy Woodpecker

Picoides pubescens

Downy seems no fluffier than its larger look-alike, the Hairy, seems hairy; *picus* is Latin for "a woodpecker," Greek *oides* is compounded from *o*, "the," and *eidos*, "similar"; *pubescens* is Latin for "downy," as in fine hairs of puberty; in older guides the now-outdated generic name is *Dendrocopus*, from Greek *dendron*, "a tree" and *kopis*, "a dagger."

Description

Bold black-and-white pattern on head, back, wings, and tail; white stripe on back, belly all white; male has small red bar on back of head; told from almost

P. Sawatzky©
1990

identical Hairy by smaller size and proportionally smaller bill; it is often doubtful who is who until the two can be compared close together; even the diagnostic black spots on white outer tail feathers of Downy (absent on Hairy) may be indistinct or not visible.

Behaviour

Typical feeding, perching posture straight up on vertical surface, clinging with the feet, propped on the stiff, pointed tail feathers; forages on tree trunks and branches, females tending to work lower trunk and large branches, males the upper trunk and smaller branches; pert, inquisitive, friendly bird around feeders, sometimes beating even chickadees to newly offered foods; call a short, sharp "kyik" or shrill rattle descending in pitch at end.

Range

Nonmigratory; in mixed, deciduous, all-aged woodlands and burns; common throughout southern British Columbia, Vancouver Island, very unusual north of line between Fort St. John and Prince Rupert.

Food

Largely insectivorous; loves suet and meat scraps, especially when it can pick them off big, raw bones; likes sunflower seeds.

Nest

In winter each bird drills its own roosting nest in dead or decay-softened trunks; entrance hole perfectly round, 3.2 cm (1.25 in) in diameter, from 1 to 15 m (3 to 50 ft) up; occasionally uses nest boxes for temporary shelter.

Comment

Why Downy males forage in the upper levels of trees and their mates the lower has been explained variously. Some dismiss it as mere male dominance, others attribute it to a provident parcelling out of foraging resources and point to the slightly longer tongue of the male as suggestive of division of the sexes at mealtime. Whatever; both search randomly for dormant insects and pupae in and under the bark of trees, sometimes flaking off the bark, sometimes drilling into the insect's refuge and spearing it with the pointed, barbed end of the tongue. Once condemned as injurious to trees, Downies and other woodpeckers, with the possible exception of the sapsuckers, are now tolerantly regarded as important controls on insects whose interests conflict with ours.

The mere presence of trees is no assurance that woodpeckers will be there. Downies require mixed-age woodlands, including a decent complement of the soft-hearted seniors that forestry types sneer at as "decadent."

REF: A(W) - 641; BC - 348; GO - 200; NG - 270; P(W) - 224

Hairy Woodpecker
Picoides villosus

"Hairy" a puzzlingly undescriptive name for a bird with so many other distinguishing features; *picus* is Latin for "a woodpecker," Greek *oides* is compounded from *o*, "the," and *eidos*, "like" (similar); *villosus* is Latin for "hairy"; in older guides the now outdated generic name is *Dendrocopos*, from Greek *dendron*, "a tree," and *kopis*, "a dagger."

Description

Robin-sized; oversized version of Downy; head, back, and wings patterned in sharply contrasting white on black; belly and outer tail feathers all white; adult male has a small red flash on back of head; bill proportionally heavier and longer than Downy's.

Behaviour

Typical woodpecker affinity for perching and feeding on vertical surfaces, especially tree trunks and suet cages; more wary than Downy, usually not as numerous; in spring, drums rapid-fire on resonant surface as part of territorial/courting ritual; call a sharp, abrupt "kyeek" as well as a rapid, strident rattle resembling the kingfisher's; during strongly-powered flight, as in takeoff or sharp turns, wings make a pronounced "whuck-whuck-whuck" noise, possibly a controllable sound used as an alarm signal.

Range

Nonmigratory; in woodlands north to the limits of tree line; widely distributed but not common throughout British Columbia, including Vancouver Island and the Charlottes; very rare in northwest corner; in winter, parks and well-treed yards furnish adequate habitat.

Food

Insectivorous, especially where prey is found in or on trees; at feeder very fond of suet and, secondarily, sunflower seeds.

Nest

Generally in live, firm wood, favours aspen, alder; hole oblong, 5 to 6 cm (2 to 2.5 in) long by 3 to 4 cm (1.25 to 1.5 in) wide.

Comment

Woodpeckers tap sharply to test the resonance of wood, very likely to detect the hollow tunnels of insects. The sudden concussions might also startle hidden insects into moving and giving away their presence to the keen ears of the bird, upon which it drills in to make a capture with its probing, barb-tipped tongue. Exterior siding sometimes excites the excavating reflex in Downies and Hairies who respond to spaces in plywood by punching out the covering plies, or who

drill holes in plastic or other coverings to check the hollow spaces behind them. This habit explains to frustrated householders a behaviour they might otherwise mistake for wilful property damage.

REF; A(W) - 702; BC - 349; GO - 200; NG - 270; P(W) - 224

White-headed Woodpecker

Picoides albolarvatus

Picoides from Latin *picus,* "a woodpecker," and Greek *oides,* "similar"; *albo* from Latin "white," *larvatus* "masked"; recent generic change from *dendrocopos,* from Greek *dendron,* "a tree," and *kopis,* "a dagger."

Description

Robin-sized; unmistakable; black all over except for pure white face, crown, and throat, wing primaries frosted at edges to form white patch in flight, white streak when folded; male has horizontal red patch on back of head.

Behaviour

Pries off loose bark in search of insects; more often seen at watering places than other woodpeckers; comes readily to feeders in winter, occasionally in company of young of the year; call a sharp "chik," or rapid "chik-ik-ik-ik-ik."

P. Sawatzky
1992 ©

Range

Nonmigratory; limited to intermountain valleys and plateaus in the three Pacific coast states and extreme south of the British Columbia interior; strongly associated with Ponderosa and Lodgepole Pine, Douglas-fir and Engelmann Spruce.

Food

Insects, seeds of Ponderosa Pine, and on heads of Common Mullein, an abundant introduced roadside weed; at feeders readily takes suet and sunflower seeds; observed affinity for water would bring it to backyard ponds and fountains.

Nest

Excavates in dead or punky-hearted tree trunks, at widely varying heights; entrance 4 to 5 cm (1.5 to 1.75 in) in diameter;

Comment

Keen birders relish the chance to add this striking bird to their Canadian lists on visits to the southern Okanagan. And while it is so limited in range in British Columbia, it has nevertheless shown a willingness to winter in the yards and orchards of lower altitudes, where, no doubt, it is a treasured visitor at feeders.

REF: A(W) - 706; BC - 350; GO - 198; NG - 266; P(W) - 224

Three-toed Woodpecker

Picoides tridactylus

Until recently, and still in some guides, "Northern (or American) Three-toed"; *picus* is Latin for "a woodpecker," Greek *oides* is compounded from *o*, "the" and *eidos*, "similar"; Greek *trias*, "three" and *daktylos*, "toe," combine to form descriptive *tridactylus*.

Description

The only other three-toed woodpecker is the closely related, and slightly larger Black-backed; three-toed is noticeably larger than Downy; adult male has yellow patch on crown, dark crown of adult female may have light flecking; back, sides, wing primaries, and marginal tail feathers thickly barred in black-and-white, although density of barring is variable; white stripe widening from back of eye down side of neck; white "moustache" from corner of mouth; wing coverts and central tail feathers are black; chin, throat, belly, are white.

Behaviour

Like its larger cousin, the Black-backed, has a reputation for being tame and trusting, and shares preference for dense growths of mature conifers growing on low, swampy ground; favours stands of fire-killed and/or drowned trees; calls a sharp "kyik" and a harsh rattle, very similar to, but softer than, the Black-back's.

Range

Nonmigratory, although occasional winter irruptions may take it far south of breeding range; in boreal, Douglas-fir, and hemlock forest in British Columbia interior, often around openings caused by lakes, muskegs, burns, clear cuts; occasional winter wanderer to lower elevations than its normal haunts.

Food

Insects, principally those found in and under bark of dead, aged trees; although a rarity at feeders, takes readily to suet where it does appear, and may develop liking for sunflower seeds.

Nest

Low hole, 1.5 to 3.7 m (5 to 12 ft) in old or dead conifer; lower edge chiselled to bevel to provide easier access; allowing for "step," hole is 4.4 cm (1.75 in) wide by 5.1 cm (2 in) high, but into tree narrows to circular 3.8 cm (1.5 in) diameter.

Comment

The Three-toed is circumpolar in distribution, unlike the Black-backed, which is exclusively North American. It feeds by drilling small round holes in bark or wood and harpooning exposed insects or grubs with its barb-tipped tongue. Nowhere throughout its extensive range is it a common bird, although its scarcity may be more apparent than real due to its preference for dense habitat at higher elevations, and its infrequent descent to habitat favoured by humans.

REF: A(W) - 704; BC - 352; GO - 200; NG - 270; P(W) - 224

Black-backed Woodpecker

Picoides arcticus

Common names have included "Arctic Three-toed," "Black-backed Three-toed"; *Picoides* compounded from Latin *picus*, "a woodpecker," and Greek *oides* compounded from *o*, "the" and *eidos*, "like" (similar); *arcticus* self-evidently "northern."

Description

Same size as Hairy; only other woodpecker with three toes is aptly-named Three-toed, all the rest having four; back, most of wings, central tail feathers, much of neck, and head, are black; sides and wing ends thickly barred; belly, throat, chin, and dash below eye are white; adult male has yellow patch on top of head, female's crown is all black; told from Three-toed by black back, otherwise difference is hard to see.

Behaviour

A scaler, rather than a driller, flakes off patches of loose bark in search of prey; normally shy and evasive, it can be unusually tame, especially around nest; calls a single, sharp "kik" and a harsh, scolding rattle; in courting season, pairs stage staccato drumming duets.

Range

Nonmigratory; throughout British Columbia interior, in subalpine coniferous forests, and upper levels of the interior Douglas-fir, western hemlock belt, often in heavy growth near bog or muskeg; favours burnt-over conifer forest with tracts of standing, dead trees; absent west of the Coast Range in British Columbia, and from Vancouver Island and the Charlottes.

Food

Scales bark off standing, fire-killed trees for insects, spiders, grubs; readily takes suet at feeders.

Nest

Usually low, from 0.6 to 4.6 m (2 to 15 ft) up in a dead snag, a post or, if in live tree, usually one with a dead heart; hole 3.8 cm (1.5 in) high by 4.4 cm (1.75 in) wide with pronounced bevel to lower rim forming a kind of step.

Comment

Not a bird easily met, partly because its black upper body and barred flanks are excellent camouflage against the dark bark of live spruce, or against the blackened trunks of the fire-killed trees it seeks out. According to *Birds of the Okanagan Valley* it is more inclined than the Three-toed to show up at lower elevations, particularly in winter, especially where it can forage on the standing trunks of a burn. Its appearance at a feeder anywhere in British Columbia should be considered a noteworthy event.

REF: A(W) - 705; BC - 352; GO - 200; NG - 270; P(W) - 224

Northern Flicker
Colaptes auratus

Woodpecker family. Until recently also "Common Flicker"; previously "Yellow-shafted" (*C. auratus*), "Red-shafted" (*C. cafer*), or "Gilded" (*C. chrysoides*); folk names have included "high-hole," "high-holder," "clape," "pigeon woodpecker," "yellow-hammer," "yarrup," "hairy wicket," "wake-up," "yawker bird," "walk-up," "ant-bird," among many others; "flicker" from Anglo Saxon *flicerian*, "fluttering of birds," although word is also highly echoic of bird's call; *colaptes* from Greek *kolapto*, "to peck with the bill, chisel"; *auratus* from Latin "golden," referring to undersides of wings and tail.

Description

Larger than robin; short-legged, solid; in flight shows bright salmon-red underwings, boldly speckled undersides, and bright white rump; bold black bib across top of breast; long, strong, slightly down-curved bill; in normal red-shafted phase neither sex has horizontal red dash on back of head; crown and neck are brownish grey; sides of head and throat grey; back and wings dark brown with horizontal black barring; male has red "moustache" from corner of mouth extending back under eye.

Behaviour

Strong, markedly undulating flight with several rapid beats on up-swoop, wings folded for down-swoop; unlike other woodpeckers, spends much time on open, grassy ground and roadsides, hopping awkwardly about searching for ants; drums during mating season, sometimes on buildings; courting couples go through elaborate "dance" duet on tree limbs, flaring wings and tail, bobbing and moving heads in circles; noisy, calls a staccato, strident "yuk-yuk-yuk-yuk," a more deliberate "wicker, wicker, wicker," or a single, loud "kleee-yer."

Range

Migratory; breeds throughout Canada, coast to coast and north to tree line; favoured habitat is open woodland, parkland, pastures, suburban yards, and

-P SAWATZKY -
1992 ©

parks; winters on Vancouver Island, the Fraser Lowlands, and upper Fraser Valley occasionally as far north as Prince George; also Okanagan and Kootenays; "red-shafted" phase predominates west of the Rockies.

Food

Ants, mostly from ground; in season fruit, nuts, seeds; suet, peanut butter and, perhaps, sunflower seeds at feeders.

Nest

Excavates hole in tree or snag with punky heartwood, thus favouring poplars; also utility poles, fenceposts, buildings, or uses natural tree cavities or nest boxes; known to use holes in banks and cliffs; excavated hole 5 cm (2 in) in diameter, from .5 to 20 m (20 in to 65 ft) up; old flicker holes are important to other birds and small mammals; starlings frequently evict flickers.

Comment

Flickers have recently been taxonomically "lumped," three former separate species downgraded to regional races and newly renamed the Northern Flicker. Except for the underwing colours that gave them their names, all three races have very similar plumage patterns, differing only in that the Yellow-shafted has a crescent of bright red encircling the back of its head, while the Red-shafted and Gilded don't, at least not as a rule.

The really important plumage difference is sex-related; all males, otherwise identical to the females, have a coloured "moustache." The Yellow-shafted's is black, the others', red. To confirm its significance, a biologist painted a moustache on a mated female flicker. Her erstwhile lifelong mate promptly attacked her and drove her away. When the offending mark of maleness was removed, he took her back. Where the races meet and interbreed, the essential moustache may come out red on one side, black on the other. Except to sometimes befuddled bird watchers, it doesn't seem to matter.

In my own experience on the southeast side of Vancouver Island, a male flicker regularly appeared to feed on winter-fast apples. Almost as far as you can get from the Continental Divide that separates his race from the Yellow-shafted, he bore all the Red-shafted marks, and in addition had a nice red blaze on the back of his head!

REF: A(W) - 642; BC - 352; GO - 194; NG - 264; P(W) - 226

Pileated Woodpecker

Dryocopus pileatus

"Pileated" from specific name which is from Latin *pileum*, "a cap," refers to bird's prominent crest; formerly "cock-of-the-woods," or "logcock," from red crest's resemblance to a rooster's comb; *dryocopus* compounded from Greek *drys*, "a tree" and *kopis*, "a dagger."

Description

Crow-sized, continent's largest woodpecker by far; with wings folded is predominantly black except for white stripe on each side of the long neck and side of face; white chin, narrow white eyebrow stripe; both sexes have conspicuous red crest, the male's being larger, and he has a red "moustache"; in flight, white lining on underside of wings flashes prominently.

Behaviour

First clue to presence is often large, vertically oblong holes freshly chipped out of trunks of trees and snags, frequently close to ground; litter of chips especially obvious in snow; very wary except where it has had a chance to become habituated to people in protected areas such as national, or large urban, parks; on quiet days in mature woodland loud, irregular whacking noise of this bird at work is usually the first active sign of its presence; call a loud, strident succession of "kyak-kyak-kyak-kyak"s often increasing in volume, similar to flicker with the sound turned up.

Range

Nonmigratory; formerly limited to substantial tracts of mature deciduous and boreal forest away from human activity, but latterly adapting to share parks and enclaves of mature woodland with people; widespread in British Columbia, more familiar in southern half and on Vancouver Island than in northern half; may be some movement from north of range in winter.

Food

Wood-boring insects, especially carpenter ants which it regurgitates to feed its nestlings; occasionally visits feeders for suet; said also to take nuts, meat scraps, and hamburger.

Nest

Hole is usually 9 to 15 m (30 to 50 ft) up in a large tree; entrance 8 to 9 cm (3 to 3.5 in) wide, somewhat longer.

Comment

Often the first outward sign that a big, apparently sound tree is harbouring carpenter ants is a Pileated's fresh, gaping hole near the base of it.

In response to early settlement and logging, populations plummeted to the point where the species was thought to be threatened. But numbers recovered, and may still be increasing, thanks to the birds' latent ability to adapt to cutover forest habitat, and to growing public revulsion against indiscriminate shooting that once claimed many of these beautiful birds.

REF; A(W) - 703; BC - 354; GO - 194; NG - 274; P(W) - 222

Crow Family

Family *Corvidae*

Crows—the corvids—are an avian success story. Masterfully versatile generalists, they can call upon a repertoire of survival skills that allows them to adapt to virtually every habitat on earth.

By being generalists, they have missed both the benefits and the risks of specialization. They are predators, of a sort, but they lack the power and speed of the flashy hawks. They feed on dead animals, but cannot soar effortlessly aloft and stay there all day, surveying a huge circle of earth, like that master scavenger, the vulture. But unlike these two, if there's no meat of any kind to be had, they simply look for something else—seeds, green shoots, insects, garbage. They have no obvious physical feature that makes them anything but oversized songbirds. Even the bulky raven faces its harsh world in the highest Arctic on dickybird feet innocent of destructive capacity. Its bill is large and businesslike, but more a handyman's tool than a specialized instrument.

If there is one thing they can claim as special, it's their intelligence. There is no trustworthy scale for measuring this attribute in humans, let alone one for rating one species of animal against another. But in comparison to other birds reacting to similar situations, the corvids do seem to be "smarter."

In this brainy tribe, crows and ravens are regarded as the most highly evolved. It is an assumption supported by their obvious ability to learn quickly and to remember, and their unusual degree of adaptability in a wide range of habitats. Convincingly, they have the highest brain-to-body weight ratio of any bird.

The popular literature repeats a seaside anecdote on how gulls and crows both attempt to feed on mussels. Neither are strong enough to smash the shells or pry them open with their beaks. Both have learned to fly aloft with a mussel and crack it by dropping it. With the gulls, however, it is a hit-and-miss operation since, as often as not, they bomb them fruitlessly onto soft mud. But the crows have learned to drop them onto the rocks.

Tufts, in *Birds of Nova Scotia,* reports nest-building ravens' pulling wool from the rumps of resting sheep.

Corvid intelligence isn't the lovable smarts of, for example, the porpoise. It is a defiant craftiness with a bent for larceny that irritates humans. Branded as pests by farmers and hunters, they have been persecuted relentlessly. They simply respond to the plots against them by becoming more skilfully evasive. Crows are noted for their uncanny ability to sense the presence of a concealed gun, and to spot the difference between a shotgun and a similarly shaped cane.

Country Bird Moves Uptown

Throughout their range in Canada several species of corvids, initially swept aside by the impact of settlement, have learned to capitalize on the changes mankind has wrought. In any northern mining or lumbering town ravens are as common as park pigeons, often hanging about the downtown business sections in such numbers as to be nuisances. Thompson, Manitoba—determined, perhaps, to adopt a positive view in spite of some misgivings—made the bird its emblem. Squadrons of "Thompson turkeys" ensure that the contents of any garbage can left open will soon be strewn about. Auto insurance claims are occasionally paid to repair dents caused by ravens' dropping bones or frozen globs of refuse onto cars from on high.

Not to be outdone, the prairie magpie has also gone urban in a big way, thanks in part to a change in human behaviour. When prairie farmers retire to town they take their shotguns with them. In earlier days they continued to do what they and their neighbours deemed a civic duty—blast any magpie that came within range. Now, however, prairie towns don't tolerate gunplay within their limits, not even if the target is the despised magpie. So the cheeky bird has moved in where it finds not only bountiful food, but protection from the wrath of its human enemies and safety from its natural predators.

Grown abundant, it is condemned for its noisiness, its destructiveness and domination of feeders, its habit of strewing refuse about, and its reputation as a destroyer of small birds' eggs and young. In cities like Calgary some irate citizens demand campaigns of eradication, others will have none of it, and controversy rages.

Likewise adaptable, and controversial, the Northwestern Crow commutes between shore and shopping centre in coastal harbours and towns of British Columbia. When not flipping through the wash line of seaweed on the beach, it dodges cars and shopping carts to forage for scraps in the middle of town.

The "Good Guy/Bad Guy" Role

In nature there is an endless interplay of actions that can be misinterpreted according to human values as either "good" or "bad," even for activities that don't relate to human interests. These biases obscure the real roles of the species they affect, in the case of the crow family making them targets of unthinking persecution.

Crows, ravens, and magpies will congregate around dead animals to pick out the eyes and feed on the rotting flesh, a behaviour finicky humans find ghoulish. Other emotions intervene; all corvids are nest predators, feeding on the eggs and nestlings of other birds. On a purely emotional level this is abhorrent; bird lovers feel pity for the bereaved parents, hunters fume over the loss of "their" game birds.

The answer for genuinely interested nature watchers is to learn more about the survival imperatives of the animals around them, to let true knowledge supplant prejudice and emotion. The important thing to keep in mind is that in nature there is no altruism and no vindictiveness, only the unbreakable rules of survival and reproduction.

Predators As Prey

It may help us overcome our judgemental prejudices to realize that the maligned crow family is as accountable to the laws of survival as any wild animal. In the game of eat-or-be-eaten, the corvids themselves, especially the young, provide food for larger predators.

Birds of the Okanagan Valley relates an observation by James Grant in late May, 1976, of a raven killing the nearly fledged young of a crow near Lavington. The tables were turned, however, in an incident recorded by L. and V. Gibbard in June, 1967, when they saw a male Northern Oriole, on guard at its nest, put the run on a would-be plundering raven.

In 1990, at Riding Mountain National Park in Manitoba, where I worked as an interpretive naturalist, the headless carcass of a fully fledged young raven was found in mid-June on the ground a few metres from the nest. Evidence pointed to a Great Horned Owl which, at that time of year, would have been feeding a nest of its own young.

On the matter of food, corvids have the most varied diet of any birds. They eat grain, green shoots from gardens, berries, dried fruit, carrion, eggs and nestlings, small terrestrial animals, insects, fish, and all manner of human refuse, and will hoard surplus food. "Pica," the Latin word for "magpie," is also a medical term describing an unusual craving for unnatural things, such as a child that eats dirt or paint.

The crow family tends to be long-lived. A raven in captivity lasted for twenty-nine years, and wild Blue Jays have survived to fifteen. This of itself does not prove a high IQ, but it is an advantage permitting both the time, in youth, to learn, and an extended adulthood in which to accumulate and apply the lessons of experience.

Finally, for what it's worth as a measure of their intelligence, this family boasts the only native Canadian birds that can be taught to imitate human speech.

❋　❋　❋

Gray Jay
Perisoreus canadensis

Lacklustre "gray" replaces "Canada" of former name; interesting that European writers describe the call of their Siberian Jay as "whisk-ee," and that the Algonquian peoples named it *wiskatjan,* "whiskey-jack" in its woodsy English version; *perisoreus* is Greek for "to heap up," i.e. to hoard; *canadensis* is Latinized "of Canada."

Description

Slightly larger than robin; off-white face and forehead shading softly into smoky grey accentuate the overall soft, puffy look; back of head, neck, and indistinct stripe encircling eye are darker grey to grey-brown; back, wings, and tail soft grey, underside lighter grey; bill of modest proportions; tail long.

Behaviour

Actions deliberate, unhurried; flight often a smooth, suspended, descending glide; accomplished mooch, training picnickers to share food by approaching them with an air of poised expectancy; not above helping itself with a well-timed grab if passive appeal doesn't work, hence the alternate bush name "camp robber"; compulsive food hoarder; call a clear, descending "quee-oo" whistle; other sounds include typical jay repertoire of squawks, chortles, and imitations.

Range

Partially migratory, in some areas readily moving from high altitude summer ranges to lower altitudes in winter; some parts of population also migrate north-south; in Canada breeds from tree line south through boreal and montane forest from coast to coast; in British Columbia occurs everywhere in the boreal and subalpine fir belts of higher altitudes; absent from the Charlottes; unusual visitor to lower elevations.

Food

Omnivorous; fruit, seeds, meat, insects, carrion; at feeder takes suet, larger seeds, table scraps.

Nest

Large, thick-walled; well lined with fine grasses, bark shreds, feathers, hair, fur, spider and insect cocoon webbing; usually 1 to 3 m (3 to 10 ft) from snow surface, but occasionally much higher; usually close to trunk of small to midsized conifer exposed to sun, almost always on south side of tree; eggs very pale greenish splattered with olive and paler grey, especially at large end.

Comment

Gray Jays have perfected food-caching to a degree that allows them not only to survive the harsh conditions of a high alpine winter, but to begin nesting well before it ends. Compulsive hoarding, familiar to campers and picnickers, is the means to this end. Their unique facility for storing food where subsequent snow won't bury it, aided by a prodigious memory, sees them and their brood through the toughest period of the winter. See Chapter 6, "Midwinter Nests," for a fuller discussion of Gray Jay nesting behaviour.

According to *Birds of the Okanagan Valley,* the Gray Jay can convincingly mimic the Northern Pygmy-owl, a much sought-after species by birders who, when "owling," imitate the call of the bird, hoping to elicit a reply. Apparently the jay is just as happy to respond in place of the desired owl.

REF: A(W) -727; BC - 381; GO - 224; NG - 302; P(W) - 256

Steller's Jay
Cyanocitta stelleri

Named after Georg Steller, German physician and expedition biologist with Bering's 1740 expedition to Alaska; *cyanocitta* from Greek *cyanos,* "blue," and *kitta,* "a jay."

Description

Large, tall-crested, dark bird; sooty head, throat, and neck blend into dark blue of body; darker flecks on wings and tail; Queen Charlotte race almost entirely black.

Behaviour

In family groups for awhile after young fledged; a confident, unafraid regular in yards, gardens, and orchards, but wary and evasive in its preferred upland habitat; voice a tuneless, raspy "yaaak-yaaak-yaaak," but imitates musical calls of other birds.

Range

In Canada, almost uniquely British Columbia's bird, a thin slice of southwestern Alberta excepted; absent from northeast of province; coastal populations non-

migratory, but interior populations partially migratory, returns from birds banded at Revelstoke coming from well into United States; found in various types of coniferous and mixed-wood forest; retreats from upper altitudes in winter when it becomes more evident in valleys and coastal lowlands.

Food

Omnivorous; insects, small vertebrates, seeds in summer, switching to acorns, pine seeds in winter; at feeder fond of peanuts, sunflower seeds, suet, baked goods, table scraps.

Nest

Well-made, bulky base of twigs, dead leaves; cup of mud and grasses, lined with fine grass, root fibres, hair, pine needles; in bush or tree, usually conifer, 2.5 to 5 m (8 to 16 ft) up, but can vary greatly, including being located in cavity in tree or even in building.

Comment

The Steller's is British Columbia's provincial bird. The literature on this largest of North American jays assures us that they are accomplished mimics, frequently leading birders on wild goose (or eagle, or owl) chases. They have even been heard to give a perfect imitation of a Common Loon.

Recently, Blue Jays have begun showing up frequently in the interior of southern British Columbia, and there are recent records of birds as far west as the west coast of Vancouver Island. Unknown here except as rare vagrants prior to the mid-1970s, they have been turning up more frequently in cities, towns, and resorts, presumably using these centres of human population as stepping-stones into Steller's territory. This population shift is also occurring in the United States, in a similar pattern. It is assumed that the abundance of winter food at feeders is aiding this advance.

The impact on the Steller's Jay could in time be profound, less from direct competition with the Blues than from the fact the two species interbreed, a phenomenon that always favours an invasive species expanding from a larger population base.

REF: A(W) - 735; BC - 382; GO - 222; NG - 302; P(W) - 254

Blue Jay

Cyanocitta cristata

"Jay" is rooted in the Latin *gaius,* "a jay"; may also be echoic of the call; *cyanos* is Greek "blue," *kitta,* "a jay"; *cristata* is Latin for "crested."

Description

Bigger than robin, smaller than Steller's Jay; gorgeously blue; bright azure patterned with black bars and white patches on wings and fan-shaped tail; back and crest a uniform purplish blue; face patterned with a grey-bordered black eye-stripe extending downward in a narrow ribbon forming a circlet over the upper breast; breast and belly smoky grey, undertail white.

Behaviour

Movements graceful; attitude alert, wary; almost always in company, probably family; hurriedly gobbles food to carry away in throat pouch to storage places; highly vocal, with repertoire of squawks, whistles, chortles, and trills to add to its standard, rasping "ja-a-a-ay" call and a clear "weedle-weedle-weedle."

Range

Partially migratory; in Canada inhabits mixed and deciduous woodland, parks, and suburbs east to foothills of Alberta; extending range west into southern British Columbia.

Food

Omnivorous, opportunistically predacious, sometime scavenger on carrion such as road kills; takes, and stashes in quantity, most feeder offerings except smallest seeds; robs eggs and nestlings of other birds.

Nest

Rather loose, shallow platform of coarse twigs; cup lined with rootlets, bark, shreds of plastic, paper, rags, and feathers.

Comment

In a famous incident a captive Blue Jay tore pieces of newspaper from the bottom of its cage and used them to fish through the bars for food pellets otherwise beyond its reach. It is a talented mimic of other birds, especially the Red-tailed Hawk, and of odd sounds like the squeaking of a rusty clothesline pulley. With patience, Blue Jays can be tamed to hand feeding, and become entertaining, ingenious scrounges.

Some observers have suggested that its taste for songbird eggs stems from its own need for calcium during the female's egg-developing stage, and that supplying oyster shell or chopped-up eggshell will diminish its drive to pilfer nests. It's a comforting thought awaiting verification.

The Blue Jay's appearance in eastern British Columbia is looking more like a permanent range expansion than a succession of isolated incursions. Individuals that have recently been observed in places like the Sunshine Coast and Tofino may be the harbingers of a massive invasion that could spell trouble for the indigenous Steller's Jay.

REF: A(E) - 552; BC - 382; GO - 222; NG - 302; P(W) - 254

Clark's Nutcracker
Nucifraga columbiana

"Clark," of Lewis and Clark(e) expedition of 1803 to northwest United States; "nutcracker" from bird's method of feeding; *nucifraga* from Latin "nut" and *frango,* "break"; *columbiana,* after river near which Clark collected type specimens.

Description

Built like half-sized crow; canvas-grey body; wing dark with white patch prominent in flight; central feathers of tail dark, outer ones white; curved dagger bill much longer than that of similar Gray Jay.

Behaviour

Slow, crowlike wingbeats; around mountain resorts a bold, persistent beggar of handouts; industrious hoarder of seeds which it buries in ground; voice a flat, grating "caaa" or "craaa."

Range

Generally nonmigratory; as with many high-altitude breeders, may make seasonal altitudinal shifts; in Canada confined to subalpine regions of West, and there largely to pine forests; in British Columbia locally very common in southern half from Bulkley Valley southward wherever White-bark and Ponderosa Pines occur; a few scattered records from northern half of the province.

Food

Omnivorous, but dependent mainly on pine seeds which it stores in great numbers prior to winter; carries seeds in throat pouch; at feeders takes peanuts, sunflower seeds, suet, table scraps.

Nest

Large bowl-shaped base of twigs, sticks, bark, built up with inner cup of bark, grass filled in with punky wood powder; inner cup lined with grass, bark, and other plant fibres; sometimes a plaster layer (mud, duff, soil) between base and inner cup; in dense conifer, often towards end of a branch.

Comment

Like the crossbills with which it shares a conifer-dependent lifestyle, the nutcracker must periodically abandon its preferred habitat when the seed crop fails.

Judged by major eruptions of these birds out of their mountains, pine seed production collapses every ten to fifteen years. Unlike crossbills, but very much like jays, the nutcracker hedges against famine by storing from twenty thousand to thirty thousand pine seeds in caches on exposed south-facing slopes where mountain winds scour off the snow, and the sun keeps the earth from freezing solid. It is aided in its hoarding by a throat pouch with a capacity of ninety or more pine seeds, plus whatever it can load into its bill. It also has a mental map grid capable of accurately relocating seed caches by orienting to nearby marks such as stones. Experimenters have moved the marks and found the bird's recovery probes changed location by the same amount. It has been seen to dig down through a foot of snow with great accuracy to recover buried seeds.

The life-giving pine crop permitting, it shares with the crossbill the ability to nest very early in the season, brooding its young in heavy, well-insulated nests and feeding them on regurgitated seeds.

REF: A(W) - 726; BC - 384; GO - 224; NG - 302; P(W) - 256

Black-billed Magpie

Pica pica

"Black-billed" as distinct from "Yellow-billed" of California; sometimes "American" Magpie; "magpie" has two roots, "mag" from the pet version of

"Margaret" (although the connection is a mystery), and "pie," possibly from same root as "piebald," an animal with a patchwork of contrasting colours, or from Middle English *pie,* "magpie"; *pica* is Latin for "a magpie."

Description

Pigeon-sized, slim; very long-tailed, strikingly beautiful; contrasting black-and-white body pattern; tail and wings are iridescent blue-green-bronze; in flight, outer wing primaries flash white, and horseshoe-shaped white mark on back is very evident.

Behaviour

All movements graceful and fluid, particularly when springing about among branches; unhurried flight almost languid, stroking the air on measured wingbeats; travels in small, loose groups; congregates around garbage dumps and road kills; call a strident, rasping "yek-yek-yek," repeated rapidly or in a single, drawn-out, ascending "yaaag?"; usually very wary and alert.

Range

Regionally and optionally migratory, especially from northern extremes of range; in North America a western native, from Alaska south to New Mexico; fall dispersal may see it well up in mountain terrain; throughout British Columbia east of Coast Ranges, north, and up, through boreal zone; prefers open land with scattered woodlots, brushy gullies, wooded valleys.

Food

Omnivorous scavenger and predator; at feeders, hauls suet away in bulk chunks until it's all gone—a good reason for dispensing it in sturdy wire screen holders with 1 cm (.5 in) or smaller mesh.

Nest

Unmistakable; huge, loosely interlaced structure of twigs, often thorns, up to 1 m (3 ft) in height woven around a cupped nest of mud and fibres, completely enclosed except for one or more side entrances; in small tree or large bush, from 2 to 5 m (6 to 16 ft) up; takes forty to fifty days to build.

Comment

This is the same species notorious in Europe as a noisy scold and thief. In Canada it is a western bird, initially driven from the Prairies by loss of bison and/or subsequent settlement. But it has reclaimed its former domain and is spreading steadily southeastward, in time possibly to establish itself in southern Ontario.

As expected of a species that is adaptively migratory, birds from the northern extremes of their range move south. Wayne Campbell (personal communication) pointed out that towns like Atlin, and its garbage dump, play host every winter to birds from Alaska.

The magpie's legendary wariness is a response to persecution for its purported depredations on game bird eggs and for pecking at wounds and warble fly sores on the backs of cattle. Sometimes, it is said, they deepen these wounds enough to injure or kill the animals which, unaccountably, seem not to be troubled by the probing bills in their live flesh. In its turn, the magpie is prey to the wintering goshawk and Great Horned Owl at a time when other game is scarce.

REF: A(W) - 564; BC - 393; GO - 224; NG - 304; P(W) - 256

American Crow
Corvus brachyrhynchos

Sometimes "common" crow; from Anglo Saxon *crawe*, "crow," imitative of call; *corvus* is Latin for "a crow"; Greek *brachys* is "short" and *rhynchos* "beak" because the crow beak is shorter than a raven's.

Description

All-black; told from raven by considerably smaller size, relatively smaller bill, lack of hackle feathers at throat, and square tail (raven's is fan-shaped); most diagnostic is voice, the raven's a variety of croaks, the crow's a basic "caw."

Behaviour

Social; out of breeding season may rove and roost in large flocks; wary, alert and sharp-eyed; flight on steady wingbeats with little gliding unless circling or coming in for a landing; forages on ground in cultivated fields, roadsides, garbage dumps; scavenges dead animals; "caw" loud, harsh; may be very noisy

especially around nest when young are begging from old birds, or when a group is "mobbing" an owl or hawk.

Range

Migratory; breeds from coastal mountains of British Columbia to Atlantic Provinces, including Newfoundland, and north to tree line; in British Columbia's Kootenays and Okanagan Valley it is nonmigratory; incidence decreases from north to south in north half of province, with only a few records from the top third; replaced by the Northwestern west of Coast Range.

Food

Totally omnivorous, taking seeds, fruit, insects, carrion, buds and shoots, eggs and nestlings; at feeder takes suet, seeds, corn, and grain.

Nest

Large bundle of coarse twigs, usually well up in major crotch on trunk or branch, obvious from a distance when tree is leafless; bowl made of shredded bark, grasses, vine stems, lined with moss, grass, fur, feathers; most frequent used-nest-of-choice by Great Horned Owls which don't make their own.

Comment

As Godfrey points out in *Birds of Canada*, if the average person were asked to name four birds, one would almost certainly be the crow.

Very likely that person could also do a fair vocal impression of a crow. And although that hoarse "caw" is the only call we associate with this plentiful bird, it is nevertheless employed with great eloquence. Its inflection, duration, frequency, pitch, volume, and tone can clearly communicate fear, alarm, suspicion, curiosity, anger, hunger, and "come hither," even to the casual ear of a listening human.

As to its clever adaptability, American clergyman and lecturer Henry Ward Beecher summed up the crow in a trenchant comparison: "If men wore feathers and wings, very few of them would be clever enough to be crows."

REF: A(W) - 685; BC - 394; GO - 226; NG - 306; P(W) - 252

Northwestern Crow
Corvus caurinus

Sometimes the "San Juan chicken" in those islands; in Old English the *crawe* was said *to crawan*, in Middle English becoming *crowe* and *crowen*, out of which evolved "to crow," which only roosters do in modern English; *corvus* is Latin for "a crow," *caurinus* for "northwestern."

Description

To all appearances a slightly smaller, more lightly built version of the American Crow.

Behaviour

Very social; a beachcomber, pulling apart high-tide windrows of seaweed, winging a few feet into the air to drop small shellfish on the rocks, hanging about seabird nesting colonies to grab eggs or young; equivalent of American Crow's "caw" is a hoarse untuned "caaa"; also dry, clicking rattle more mechanical than vocal.

Range

Coastal strip, and adjacent islands, from United States border on mainland, and Victoria on Vancouver Island, northward along Alaska panhandle to south Alaska coast.

Food

Omnivorous, range dictating that shellfish, crabs, marine carrion constitute bulk of diet; garbage; grain, especially corn; fruit.

Nest

Nest a bulky mass of twigs under large cup of grass, mud; inner lining of fine grass, bark fibres, hair; in tree or shrub at varying heights, on rocky ledge, occasionally on ground under boulder or stump; often nests in loose associations.

Comment

Much of the literature on this bird hedges on whether or not it should be considered a race of the American Crow rather than a separate species. Where the two meet in the Puget Sound area they are said to interbreed readily.

Among most coastal householders, resort owners, and fruit growers this bird is an unwelcome, noisy nuisance. Bird lovers in condominiums are often forbidden to put out feeders because they might attract crows. Some indeed do; in winter one flock of seven calls regularly at my yard between scavenging sessions on the shore about a kilometre away. The attraction is the hen scratch I scatter on the ground some distance from the house. They walk through it, picking out the kernels of corn with their tweezer beaks and flying off with them. Their unfailing good manners belie their bad reputation; they have never come near the feeders, and when not searching for corn sit quietly in the trees. Their presence doesn't upset the small birds, nor does it intimidate the California Quail that tiptoe out of the adjacent cover mornings and evenings to pick through the grain. Evidently close-mouthed, they have kept our relationship private. Perhaps a corvine sense of discretion tells them that bringing along a mob of freeloaders would spoil a good thing.

REF: A(W) - 754; BC - 395; GO - 226; NG - 306; P(W) - 252

Common Raven

Corvus corax

Sometimes "Northern" Raven; "Raven" from Anglo Saxon *hraefn*, "raven"; *corvus* is Latin for "crow," *corax* Greek for "a raven," akin to *krazo*, "croak."

Description

All black; distinguished from crow by larger size, more massive bill, shaggy throat feathers, wedged tail (crow's is squared off), and voice, a grating, guttural, resonant "cronk."

Behaviour

Usually seen in pairs or small family groups, except at food sources like garbage dumps where it may congregate by the dozens; more inclined than crow to circle aloft and soar, and frequently indulges in rolling, tumbling, and diving aerial games; voice a highly variable repertoire of throaty honks, squawks, and an unexpectedly musical, bell-like "tok"; fur traders called it "barking crow"; vulturelike in ability to detect carrion and kills.

Range

Nonmigratory; worldwide in northern hemisphere; in Canada from highest Arctic islands throughout northern continental mainland in boreal, sub-boreal and montane forests; found virtually everywhere throughout British Columbia, from balmiest seacoasts to the highest glaciers.

Food

"Kills rabbits and birds" says a British field guide; people who feed birds where ravens are present discover they have a voracious capacity for suet and for wrecking all but the sturdiest dispensers.

Nest

Begins spectacular courtship aerobatics around end of March; nest a large mass of sticks and twigs on cliff ledges or in trees (usually large conifers); may build new nest on top of last year's.

Comment

In what must be something of a record, the two most recent Christmas Bird Counts for Prudhoe Bay, Alaska, which reposes at 70° 19' north latitude, recorded only one species. Guess who?

On a number of occasions I have noted that most ravens approaching a scrap of food in the snow for the first time go through an elaborate routine. Surveillance comes first, from varying angles and elevations. The ground approach proceeds by hesitant stages and nervous retreats, ever nearer until the bird is close enough to stretch forward, stab and recoil, and pause. Slightly reassured it repeatedly

P.SAWATZKY
1991 ©

jabs, bounds back, and springs up on flapping wings until the prize is finally snatched and yanked back or flipped overhead.

Students of ravens say it is a test to make sure potential carrion is really dead. Possibly so, but I call it the "trap dance," acquired from generations of ancestors that learned to rob the still-ubiquitous leghold trap of its bait without falling into the hidden, snapping jaws.

REF: A(W) - 685; BC - 396; GO - 226; NG - 306; P(W) - 252

Titmice

Family *Paridae*

The short form for "titmouse" makes North Americans flinch. But "tit" in this case is from the Norse *tittre*, a general term for anything small or little. Perhaps via the Vikings and their well-known practice of dropping in to stay, the word became Middle English *tit*, meaning "small." "Mouse" is a case of linguistic mistaken identity, for it has nothing to do with mice, arising instead from the Anglo-Saxon *mase* or *mose*, a term for small birds. It would be a quibble rendered hopeless by time and long custom to point out that the plural should really be "titmouses."

Titmice are a widespread family of forty-six species, ten of them in North America—four of these in British Columbia. The Bushtit, name and appearance notwithstanding, isn't a member of this family. Worldwide, they inhabit every zone from subarctic to tropical, missing only Australia, New Zealand, and South America. Although in some cases separated by great chunks of geography, the family resemblance between our chickadees and several species of Eurasian tits is obvious; the Marsh, Sombre, and Willow tits could pass at first glance as Black-capped Chickadees. The Marsh Tit's call includes a "chikka-dee-dee-dee," but a sneeze-like "pitchoo" and a nasal "chay" would give away the disguise. The Siberian Tit could pass as a Boreal, and in fact shares Boreal territory in central Alaska, neighbouring Yukon, and Northwest Territories.

The best-known titmouse in North America is the spritely little Tufted, occupying the eastern and southeastern United States and down into Mexico. It was first spotted in Canada at Point Pelee in 1914. Since then it has become an increasingly frequent visitor and now is classed as a permanent but unusual resident of southernmost Ontario.

Snake In The Hole

Most titmice, including all chickadees, are cavity nesters, enjoying the advantages of this more secure housing by, in the case of the Eurasian titmice, rearing large broods of eight to ten. But, as pointed out in the section on woodpeckers, a hole is also a trap for brooding females. How do you get away, when a squirrel or weasel is filling the hole and there's no fire exit? In the titmouse family brooding females, when threatened on the nest, will open their mouths, hiss loudly and move their heads back and forth in a manner clearly imitative of a snake's threat gestures. If this bluff doesn't scare off the predator altogether, it might at least make it hesitate just long enough for a brooding chickadee to make a last-chance escape.

All members of the family share the trusting nature and the bold, inquisitive behaviour that make our chickadees such favourites at feeders. The urge to examine anything new that comes to their attention is one adaptation to a harsh environment where opportunism in the search for food can mean the difference between survival and starvation.

Along with this exploratory bent goes a good measure of ingenuity. An experimenter in Britain discovered that tits learned to retrieve bits of food on the end of a long string tied to a perch. The birds would haul in with their beaks, clamp the loose loop under one foot, haul in again, and repeat the move until the prize was reeled in. John V. Dennis in his book *A Complete Guide to Bird Feeding* notes that he failed in his own efforts to duplicate this test on his Tufted Titmice and Carolina Chickadees. They demonstrated an ingenuity of their own by simply fluttering directly to the end of the string and hanging on there with both feet while they ate the bait.

It has long been noted that in winter several species of birds habitually forage in each other's company. These mixed "guilds" include chickadees, nuthatches, woodpeckers, kinglets, and siskins. With more eyes on the alert there is better security against predators. An additional benefit may be that the food search of one species uncovers sources for another. Given the chickadees' opportunistic ways, one wouldn't be surprised if they turned out to be the ones that profited most from these integrated outings.

❊ ❊ ❊

Black-capped Chickadee
Parus atricapillus

Titmouse family. "Chickadee" imitates call, although "chickadee-dee-dee" would be more accurate; *parus* is Latin for "titmouse," *ater* for "black," *capillus* for "hair of the head."

Description

Very small and active, with tiny bill; body plumage soft and fluffy; crown, back of neck, throat and bib black; cheeks and sides of neck white; back is grey-beige; wings and tail slate-grey with edges of feathers lightly frosted; flanks tinged with buff, belly off-white; sexes identical.

Behaviour

Acrobatic, hyperactive, excitable, and vocal; undeterred by cold weather; usually the first "customer" at new feeders; feeds by fluttering hurriedly to feeder, selecting a seed, flying off; cracks sunflower seeds by clutching them tightly against perch with one foot and hammering them open with beak; in winter travels in family groups; famous "chicka-dee-dee" call augmented in late winter with clear, slow "seeeee-fee-bee" whistle resembling White-throated Sparrow song, first note higher than other two; also soft twitter.

Range

Nonmigratory; common coast to coast in Canada from tree line south; throughout British Columbia, but only in rare, isolated occurrences in coastal strip west of the Coast Range and on Vancouver Island; absent from the Charlottes.

Food

Insectivorous by preference, scouring winter twigs and bark for eggs, pupae, and dormant adults, but supplementing this with weed seeds; in the wild picks scraps from remains of predator kills; at feeder is keen on sunflower seeds, nuts, peanut butter, suet, much of which it stashes away.

Nest

Nests, and shelters in winter, in tree holes cleaned out of punky knotholes; in winter adults huddle together in holes; can sometimes be tricked into using nest box if it is first filled with wood shavings.

Comment

These beady-eyed charmers have done more than any other bird to convert indifferent householders into dedicated bird feeders. Their unquenchable, bubbly good nature is often the only evidence of life on the worst winter days. A light "tap-tapping" from the edge of the shelf is familiar to those with windowsill feeders—a chickadee is hammering open a sunflower seed. Clean around feeders, they don't congregate on platforms in a squabbling, defecating bunch as House Sparrows and finches do. Compulsively inquisitive and trusting, they are the easiest of birds to "tame," learning quickly to take seeds out of hand, then to search clothing, lips, and ears for hidden tidbits.

REF: A(W) - 663; BC - 398; GO - 228; NG - 310; P(W) - 258

Mountain Chickadee

Parus gambeli

Titmouse family. *Parus* Latin for "titmouse"; *gambeli* from Wm. Gambel, first ornithologist to spend several years, in the 1840s, in California.

Description

Only chickadee with striped face, dark line through eye, white stripe over it; otherwise very similar to Black-capped.

Behaviour

In all respects a chickadee; tends to move and forage in tree crowns rather than in lower vegetation; voice huskier than Black-capped's, similar in tone to Chestnut-backed's, a slightly hoarse "tzik-a-zee-zee."

Range

Nonmigratory; resident in the mountains of western North America from Mexican border to Alaska; rare in northeast British Columbia; absent as a resident from wet coastal forests and from Vancouver Island; no records from the Charlottes; mainly a highland breeder, favouring conifer forest up to tree line, but in the Cariboo region is an occasional nester in nest boxes, even those in lowland valleys; in winter descends to lowland woods, orchards, and residential areas.

Food

Insects, seeds; at feeders seeds, suet.

Nest

In a cavity; digs its own, but more ready than other chickadees to nest in boxes and vacated woodpecker holes; nest a thick pile of moss, grass, plant fibres, fur.

Comment

Like other chickadees this one readily joins "guilds" of other species in winter, foraging in a loose flock through the woods; at this time it is found in the company of whatever other species of chickadee may be resident in the area.

Nest holes are essential to the breeding success of species that use them, especially if they cannot dig their own. A vivid illustration of this is recounted in the *Book of North American Birds*, a *Reader's Digest* publication. Arizona observers recorded an attempt by a pair of Violet-green Swallows to usurp a Mountain Chickadee hole while the owners were out. The pitched battle that broke out upon the chickadees' return lasted for over an hour. The birds fought in the air, grappled on the ground, pecking and buffeting. Several times a swallow grabbed a chickadee by a wing or foot and yanked it out of the hole. The chickadees eventually won, leaving the homeless swallows to try their luck elsewhere.

REF: A(W) - 733; BC - 399; GO - 228; NG - 310; P(W) - 258

Boreal Chickadee

Parus hudsonicus

Titmouse family. "Boreal" means "of the north," "chickadee" imitates its call; *Parus* is Latin for "titmouse" and *hudsonicus* "of Hudson Bay."

Description

Similar in size and plumage pattern to Black-capped; colouration resembles the Chestnut-backed, but lacks brown back; chin and throat black, but cap dark brown; flanks a ruddy brown wash; overall colour tends to beige rather than grey.

Behaviour

Shares acrobatic, fluttery energy of all its kind, but less trusting, more subdued; often forages with Black-capped, nuthatches, and smaller woodpeckers; call

definitely a chickadee's but thinner, wheezy "sik-a-day-day," drawled out, like slow Black-capped with laryngitis.

Range

Nonmigratory; most northerly chickadee; found through boreal forest to southern tundra; in alpine country favours boreal zone and is thus more a "mountain" bird than the Mountain Chickadee, infrequently descending to elevations much below the Ponderosa Pine, subalpine fir zone.

Food

Omnivorous; winter gleaner of small branches and twigs for dormant insects, larvae and eggs, and scraps from predator kills; comes less readily to feeders than other chickadees; once there, shares its cousin's delight with sunflower seeds, suet, and peanut butter.

Nest

Hole cleared out in decayed stub of conifer or birch, often quite low, almost never higher than 3 m (10 ft); prefers swampier, more enclosed habitat than Black-capped.

Comment

Of the two species of chickadees whose range straddles the top of the continent, the Boreal extends its range farthest north. Where it occurs south of its major range, in disjunct pockets of woodland, the woodlands invariably turn out to be boreal relics. Some authors suggest that its habit of foraging in the interiors of dense spruce trees, and of coming less readily to the tips of branches, make it seem less plentiful than the Black-capped. This habit, and its affinity for high elevations in British Columbia, combine to make the Boreal seem scarcer than it really is.

REF: A(W) - 744; BC - 400; GO -228; NG - 312; P(W) - 258

Chestnut-backed Chickadee

Parus rufescens

Titmouse family. *Parus* Latin for "titmouse"; *rufescens* Latin for "reddish."

Description

Smaller than other chickadees; distinguished from them by rich chestnut sides and back; black on crown rather faded out, brownish, otherwise the head and throat same as Black-capped.

Behaviour

Typical chickadee; in natural surroundings tends to forage higher in trees than Black-capped; least musical of chickadees; voice hoarse, shrill; "tzeek-a-zee-zee" call delivered with agitated rapidity; most frequent utterance a nervous "tzee-deee."

Range

In a strip along the west coast of the continent; inland in northern Washington, Idaho, up into East Kootenays as far as Revelstoke; rare in the Peace River, occurring up to Fort St. John at feeders; population centre in British Columbia is in the coastal forests west of the Coast Ranges, Vancouver Island, and the Charlottes; Vancouver Island's principal resident chickadee; inland, favours heavy Columbian forest.

Food

Insects, seeds, occasional fruit; at feeders sunflower seeds, suet.

Nest

In stub or dead tree, usually low, rarely more than 3m (10') high, nest a cup of plant fibres, hair, fur, feathers on a thick base of moss.

Comment

In certain favoured areas of British Columbia it's possible to see four chickadee species at once. In the Kootenays, the Cariboo, and somewhat further north, the Boreal and Chestnut-backed join the Mountain and Black-capped. Around Revelstoke it isn't unusual for the four to

- P. SAWATZKY -
1992 ©

show up at the same feeder. In the 1990 Christmas Bird Count the distinction of recording four species on the same day fell to the Burns Lake-Francois Lake counters.

REF: A(W) - 744; BC - 401; GO - 228; NG - 312; P(W) - 258

Bushtit Family

Family *Aegithalidae*

or *Paridae*

The *Aegithalidae* aren't a plenteous family. In the two genera found worldwide—the Longtailed Tits and Bushtits—there are only seven species. Just one of these occurs in the Western Hemisphere, undoubtedly explaining why the first part of its former name, "common," was recently acknowledged to be redundant in North America, and dropped. You'll find "Common Bushtit" in all but the more recent guides. These may also list the Bushtit as a member of the *Paridae* family, the one that includes the chickadees and the verdin. There is still debate over where it truly belongs.

In the meantime, we can be happy that British Columbia is the place in Canada where this lone New World bushtit can be found. It is a recent arrival; Godfrey gives the first nesting record for the province as 1937, in Victoria. A year later it was noted on Lopez Island in the San Juans. Since then it's been steadily increasing its range eastward and northward.

Bushtits are almost as tiny as kinglets. Those of us who have seen kinglets up close, or strained to pinpoint the sources of their wispy little peeps falling from the trees above, can appreciate how small they are. There is a ventriloquistic effect to sounds that strain the upper limits of (in my case) the middle-aged ear, much as you might crane upward and swivel and tilt your head for a sonic fix. When you mingle another bit of a bird with the two kinglet species, the challenge to the middle-aged ear and eye, to say nothing of the middle-aged neck, is considerable.

The field guides try to help by pointing out that while kinglets have marks that are difficult to see, Bushtits are even less distinguished. Up close, assuming you can keep them in your binoculars long enough for a good look, they are devoid of any obvious pattern or colour deserving the term "field mark."

As if to compensate for being a diminutive grey-brown puff of feathers, the Bushtit constructs one of the most impressive nests you're likely to encounter. It is a well-woven pouch of fine materials hung from a thin branch; it may take the pair from two weeks to over a month and a half to build. Although there is no real effort to conceal the nest, if it's disturbed at any time during construction, egg-laying or incubation, the pair will desert, break up, and try again with new mates. After the young have fledged and left the nest, the old pair may still use it as a winter roost.

Nest-building skill runs in the family. The Cape Penduline Tit of Africa makes one with a dummy entrance in the side that leads to a dummy nest chamber. The real entrance is a woven tube above the decoy hole that the bird closes in its passage to and from the real nest chamber below the false floor of the fake chamber. Some African tribespeople collect penduline nests and use them for purses and carrying pouches.

❋ ❋ ❋

Bushtit

Psaltriparus minimus

Formerly "common bushtit"; *psaltriparus* from Greek *psaltria*, "a harpist," and Latin *parus*, "a titmouse"; *minimus* is Latin for "least."

Description

Small; tiny bill, long tail; grey-brown overall, with no obvious field marks; adult female has straw-coloured iris, male's is dark.

Behaviour

Ceaselessly acrobatic, flitting, hanging, pecking on twigs, branches, and leaves from low shrubs on up to tall trees; except during breeding season travels in busy, dispersed groups, constantly calling; frequent members of mixed foraging "guilds" with other species; voice a thin, high, "tseep"or lisping, nervous twitter.

Range

The mountainous west and southwest of North America, down into Central America; spread to British Columbia from northwest Washington, now present on Vancouver Island north to Sayward; in Vancouver area and lower Fraser valley east to Hope; have been confirmed as far east as the Shushwap area.

Food

Insect eggs, larvae, pupae, and adults; spiders; some fruit; found to be keen on suet, peanut butter, or mixtures of two at feeders.

Nest

Woven pouch hung from small twigs; 17 to 25 cm (7 to 10 in) deep, 8 to 10 cm (3 to 4 in) wide at bottom; entrance through side at top; fine fibres, plant down, algae, cocoon silk, felted and bonded with spider webbing; thickly lined with small feathers; wall as much as 1 cm (.5 in) thick at bottom.

Comment

Vancouver Island naturalist Bill Merilees in his book *Attracting Backyard Wildlife* relates his observation of Bushtits flying repeatedly through the spray from lawn sprinklers until their feathers got so soaked they had to dry off before they could fly again.

Bushtits were until recently not regarded as likely feeder birds, but have now established themselves in some areas as regular visitants. Wayne Campbell, in a personal communication, said that in the Victoria area one of the most frequent phone enquiries he has had in the last few years has been about "a small, plain bird with a long tail eating suet at my feeder."

For his part, Bill Merilees has had them come to his yard in Nanaimo to feed on a blend of dripping fat, peanut butter, and rolled oats pushed into holes drilled in a small tree trunk.

REF: A(W) - 662; BC - 403; GO - 232; NG - 312; P(W) - 260

Nuthatches

Family *Sittidae*

In one of the many introductions to birding books that he has written over the years, Roger Tory Peterson attributed the base level of interest in birds to ". . . the white-breasted nuthatch type of bird watcher who feeds birds on the shelf outside the kitchen window and goes no farther afield."

I took this as a tribute to the bird, and to the fact that it is one of the most consistent of visitors to winter feeding stations, often the first one to acknowledge a newly placed offering. For many of us, the faithful nuthatch is second in our affections only to the irrepressibly cheerful chickadee.

Nuthatch "faithfulness" extends through their mutually held territory to each other, and is a year-round bond. The sentiments of their human hosts notwithstanding, this is simply a matter of their behaving in their own reproductive interests. Constancy may be a response to their need for ready-made tree holes to nest in. Safe, secure holes in trees, particularly if you are in the second-hand market, are a scarce item. The absence of a suitable hole means that cavity nesters cannot breed. It is therefore crucial for those who already have a territory, nest site included, to hang onto it. They can maintain better security if they stay on their turf and have a mate to help run off pushy intruders.

"No Trespassing"

Nuthatches aren't noticeably quarrelsome at feeders, but confronting an aroused one near its nest is something trespassers don't do lightly. The body language is eloquent; wings and tail are raised and flared, exposing otherwise concealed patterns of white that are a warning flash that cannot escape notice. The stiletto bill and the beady eyes are directed at the enemy with no-nonsense intensity. The agitated body is cocked toward the adversary and rotated jerkily back and forth, like a mechanical toy. The threat is unmistakable.

I once watched two embattled nuthatches confront both Grey and Red Squirrels over possession of a disused flicker hole in an old aspen in my yard. After much skirmishing it was the doughty birds that raised their brood in the old tree that summer.

The European version of the Red-breasted Nuthatch adds to the security of its nest hole by plastering the entrance with mud until it is barely able to squeeze in. This serves to keep out larger preemptors, especially starlings. Our Red-breasted smears spruce, pine, or fir gum around the entrance hole, very likely a behavioural relic from its Eurasian ancestor, modified, perhaps, because our species has evolved on a continent free of starlings until very recently. The pungent gum would mask the scent of the nest, and its gooiness repel trespassers. One reference noted that a nuthatch itself was found dead in the entrance to its nest, stuck in the gum.

A further variant on this behaviour is the White-breasted's habit of nabbing blister beetles or ants and rubbing them around the bark near its nest hole. Both insects emit repellent chemicals when manhandled. The strong-smelling, irritant vapours thus deposited could be a way of masquerading the nest's telltale scent, or of deterring nest-robbers like squirrels.

In common with many overwintering birds, all three of our nuthatch species store surplus food. A feeder with a generous supply of sunflower seeds can trigger a marathon of activity, as happened with a solitary male Red-breasted that arrived at my city windowsill early one October. He made a collecting flight from the shelf to nearby oaks once every forty-five seconds on average for extended periods. He must have had hundreds and hundreds of seeds poked into the rough bark of the oaks. Then he abruptly vanished, never to reap the rewards of his labours. I could only guess whether his disappearance was a decision to resume his journey south, or the intervention of a neighbour's cat.

There are twenty-one species of nuthatches throughout the world. They are unique in their insistence on climbing *down* trees (or rocks or walls) rather than up, and for doing so headfirst. This adaptive "idea" of going upside-down to search for food gave some ancestral proto-nuthatch access to a new niche, a distinct edge in a world where, presumably, a host of conventional tree climbers already had the "from-the-bottom-up" niches filled. The descendants fortunate enough to inherit the knack gradually created a race of their kind and, over time, a number of separate species.

Refinements

Nuthatches share with a lot of other scanners and probers a white chin and/or breast. The glow reflected off this bright surface into shadowy cracks and holes would throw useful light onto food items concealed in them.

If you look closely at a nuthatch fixed in place you will see that it has one leg out behind, on the "up" side, with the oversized hind claw firmly hooked onto the surface. The other foot is placed well forward, i.e., down, for steadying support.

There are other refinements that the nuthatch brings to its trade. One of them has to be a highly developed skill at selecting cracks and notches that will hold a nut or seed in place solidly enough for the deft bill to hack apart. The Brown-headed Nuthatch of the southeast United States even uses bits of bark as tools to pry up loose flakes in its search for hidden insects. Nuthatches will also attempt to cover hidden seeds with bits of bark or shreds of lichen, if they are available.

Of the four species of nuthatches found in North America, only one—the Red-breasted—is migratory. But even this species is an irregular nomad, part of the population electing in some winters to stay behind or to migrate only part way. In such times bird feeders in the southerly parts of the species' breeding range have an unusual and welcome wintertime guest.

Unattached White-breasteds will also drift south during their first winter if the prospects in their natal surroundings aren't too good. It would be less easy to detect such a population shift, since the breeding range of the White-breasted extends to the Gulf of Mexico and well down into Mexico. Who, then, are the locals, who the wintering northerners?

✳ ✳ ✳

Red-breasted Nuthatch

Sitta canadensis

"Nuthatch" from "nuthack," original name brought to Americas by English colonists; *Sitta* from Greek *sitte*, "nut-hatch"; *canadensis*, Latinized "of Canada," reflecting major range of bird.

Description

Shares slate-blue back, wings, and tail of larger White-breasted; distinguished from it by smaller size and by narrow black line through the eye and white line above eye; breast, belly, flanks, thighs, and tail coverts pale rust to brick-red, varying with individuals; sexes similar, but female's crown is dark grey, ruddy parts are paler.

Behaviour

Very similar to White-breasted, foraging head-down on tree bark; a busy, businesslike but sometimes dithery feeder bird; diligent hoarder of larger seeds and suet; voice similar to White-breasted but weaker and higher-pitched, a thin, nasal "yank-yank"; also makes a clear, soft note, "hit," very high, repeated several times.

Range

Conditionally migratory, depending on weather; found throughout boreal forest right up to tree line; much more a denizen of coniferous forests than White-breasted; scattered irregularly throughout British Columbia, including Vancouver and Queen Charlotte islands; much more likely to migrate from colder/higher zones of interior when winters are severe.

Food

Natural summer food insects and spiders; in winter, insect dormants and eggs, seeds of conifers, bits from predator kills; in the wild forages in company of chickadees, White-breasted, and Pygmy cousins; at feeder a lover of sunflower seeds and suet.

Nest

Either ready-made cavity in tree or one excavated in punky wood, hence height highly variable; occasionally uses nest boxes; entrance smeared with pine, spruce, or fir gum; female reported to fly directly into hole, presumably to avoid contacting resin.

Comment

The little Red-breasted closely resembles the European Nuthatch, *Sitta europaea*, with which it shares the habit of plastering the rim of its nest hole. Observers note that by the end of the nesting season parent Red-breasteds acquire a very tatty appearance from the resin stuck on their feathers.

REF: A(W) - 707; BC - 404; GO - 234; NG - 314; P(W) - 262

White-breasted Nuthatch

Sitta carolinensis

Seventeenth century British colonists brought "nuthack" with them, descriptive of familiar European bird's habit of wedging nuts into cracks, hacking husks off with bill; with dialectic drift it became "nuthatch"; *sitta* from Greek *sitte*, "nuthatch"; *carolinensis*, "of Carolina," origin of type specimens.

Description

Sparrow-sized; large head, short neck, stubby tail impart compact, torpedo shape; crown and back of neck black; bill slender, sharp, slightly upturned; dark eye prominent in white face; throat and breast white; back slate-blue; wings a subdued pattern of slate-blue, with black check marks and lines, and frosted feather edges; thighs and undertail brick-red; sexes similar, except female's head is grey.

Behaviour

Perches, feeds, and forages head-down on vertical surfaces; stance squat, scans world with neck craned back; cracks nuts and large seeds by wedging them into crevices, whacking at them to chip off husks; winter call a flat, nasal note repeated urgently several times, best imitated by a falsetto "yaank" whilst holding nose.

Range

Migratory from northern parts of range, in southern British Columbia much more a year-round resident; southern Canada is northern margin of continental range; found throughout southern British Columbia, including Vancouver Island where it favours coniferous woodlands.

Food

Searches tree trunks for spiders, and insects in all stages; nuts, some berries, and larger seeds; not fussy at feeders, taking sunflower seeds, peanuts, suet, baked goods, and some kinds of table scraps; diligent hoarder, jamming seeds into cracks in bark; will readily try different foods, often beating even chickadees to feeders to sample new offerings.

Nest

In tree cavities, usually those ready-made by decay or woodpeckers; occasionally accepts nest boxes or uses cavities in buildings.

Comment

This family's habitual upside-down position is its most obvious "field mark,"

P. SAWATZKY ©
1990

since nuthatches are the only birds able to move easily down vertical surfaces headfirst; even the tree-adapted woodpeckers hitch awkwardly backward when descending. This habit, plus their trim shape, air of urgent busyness around feeders, and bold plumage pattern make them unmistakable. The main challenge is spotting the difference between the White-breasted and Red-breasted, where they coexist.

REF: A(W) - 708; BC - 405; GO - 234; NG - 314; P(W) - 262

Pygmy Nuthatch

Sitta pygmaea

Sitta from Greek "nuthatch"; *pygmaea* from Latin *pygmaeus*, "a pygmy," this being the smallest North American nuthatch.

Description

Squat, compact, very short-tailed; head to beneath eye, and hindneck, grey-brown; back and tail slate-blue, wings slate with frosting of light blue-grey; sides of face and throat white, underparts cream-buff; whitish mark as if brushed lightly on back of neck.

Behaviour

Social outside of breeding season, sometimes in large groups; perches and forages head-down on tree trunks; busy, energetic, vocal, often chattering continuously; voice a rapid, piping "pit-pit-pit" and, as Peterson's Guide describes it, a "pit-pi-dit-pi-dit"; also a high, extended "seeeeee-dee."

Range

Nonmigratory; scattered through pine forest areas of western United States, Mexico; northern edge of range extends into south-central British Columbia where it is plentiful and very closely associated with Ponderosa Pine, Douglas-fir and Lodgepole Pine biome; found occasionally as far north as Peace River, and in the southwest mainland and on Vancouver Island.

Food

Insects at all stages, occasionally hawking them like a flycatcher; seeds, mainly of pine; at feeder takes seeds, suet.

Nest

In cavity, usually self-made, generally 6 m (20 ft) or more up a tree, snag or post; willing to use second-hand hole, including nest boxes; interior well padded with bark shreds, plant fibres, moss, hair, wool, leaves, and feathers.

Comment

This busy little stub-tail has the peculiar habit of cramming any cracks or holes around its nest with hair or fur, finding a ready source of it in owl castings.

Where the pines are—Ponderosa, Yellow—is where this bird is. *Birds of the Okanagan Valley* notes that winter suet feeders set up near stands of Ponderosa Pine often have Pygmy Nuthatches "crawling over them like hungry mice."

REF: A(W) - 709; BC - 406; GO - 234; NG - 314; P(W) - 262

Creepers

Family *Certhiidae*

This family has six species in two genera, only one of which is represented in North America. Until the 1970s our little Brown Creeper was *Certhia familiaris,* and considered to be circumpolar, the same bird the English call the treecreeper. However, the American Ornithologists' Union decided that the North American bird was a separate species and changed the name to *Certhia americana.* This, in a roundabout way, explains why older field guides label this species *C. familiaris.*

While many of our birds, especially wintering species like Downy and Hairy Woodpeckers, and chickadees, are foragers in and under bark, the Brown Creeper is the most dependent bird of all on tree bark. It not only searches on it for food, but uses it for winter roosting and for nesting. Other cavity nesters may now and then use the shelter of a buckled slab of bark if nothing else is available, but the creeper will rarely use anything else.

Some writers note that if you nail a slab of bark to a tree by the ends, being careful to hump it outward in the middle to leave a decent space of several inches between it and the trunk, the Brown Creeper might use the contrived cranny as a winter roost, or even as a nest. I wonder if the sole of an old rubber boot, or some other suitable discard, would be an acceptable substitute for the bark providing it blended unobtrusively with the surface of the tree.

As befits a bird that spends its active hours hitching itself ever upward, the creeper's feet are long-clawed and strong. It also shares with woodpeckers a tail equipped with strong, pointed hackles that serve as a brace while the feet are clamped into the bark. They very likely also snaggle into the surface, preventing backslide when the bird hitches upward, which it does by moving both feet simultaneously in a quick hop. Woodpeckers and nuthatches, in contrast, move their feet in sequence, in a very quick motion that seems like a hop, but is in fact a very quick step.

Closet Machismo

Surprising for one so timid and retiring, the male turns into an exhibitionist like the rest of us during courting time. He woos his prospective mate with a burst of song, described in Noble Proctor's *Song Birds* as "a wonderful, descending musical jumble of notes," a generous review of a talent most other critics classify as meagre. Then this drab little elf turns athletic with a fast, spiral flight upward around the tree trunk he has selected for his display. The female may join in this flight, allowing herself to be pursued in the same dizzy spiral.

If, ultimately, she is sufficiently impressed, the two of them go to work building a nest behind his preselected slab of loose bark. He helps fetch the raw materials, she does the weaving; the project can take as little as six days, or as long as a month. Nests are situated from 1.5 to 4.6 m (5 to 15 ft) up. Observers report that nest tending is done with typical creeper reserve. An adult lands below it, spirals upward in those rapid, jerky little hitches until, with one quick hop, it abruptly vanishes behind its shield of bark.

❈ ❈ ❈

Brown Creeper
Certhia americana

"Creeper" from the way it moves close against the bark of trees as it forages; *certhia* from Latin *certhius*, "a creeper," and *americana*, latinized "of America"; in older guides species name is *familiaris*, Latin for "homelike," hence friendly.

Description
Very small, slim, with slender, down-curved bill, longish tail with stiff, pointed feathers flared slightly against the bark; upper plumage a camouflage pattern of buff spots, streaks, and lines on a brown base; belly, breast and chin are white.

Behaviour
Secretive and solitary; constantly searches bark of larger trees by starting near the base, hitching upward in short, quick jumps in a spiral around trunk until it

is well up, then flying quickly down to base of another tree; favours mature trees, especially in damp, mossy woodlands; call a very high, thin "tsee," like a Golden-crowned Kinglet but clearer, slower; song as described in the Peterson Guide is a thin, sibilant "see-ti-wee-tu-wee," translated to "trees, trees, trees, see the trees."

Range

In Canada breeds coast to coast in the southern boreal woods and the belt of mixed-wood forest south of it; scattered through southern two-thirds of interior British Columbia and up the Coast Ranges and coast to Stikine River; on Vancouver Island and Queen Charlottes; favours old growth and mature woods, both deciduous and coniferous, including woodlots, well-treed urban areas and parks; along the coast it is considered nonmigratory, but is classed as partially migratory to fully migratory in the interior.

Food

Close scanner of bark for insect eggs, pupae, and adults, using its sharp, decurved bill as a fine probe; rare visitor to feeders, where it takes suet; may be coaxed to specific trees if bark is smeared with suet or peanut butter.

Nest

Unique in that it almost invariably nests behind or under loosened slabs of bark on dead trees; nest may be compressed considerably by confines of space and reveal a sharply upturned crescent shape when exposed; base of twigs, grass stems, and bark shreds often arranged to block off most access to the space beneath the bark; lining of fine bark threads, grass, root fibres, spider silk, mosses, and occasional feathers.

Comment

This cryptic little bird is professionally inconspicuous, flattened to patterned bark, making little noise and no disturbance. In the shady woods it prefers, where the light is dappled and dim, the bird is often spotted just as it spirals out of sight around some distant tree trunk. It is understandable, then, that this recluse is often listed as "scarce" or "infrequent." Some observers allow that its "uncommon" status may be more an apparent scarcity than a real one. "Keep looking" is the word.

Getting creepers to a feeding station is a challenge. Some birders note that they seem to pay more attention to trees in the vicinity of feeders, possibly to glean fragments of seeds and fat left on the bark where other birds wiped their bills. It follows that smearing food lightly on rough-barked trees, and using suet, peanut butter, cheese, chopped egg, or a blend of these that caters to an insect-eater's diet, might establish a creeper as one of your regular visitors.

REF: A(W) - 709; BC - 406; GO - 234; NG - 314; P(W) - 262

Kinglets

Family *Muscicapidae,*
Subfamily *Sylviinae*

Latin *musca* means "a fly," *capere,* "to take," hence "flycatcher"; Latin *silva* is "a woods," *sylviinae,* "of the woods."

It would take approximately one hundred Ruby-crowned Kinglets to make a pound. I have never had the unhappy task of weighing a dead one, but several references assure me that they run from just under 4 to 4.5 grams, the greater figure just equalling .16 oz. The Golden-crowned is even tinier, and is the smallest songbird in Canada. Bird banders inform me that Ruby-crowneds take the smallest-size leg-band, but even that size is too big for Golden-crowneds. Hummingbirds are smaller, but they're not songbirds.

For most British Columbians, even those who live in mixed or coniferous woodlands, kinglets are not obvious birds. In summer they favour a heavy cover of evergreens, often back among the muskeg and mosquitoes that so effectively deter humans. Even when the two do meet, the birds are so small, so busy and unobtrusive, and often so far up in tall conifers that they aren't noticed. Their tiny nests are built away up near the roof of the evergreen canopy, so masterfully concealed that finding one is a rare accomplishment.

Although they are related to the thrush family, only the Ruby-crowned is noted as a singer, astonishing people who hear it that so small a creature can generate so much volume. But the Golden-crowned has a weak, small voice that easily gets lost in its dense evergreen habitat.

Gathered in larger flocks, and with fewer of the bigger, noisier, and more colourful birds around to distract the eye, they are more noticeable in winter. The Golden-crowned routinely includes southern and coastal British Columbia in its wintering range, occasionally in abundance. The Ruby-crowned, the more strongly migratory of the two, winters in the southwest of the province.

In winter the Golden-crowned can be observed foraging through the woods in mixed collections of chickadees, Downy and Hairy Woodpeckers, and nuthatches. John Dennis, in his *A Complete Guide to Bird Feeding*, says it may occasionally follow these to feeders, but that it rarely becomes a regular. When it does show up, Mr. Dennis points out, it outperforms even the chickadee in its ability to get food from awkward places. It is at a feeder that one can best observe the details of this animated little bird's drab plumage, and appreciate its miniature proportions which make a chickadee look bulky in comparison.

Although the Ruby-crowned turns up regularly in small numbers in a significant number of Christmas Bird Counts in the province, particularly along the coast, it's the Golden-crowned that is the major winterer of the two. Neither is noted for its affinity for feeders, so it was felt that giving a species account of the Golden-crowned would suffice for this family in British Columbia.

❄ ❄ ❄

Golden-crowned Kinglet
Regulus satrapa

Old World warbler, gnatcatcher, and kinglet subfamily; in larger family that also includes thrushes. "Golden-crowned" from small dash of yellow on crown, "kinglet" meaning "little king"; *Regulus* Latin for "little king," Greek *satrapa* meaning "a ruler," i.e. one who wears a golden crown; an example of taxonomists' maximizing a single feature on an otherwise undistinguished little bird.

Description

Tiny; olive-green and greyish; short-tailed; delicate, fine-pointed bill; two-toned crown stripe, bright orange in centre bordered by yellow edged in black, visible only at close range or when raised in display; off-white line over eye; legs proportionately much thinner than any other small wintering bird; sexes alike, but female has no orange in crown.

Behaviour

Tirelessly flitting about, usually near tips of branches, often well up in conifers; so active, field marks other than diminutive size difficult to see; constantly flicks wings; often forages by hovering near twig tips; call a hurried, thin, high-pitched

"tsee-tsee-tsee"; song a very high, weak, rapid trill, preceded by an almost inaudible, ascending series of about four "tsee" notes.

Range

Migratory; in Canada breeds in boreal forest and adjacent mixed forests, coast to coast; winters in British Columbia's southern interior north to Smithers and along the coast north through Prince Rupert to Valdez, Alaska in some winters.

Food

Insects, eggs, larvae and pupae gleaned from twigs, needles; sap from sapsucker tap-holes; rare feeder visitor, then taking only suet and perhaps peanut butter.

Nest

A neat little suspended pouch cunningly hidden beneath foliage at tip of evergreen bough, often very high; well camouflaged with moss and lichen; feathers in lining are set so tops will fold down over eggs when parent is away.

Comment

Godfrey in *Birds of Canada* wonders at such ". . . feathered mites happily wintering in Canada when many larger species have gone south to warmer climates." No doubt the physics of size and wind chill foredoom many of these undersized bundles of energy to winter kill. But heavy losses are quickly replaced; each female that survives to mate and nest can brood up to ten eggs snuggled into her tiny nest in two layers.

REF: A(W) - 735; BC - 416; GO - 252; NG - 322; P(W) - 268

Thrushes

Family *Muscicapidae,*

Subfamily *Turdinae*

The *Muscicapidae* family includes Old World warblers, kinglets, gnatcatchers, Old World flycatchers, and the thrushes and their allies. As well as those we call thrushes, the subfamily *Turdinae* includes bluebirds, solitaires, and our robin which is in the genus *Turdus,* the true thrushes. There are over sixty species in this genus and they are found on every continent except Australia. No other single genus of songbird is so widespread, and wherever they occur, there is at least one species that is a common yard and garden bird.

The niceties of bird nomenclature didn't trouble the minds of English immigrants piling off the boats to tame seventeenth century America. Thus, any bird with a reddish breast, or even a suggestion of ruddiness about it, was dubbed a "robin" after the familiar red-breasted bird of British fields and gardens. At one time the Eastern Bluebird was a "robin," the towhee was a "ground robin," the oriole was a "golden robin," the Cedar Waxwing a "Canadian robin."

The American Robin vies with the Red-winged Blackbird as the most common bird in North America, and with the House Sparrow as the most familiar. Unlike the sparrow, it is not a human-dependent street bird. It's just as much at home in the rain forests of the west coast or the upper reaches of the boreal-tundra transition zone as it is dodging lawn sprinklers in suburbia. But people so associate it with the latter scene that their first reaction on encountering it in the wilderness is a surprised: "What is *our* robin doing away out here?"

"Cheer-up!"

The thrushes are noted for their great voices, and although the American Robin isn't rated as the greatest songster of them all, its dawn carol is one of the best-known and loved of nature's sounds. It isn't a continuous cascade of warbling, like the finches, but a series of clear, whistled phrases, separated by the briefest pauses. To some, the clipped phrases sound like football signals and they have nicknamed the robin the "quarterback bird."

In *The Birds of Manitoba* (1891), Ernest Thompson (Seton) commented on a variation in bird song that can be readily observed in robins since their voices are so loud, and they sing from regular vantage points. At times a bird will abruptly change to a muted, distant-sounding voice. Seton noted that a singing male, if slightly disturbed by something close at hand, would keep on singing, but with his bill shut. He said he had noted this habit in several other species.

Sex and Violence

Lust and property-line disputes have been sources of bloodshed among humans for as long as our history can recall. Put them together, and you have the potential for rivalry of awesome, or farcical, proportions.

Male robins compete with such frenzy in the territorial/mating game that at times they behave as if completely addled. In addition to wild low-level pursuits on the wing, accompanied by rapid "git! git! git!" shrieked at trespassers, male robins have worked themselves into frazzles attacking their reflections in windows, windshields, hubcaps, and rear-view mirrors. The cue to aggression being the ruddy breast of a male rival, they have tackled similar-coloured socks, handkerchiefs, and other items on clotheslines, and ornaments and discarded toys on the lawn.

Although the female robin selects the site, builds the nest, and does all the brooding, the male nevertheless proves to be a dutiful helpmate, feeding the nestlings and assuming full babysitting chores when his mate builds a new nest and starts brooding a second clutch. The harassed male can then be seen scouring lawns for food, with his brood dogging his heels, begging loudly when he pulls up an earthworm. These fledglings reveal their species' thrush ancestry; their breasts are dappled with brown spots on a washed-out background.

At this time there are a couple of things that can be done to give your robin family a hand. Keeping the cat (if you have one) shut in until the baby robins get over the "stupid" stage of life may help at least one or two make it onto the wing. It may also be a real help to nest-building, if the midseason weather is dry, to leave a pie plate of good stiff mud on or near the birdbath, or to turn on the lawn sprinkler where it will create a nice muddy puddle.

Foraging robin pairs recently demonstrated that new knowledge about animal behaviour doesn't have to come from costly expeditions to remote sites. By watching four pairs of robins working the lawns of a Kansas college campus, an observer discovered that they subdivided their territories roughly in half along an east-west axis when searching for food. The female always searched one half, the male the other. Such an arrangement would minimize competition between the two, avoid overlapping searches, and therefore enhance foraging efficiency.

In common with other thrushes, robins are omnivorous to a certain degree in that they freely switch from preying on invertebrates, principally earthworms, to gathering fruit and berries. They do not seem to be very interested in seeds. Their liking for soft fruits has frequently brought them to grief with gardeners and fruit growers. Loyd Groutage of Castlegar suggested in a personal communication that they go after succulent strawberries in part for the moisture, and that supplying drinking water nearby might diminish their thirst for berries.

The Varied Thrush, a British Columbia cousin of the robin, normally confines itself to the west rim of the continent. But every now and then flocks of them rove eastward in the fall. They end up startling the heck out of birders on the Prairies, in Ontario, and eastward. On at least two occasions, as noted by Tufts in *Birds of Nova Scotia*, they've strayed all the way to Sable Island, where lone males showed up briefly on October 29, 1968, and on January 12, 1977.

In a personal communication, F. Helleiner of Peterborough points out that this bird has become "almost an annual discovery (sometimes several) in Ontario, invariably in winter and almost always at feeders."

❊   ❊   ❊

American Robin

Turdus migratorius

Thrush family. "Robin" is the diminutive of "Robert" and of French origin; in England "redbreast" was original name, then "robin redbreast," then "redbreast" was dropped; *turdus* is Latin for "a thrush," *migrator* for "wanderer."

Description

Rather leggy, long-tailed bird; dark grey tail, back, and wings, darker head; brick-red breast and belly; chin light with dark, vertical streaks; broken white eye-ring; lower belly and undertail coverts white; beak yellow; female same as male but paler.

Behaviour

Most commonly seen hunting worms on lawns, alternately tipping forward to scan the grass intently or standing erect when alert for danger; runs or hops; song famous as harbinger of spring, a loud, clear, distinctly separated series of "cheery, cheery, cheer up, cheerily" phrases; call of alarm a sudden "cheep!" or rapidly repeated "git-git-git."

Range

Partial migrator in British Columbia; in Canada breeds from coast to coast, north to beyond the tree line; common throughout British Columbia, from coastal lowlands to subalpine meadows; some birds winter along coasts and in southern interior; a race in the southwest is definitely nonmigratory.

Food

Mixture of insects, earthworms, and fruit; may be encouraged to feeders with raisins, berries, fresh or dried fruit, shredded coconut; some observers note some robins' eagerness for peanut butter; early spring migrants may resort to feeders only if driven by hunger when late snows blanket natural food sources.

Nest

Substantial base of twigs, straws, and stems, mortared from inside with heavy layer of mud formed into deep, round cup; inner lining of fine grasses; in fork of tree or solid branch, in tangle of vines, or on ledge or beam about buildings; from 2 to 10 m (6 to 30+ ft) above ground.

Comment

Basically a bird of open forests and edges, the robin benefited wherever logging and agriculture wiped out all but small patches of presettlement forest. Whatever its historic niche, today's robin behaves almost like two different species, one a bold familiar of lawns and rooftops, the other a shy wilderness recluse.

REF: A(W) - 587; BC - 429; GO - 244; NG - 330; P(W) - 274

Varied Thrush

Ixoreus naevius

Also sometimes "winter robin," "Oregon robin"; "varied" suggests more multi-coloured or patterned plumage than that of most thrushes; *ixoreus* from Greek *ixos*, "mistletoe," and *oreos*, "mountain," from a European mountain thrush associated with mistletoe berries; *naevius* is Latin for "spotted" or "varied."

Description

Shape and size very close to robin; male upper parts slate-blue, underparts orange with black band across breast; wings blue with two orange bars, orange frosting on edge of primaries; wide black patch on side of face, orange eyebrow strip; female duller-coloured, with khaki brown in place of male's blue.

Behaviour

Social outside breeding season and in migration; sometimes forages on lawns for worms, hopping like a robin, otherwise feeds in shrubs and trees; flight more undulating than robin's; song a sustained, trilled note, swelling in volume, then fading into a silent pause, then repeated on a different pitch; call a low "took" or soft buzz.

Range

Migratory in interior of province, nonmigratory along the coast; breeds from Alaska to extreme northwest California, throughout British Columbia, although a rare breeder in northeast; breeding habitat is dense, coniferous, moist forest; both migrants and residents found in winter along the coast, including Vancouver Island and Queen Charlottes; a frequent but very erratic winterer in the southern interior.

Food

Snails, worms, insects, berries in summer; dried or frozen berries and fruit, and acorns in winter; attracted to yards and orchards in winter by berry bushes, orchard fruit left on trees; may visit feeders for raisins, apples, suet.

Nest

From 2 to 7 m (6 to 20 ft) up, usually in conifer concealed next to trunk; bulky base of twigs, weed and grass stems, dead leaves, bark shreds; cup of mud, grasses, moss, and dead leaves collected wet which dry into papier-mache consistency; lined with fine, dry grasses.

Comment

It is interesting to note the varying attempts by authors to describe the song of this bird of the deep woods: "Unmusical," "eerie," "remarkable," "bell-like," "buzzing," "matchless truth and purity of tone," etc. One writer suggests that the sound can be approximated by combining a whistle with a muted hum.

This western thrush is becoming a notable winter vagabond on the Prairies and eastward. During fall migration errant flocks may make a left turn over the Rockies and startle the heck out of delighted bird feeders on the Prairies, in Ontario, and south-eastward. As mentioned in the thrush family account, there are even two records for Sable Island, that lonely sandbank in the Atlantic, a hundred kilometres off the Nova Scotia coast.

The berries of Mountain Ash are a strong attractant for this bird. But Wayne Campbell relayed the observation that in his yard in Victoria it fed most readily on berries that had been knocked to the ground by preceding flocks of starlings. If follows that pulling the berries off the tree and scattering them generously on the ground beneath it will enhance your chances of attracting Varied Thrushes.

REF: A(W) - 720; BC - 431; GO - 246; NG - 328; P(W) - 274

Waxwings

Family *Bombycillidae*

There are only three species of true waxwings in the world. Two, the Cedar and Bohemian, occur in British Columbia. Their closest relatives in North America are the Silky Flycatchers, a connection acknowledged in the waxwing family name: *Bombycillidae* is a compound of Greek and pseudo-Latin meaning "silktail."

If you see a waxwing in midsummer it will likely be perched on a prominent lookout launching aerial pursuits of flying insects. This easygoing fruit-eater turns out to be a very adept flycatcher, agile enough to capture even swift and manoeuvrable dragonflies.

The flycatching is a response to the needs of its new hatchlings. They require a starter diet high in protein, a demand fruit cannot fill. After a few days of the booster menu, fruit gradually replaces insects. A parent waxwing transports berries in its crop; a Cedar Waxwing was seen to disgorge thirty chokecherries at the nest, popping them one after another into the waiting gapes of its young.

While their breeding ranges overlap hugely in British Columbia, the Cedar tends to be the representative species the farther south you go, the Bohemian, the farther north.

In the fall, both migrate—the Cedar to more benign southern holdings, the Bohemian into what had been the summer range of the Cedar. A winter waxwing in British Columbia is probably a Bohemian, although some Cedars stay on in the southern and southwest parts of the province. Both birds travel widely; banding shows that Bohemian Waxwings banded in Saskatoon came from breeding areas west of the Rockies. In *Birds of Prince Edward County* (Ontario) Sprague and Weir note that a Cedar Waxwing banded there on the nest in August, 1980 was shot February 13, 1981 in Morelia, Mexico, 3450 km (2140 mi) distant.

Avian Dandy

Both waxwings present a natty figure, impeccable in sleek plumage that always looks as if the wearer is freshly groomed for a formal night out. The colours are tastefully subtle, with shades of rich grey-brown melting into fawns with a suggestion of saffron. The few highlights—most noticeably the jaunty crest, complemented by a velvet-black line through the eye, a natty bar of deep yellow at the end of the tail, and a tiny daub of red on the wing—accentuate the overall statement of restrained elegance.

About thirty years ago birders started noticing the occasional Cedar Waxwing with orange instead of yellow at the end of the tail. In the intervening years the incidence of orange-tipped waxwings has markedly increased. The most plausible explanation is that the colour comes from pigments in the berries of ornamental yew which has come into fashionable use as a landscape shrub over the last thirty years, and which is a favourite winter food of waxwings.

For all its nattiness, the waxwing personality is that of a friendly, easygoing wayfarer, fond of dining well in good company, as polite as it is handsome. In *The*

Wonder of Canadian Birds Candace Savage notes that its beguiling trustfulness is shown in accounts of their taking bits of string from outstretched hands, and of trying to pull hair from a person's head, all in the interests of collecting nesting materials.

The "Plume Trade"

Incredible though it seems to us now, at one time millions of songbirds, and others, were shot indiscriminately every year to supply feathers for women's hats. The brutality and waste of the "plume trade" outraged many, but the influence and money of the fashion industry frustrated all efforts to put a stop to it.

Then Frank Chapman, ornithologist for the American Museum of Natural History, staged an inspired protest that helped change the course of nature preservation in North America. He went "birding" on the streets of Manhattan, recording the feathers in women's hats. Prominent among the forty species he listed, and subsequently published, were Northern Flicker, Snow Bunting, Northern Bobwhite, and Common Tern. But the most frequent victim was the Cedar Waxwing, a bizarre tribute to its elegant beauty. The sharp-eyed Chapman noted only one Bohemian plume in his fashion-parade inventory. There would undoubtedly have been more except that its remote breeding range kept it safe from the feather hunters' birdshot.

Nature-lovers of the day, spurred by Chapman's imaginative protest, launched an impassioned campaign appealing to the conscience of the fashionable to stop wearing feathers of wild birds. The plume and millinery industry fought back, claiming that 83,000 American workers would be plunged into destitution if the plume hunt were stopped. They dismissed the charges of cruelty, and of the threatened extinction of certain species, with a barrage of dubious assurances. The rhetoric of the times rings familiar to bystanders in today's controversy over the trapping that supplies wild furs for the fashion industry.

The bird preservationists eventually won out. Fashions changed, and the thousands of "threatened" workers were promptly put to work turning out featherless headgear. Birds such as Snowy Egrets slowly recovered from the brink of extinction.

Feathered Gourmands

Birds that feed on fruit trade quality for quantity, fruit being less nutritious than insects and most seeds, but often available in great abundance. Waxwings feeding on cotoneaster berries consume three times their weight of them every day. To process such bulk they have a short gut designed for fast through-put; passage from beak to car top can take as little as sixteen minutes. The need to eat hugely has gained waxwings an undeserved reputation for gluttony. They are often seen gorging on fruit and then lolling about like overstuffed Christmas-dinner guests.

Now and then this feeding pattern brings them to embarrassment when they encounter fall fruit that has fermented. Householders then report, in some alarm, that their ornamental crab is full of birds fluttering and falling about for all the world as if they were drunk, which indeed they are.

The "wax" that gives the birds their name is exuded from the tips of the feather shafts of the secondaries on the wings of both sexes. Its presence varies considerably, being nonexistent to sparse in young birds, most pronounced in breeding adults. Although it is an obscure field mark, among the birds themselves it may function as a badge of fitness and maturity.

❄ ❄ ❄

Bohemian Waxwing
Bombycilla garrulus

Common name likely arising from vagabond "bohemian" winter wanderings, rather than from any link to west Czechoslovakia where they are only occasional visitors; "waxwing" from tips of secondary wing feathers which seem to have been dipped in red wax; formerly called "silktail"; Greek *bombyx*, "silk"; *cilla* is invention from Middle Latin coined, mistakenly, to mean "tail"; *garrulus*, from Latin *garrula*, "chattering," waxwing's crest making it resemble European jay, *Garrulus glandarius*.

Description

Starling-sized; elegant, smooth plumage a subtle blend of soft greys and rich ochres; trim, sharp-tipped crest, narrow black mask through eyes, black chin; bill small, black; tiny cluster of waxy tips on wing secondaries are difficult to spot; best told from smaller, more slender Cedar Waxwing by cinnamon undertail coverts, white bar and flecking on dark wings, and by broader yellow band at end of tail.

Behaviour

Social; busy flocks in winter mob fruit-bearing trees like Mountain Ash or ornamental crabapple; constant calling while feeding or in flight; tame; share with Cedars the habit of sitting in a close row on a branch passing a berry or bright object back and forth; call a weak, trilling, slightly buzzy "tzeee."

Range

Throughout northern hemisphere; in Canada breeds through northwestern boreal zone, northern limit of range coinciding roughly with tree line from Alaska to west shore of Hudson Bay; western limit the Coast Ranges of British Columbia, hence absent as breeder from Vancouver Island and Charlottes; irregular winter nomad throughout southern two-thirds of the province; ornamental fruit and berry trees draw it to yards and suburbs.

Food

Fruit-eater, insectivorous when feeding nestlings; might visit feeding stations to try frozen crabapples, apples, berries, or raisins, prunes, and dates; best attractants are berry or fruit-bearing trees that hold fruit over winter.

Nest

Usually in conifer on forest edge near clearing, lake, or marsh; 1.5 to 6 m (5 to 20 ft) up; cup of conifer twigs, lichens, and grass, lined with hair, down.

Comment

Looking at the range map for the Bohemian, it is easy to speculate that it could be a recent arrival from Siberia, spreading south and east from a toehold in Alaska. Why, for example, doesn't it breed east of Hudson Bay and in Newfoundland where the habitat is very similar to the western boreal zone? Cedar Waxwings breed in a broad band right across the continent. Are they much earlier arrivals from the same stock that evolved into a separate species?

Should a flock appear to feed on the winter-fast fruit of a nearby tree, get out the binoculars promptly and give their beauty, and their busy sociability, a long look. They travel far and wide in search of food, and once having plucked every berry, they will not be back again.

REF: A(W) - 747; BC - 439; GO - 258; NG - 344; P(W) - 282

Cedar Waxwing

Bombycilla cedrorum

Has been called "cedar bird" from association with this tree, and "cherry bird" for its diet of fruit; like Bohemian, secondary wing feathers bear red tips resembling the wax once used to seal envelopes; Greek *bombyx* means "silk" in reference to family link to silktails, *cilla* is a Latin nonword supposed to mean "tail."

Description

Smaller than robin, slimmer than Bohemian; plumage silky, smooth; obvious crest is sharp-pointed, backswept; colour predominantly a blending of soft browns melting to fawns, beiges, and khaki; narrow satin-black face mask elegantly lined in off-white, chin dark; belly and flanks pale yellow; undertail coverts white and unusually long, extending well toward end of tail; rump and base of tail grey; squared-off tail has a wide, dark, subterminal band; terminal band is bright yellow or saffron; unlike Bohemian, darkish wings have no bars or yellow check marks; "song" a lispy, trilled "tzeee" in a metallic monotone.

Behaviour

Sweeps about in fast-flying flocks, constantly calling; settles into fruit trees or berry bushes, feeding busily in an amiable, well-mannered scramble; may grab berries on the wing by hovering at bunches; may eat plucked berry by tossing it into the air and catching it; quite tame, especially when preoccupied with feeding.

Range

Migratory; a North American species, breeding in a wide band across the continent from coast to coast; nests throughout British Columbia except for extreme north and northwest, and the Charlottes; uncommon in winter in extreme southern interior, more frequent in extreme southwest, and southeast of Vancouver Island.

Food

Fruit, petals, and buds in season; during nesting reverts to flycatcher ancestry to feed young for a few days before gradually switching to fruit; may come to feeders for raisins, frozen berries, or dried fruit, and to yards and orchards for winter-fast fruit, berries.

Nest

In open woods, hedges, orchards, shelter belts; on horizontal limb well away from trunk, 2 to 6 m (6 to 20 ft) up; a bulky, loose base of twigs, weed stems, and grass; cup of grass and plant fibres lined with rootlets, fine grasses, plant down; might appear at first glance to be a clump of debris caught by chance in a cleft in a branch; occasionally nests close together in the same, or nearby, trees.

Comment

Both our waxwings have inspired lyrical prose out of generations of authors, not only about their beauty but about their charming manners. In an ornamental crabapple in winter, or around a bath in summer, they graciously share space and wait turns. Courting couples sit close together, passing a petal or berry back and forth, accompanying the gift-giving with a sedate little side-step dance. Their devotion doesn't end with ritual; if one of a couple is killed, the survivor may call disconsolately for days.

Among the many birds that people regularly rescue and adopt, a disproportionate number seem to be waxwings. Their dietary needs of fruit are easily met, and their placid nature allows them to adjust to captivity without too much stress.

REF: A(W) - 748; BC - 440; GO - 258; NG - 344; P(W) - 282

Shrikes

Family *Laniidae*

Many people who have never seen a shrike nevertheless know of the "butcher bird's" ghoulish habit of impaling the bodies of its victims on thorns and barbed wire. The skewered remains are thus easier to dismember, since shrikes lack the powerful feet and sharp talons of full-scale raptors.

A secure meat hook makes it easier to pull larger prey apart, but is it crucial? Crows and ravens, likewise handicapped with dickybird feet, nevertheless use them very effectively to hold down large food items while they tug at them. The shrike's feet are at least as heavy, proportionately, as a crow's.

The idea that shrikes are compensating for weak feet, and that hawthorn shrubs festooned with little carcasses represent a food cache or larder, are firmly rooted in popular nature lore. But it has been convincingly challenged by researchers in Israel. The June, 1989 issue of *BBC Wildlife* recounts a study by Reuven Yosef and Berry Pinshow of the Ben-Gurion University of the Negev. They point out that if the collection of prey is a larder, it's a very poor one since it's obvious to every passing scavenger and raider. And while shrikes of both sexes do employ thorns and barbs as meat hooks to dismember large prey, this may be more an incidental convenience than a necessity, since males also impale small, fragile items like crickets, and even inedible things such as snail shells.

Working with resident Great Grey Shrikes, the same *Lanius excubitor* we call the Northern, the two men have demonstrated convincingly that the impaling habit could have arisen from courting behaviour in which males use it to display food items. The more conspicuous and well-stocked his display is, the better able a male is to attract a female. For a year Yosef and Pinshow manipulated the displays of males in a cluster of territories, consistently depleting some, augmenting others, leaving a control group untouched.

When returning migrant females sized up the prospective mates, the ones with the boosted caches were chosen first, pairing an average of a month earlier than males in the control group. Subsequent nesting success was also markedly improved. The unfortunates whose caches were cleaned out every week all failed to mate and abandoned their territories.

One persuasive conclusion from this is that a good cache advertises to cruising females that the displaying male is more able to obtain food, whether by better hunting skill, his ability to recognize and defend a superior territory, or both. Either way, he will not only be a better provider for his offspring, but will pass to them genes reinforcing these traits.

One-On-One

The Northern Shrike is one of the relatively few predators that kills prey, one-on-one, that is close to its own size, and whose weapons are not so obviously superior to that of its prey. They have better success with smaller birds, but will attack and kill larger species. They have been seen pursuing robins, and there are accounts of their killing Evening Grosbeaks. It isn't known whether they have the skill of predators such as wolves in assessing a flock of prey animals and quickly picking out the most vulnerable individual.

It is postulated that the shrike relies in part on its resemblance to an unthreatening songbird, the ultimate camouflage, to get close enough to a potential victim and pounce or launch pursuit from close quarters. Certainly this disguise doesn't fool all birds; on the infrequent occasions when a shrike has appeared at my feeder, the reaction of the regulars has been one of alarm and/or panic. Other observers, however, report that victims will sometimes remain as if mesmerized as a shrike makes its fatal approach.

Failing a quick grab, pursuit on the wing can be a protracted race. If the victim is overtaken and buffeted to the ground, the shrike hammers at its head with its heavy bill, employing an unusually strong set of neck muscles. Having knocked the victim senseless, it can then dislocate the neck or pierce the skull with a well-placed bite. It may then hang up the body, a skill that begins as an instinctive reaction. In Robert Burton's *Bird Behaviour* it is reported that young Loggerhead shrikes, at twenty-two days of age, start to hold food in their bills and to draw it along a perch in random fashion. If the food happens to catch on a twig or crotch the bird immediately concentrates on dragging it repeatedly over the obstacle. In this way it very quickly learns to direct its dragging action to the right places.

❄ ❄ ❄

Northern Shrike
Lanius excubitor

"Northern" as distinct from the Loggerhead, a more southerly-occurring relative; "shrike" from Anglo-Saxon *sric*, "a shrieker"; also "butcher bird" from habit of impaling or hanging prey on thorns or barbed wire; *lanius* from Latin "a butcher" and *excubitor*, "a sentinel."

Description

Robin-sized; black-masked, boldly patterned in off-white, grey, and black; belly, rump, undertail coverts white; wings black with white patch and frosting at ends of longest flight feathers; fan-shaped tail black with white edges; crown, nape, and back smoke-grey; large head; heavy, straight, dark bill with sharp, pronounced hook; light lines on breast of juvenile are very faint or absent in adult; sexes identical.

Behaviour

Perches quietly on utility wires, dead branch, fence post, alert for prey beneath; pumps tail upward; undulating flight on rapidly beating wings often low, ending in a sharp swoop up to perch; may hover, kestrel-style, when hunting over grassy cover; chases small birds in pell-mell pursuit, occasionally around feeding stations; call a harsh "shek" or "shak," song an extended medley of warbles, whistles, and phrases from other birds' songs mixed with discordant notes.

Range

Erratically migratory; breeds from Alaska to northern Labrador in northern

P.SALVATSKI ©
1990

reaches of boreal forest to tree line, including extreme northwest British Columbia; regular winter resident throughout the southern part of the province, including Vancouver Island and Queen Charlotte islands.

Food

Predatory on small birds, mice, and large insects which it may capture on the wing; may take suet at feeding stations.

Nest

Bulky, on foundation of twigs, cup lined with roots, hair, feathers; prefers dense conifers, height dependent on size of available trees; favours proximity of thorn-bearing shrubs.

Comment

Shrikes rarely visit feeding stations for the usual purpose; rather, they are attracted by the concentration of other birds. When one does call it is an event fraught with potential for life-and-death drama at close quarters. Lacking talons, and a significant size advantage, the shrike kills in an often protracted struggle in which the prey is buffeted to the ground and bludgeoned on the head with the heavy bill. A detached view of predator-prey relationships is hard to sustain if one sees a beloved bird so brutally assaulted. But the shrike, and its prey, are following aeons of behavioural adaptation. Anyone witnessing a shrike kill should definitely *not* react to it as an emergency to be interrupted, but as a firsthand look at a dramatic episode of nature that few have been privileged to witness.

REF: A(W) - 728; BC - 450; GO - 260; NG - 334; P(W) - 280

Starlings

Family *Sturnidae*

The scene is Vancouver's Granville Island Market on a warm June afternoon. The bird is obviously a pro, in one of the best locations, working a crowd pulled in by a duo of musicians. Their supplication is passive—the inevitable guitar cases open on the tiles in front of them. But the starling is not into passive appeals, nor random searching like the pigeons that swoop and flap from place to place, scrambling for food fallout. This guy is organized. He starts at one end of the front row of spectators, strutting briskly along, moving in close, pausing briefly but deliberately to fix each person with a beady eye. He is less like a panhandler than an usher taking up collection in church. Most of the crowd has munchies, and the bird does well—I throw him a chunk of my tempura.

I'm at best a grudging admirer of starlings. But even well-entrenched prejudice cannot blind me to the beauty of this clever, businesslike bird; the lowering afternoon sun lights up the mixed iridescence of his head and neck feathers, the satin-black body plumage is immaculate. The bright yellow bill, and the copper-pink feet and legs show up strikingly against the dark, mud-coloured slate.

The European, or Common Starling is a scion of an Old World family of 103, 106, 111, or 130 species, depending on which authority you read. There are three in North America, all of them imports. Near Homestead, Florida, is a tiny enclave of Hill Mynas, descendants of escaped cage birds. The Crested Myna was introduced in Vancouver in 1895. It spread only to nearby portions of Vancouver Island where it hung on for many years, but hasn't been seen there recently. Apparently its tropical habit of not incubating its eggs for extended periods during midday has inhibited its reproductive success.

No such laxity inhibits the Common Starling; it is a determined, opportunistic breeder. With little hesitation it will attack birds as large as flickers and evict them from their nest holes. Observers have noticed that the starlings appear to wait patiently until the flickers have completed the excavation before making their move.

In combat with other species the starling uses a hold perfected for battle with its own kind. If one of a battling pair can get onto the other's back it locks its feet into its opponent's feathers, grabs it by the back of the neck with its beak, and hangs on, sometimes for as long as half an hour. This trick, combined with the fact that starlings work well as a tag team to gang up on opponents, enables them to vanquish bigger birds like flickers. The little starlings the pair then raises in the usurped premises are—wouldn't you know it—noted in their turn for being unusually hardy.

Shakespeare was inadvertently responsible for adding this ubiquitous nuisance to North America, although direct blame rests with a group called the American Acclimatization Society. Its self-appointed aim was to introduce to America every bird mentioned in Shakespeare's works. Regrettably, in *Henry IV*, Hotspur proclaimed: "Nay, I'll have a starling shall be taught to speak nothing but

'Mortimer'. . . ." Accordingly, the Society ordered up a few cagefuls and turned them loose in Central Park, New York on March 6, 1890. The initial eighty releasees were joined in April of 1891 by twenty pairs of reinforcements.

Surprisingly, previous attempts to start the scourge had failed. However earnestly we might now wish it, do-gooders of the time didn't recognize the initial failures as the disguised blessings they were. As early as 1872, according to Tufts in *Birds of Nova Scotia*, there was a release in Ohio, and others, preceding the infamous sixth of March in Central Park.

Whirlwind Takeover

The plague incubated in New York for six years before breaking out. It first swept the southern expanses of the continent, taking only a little more time to invade the environmentally harsher north. The first report in Canada was at Niagara Falls, in 1914. The first recorded nesting was at Burlington, Ontario, in 1922. In northern Ontario a dead starling was found at York Factory on Hudson Bay in 1931. By 1937 they were nesting in Thunder Bay. The first report for Manitoba was 1925, the first for Saskatchewan at Mitchellton in 1936. They arrived in British Columbia in the mid-1940s.

Like House Sparrows, starlings are largely dependent on humans for their well-being and do not nest much beyond the confines of towns and farmyards. In breeding atlas maps that indicate the density of individual species, the dots for the starling may literally blacken settled areas. In places, however, there will be conspicuous holes of non-occurrence which turn out to be large parks where back country has been preserved from development.

Although common as winter stay-overs in British Columbia (more plentiful the further south you get), the majority migrates, congregating with grackles and blackbirds to forage in the marshes, shorelines, and agricultural lands of the southern United States. The size of some of these integrated flocks is mind-boggling, by credible estimate the largest numbering seventy million. At roosts, branches break under the weight of the clamorous horde, and the accumulation of droppings beneath the trees sterilizes the soil.

The starling musters the standard adaptive repertoire that helps successful invasive species thrive—hardiness, assertive opportunism, a high birth rate, absence of homeland pathogens, and adaptability. Except for the reprieve from pathogens, these are attributes possessed by native birds the starling has displaced. What, then, confers its competitive edge?

Firstly it arrived preconditioned to life with mankind, an adaptive move similar native birds like grackles are only now beginning to make. The second could be its unusual jaw musculature. Logically, most creatures that grip or chew with their mouths have powerful biting muscles; those required to open the jaws are relatively weak. But the starling jaw has two-way power. Pushed into your lawn, the bill can be forced open. Simultaneously the eyes are rotated forward to provide binocular vision down the hole. This "gaping" enables the bird to detect immobile as well as active prey.

Only a few members of the starling family possess this capability, and among the very few other songbirds that have it are the starling's wintering companions—

grackles and blackbirds. Most soil-dwelling invertebrates are dormant in winter, and inactive, a food source starlings are better-equipped to exploit than other birds, and at a critical time of year.

There is a further, gender-based refinement to the starling's winter feeding pattern. Males will flock to garbage dumps and feedlots where grain and other high-carbohydrate food is the most likely fare. But the females go their separate way to seek out invertebrates, rich in protein which is stored in the pectoral muscles in reserve for the demands of egg laying later on.

Booby-trapped Nests

Species of birds that breed in used cavities and old nests, either their own or others', save labour and time, and the uncertainties of relocating. But their offspring run the risk of inheriting the swarm of lice, mites, and bacteria that multiplied during the tenure of the previous clutch. Some birds habitually add fresh sprigs of greenery to the nest during incubation and prefledging. It turns out that the plants selected for this, such as yarrow, agrimony, and cedar, have fumigant properties that inhibit bacterial and parasitic growth. How do the birds know which plants to select?

Two Pennsylvania researchers—L. Clark and C. A. Smeraski—discovered that during the nesting season starlings develop a sense of smell comparable to that of a rat or rabbit. They use this to sniff out aromatic green plants that have fumigant effects when brought into the nest cavity. After the nesting season, their olfactory powers diminish to the very low level they share with most birds.

Starlings wouldn't be starlings if they simply dealt with the pathogens in the usual way and then left the nest; they use the pathogens to sabotage potential competitors. Like most birds they keep the nest clean of droppings up to the time the young begin to feather. At that point they stop both housecleaning and adding fumigant greenery. Thereafter, to quote *The Birder's Handbook*, the nest hole becomes heavily fouled and resembles "a pest-ridden compost," swarming with lice and thousands of mites. The older starling fledglings are hardy enough to tolerate such infestations. But what they leave behind is a biological "booby trap" fatal to the more fragile newly hatched young of any competing species that might reuse the nest.

Like the crow family, starlings have a reputation for "smarts." As cage birds they can be taught, as Hotspur proclaimed to our regret, to imitate human speech. In traps that securely confine other birds, starlings have been observed to take as little as two minutes to get out by lifting drop-doors or pulling hinged ones inward.

On a positive note, starlings probe out and eat the larvae and pupae of the Gypsy Moth and Japanese Beetle, introduced pests that most other birds do not prey on. It is also suggested that their probing bills spread the spores of insect diseases.

A final note on starling ingenuity: On a winter visit to Toronto in 1992 I bought a small bag of bird seed at the corner shop for my hosts and set up a feeder for them. The bag dribbled seeds on the kitchen floor, however, and when I looked more closely found that one side was punched with little holes in the clear plastic. Later, on a stroll past the same shop I noticed a starling on the sidewalk near the pile of seed bags, and stopped to watch. When not dodging the dogs and the passing feet it hopped among the bags, punched its dagger of a bill through the plastic, gaped it open and dipped up millet with its tongue.

❊ ❊ ❊

European Starling
Sturnus vulgaris

"Starling" from Anglo-Saxon *staer*, "star," plus diminutive "ling," possibly from fanciful likening of delta-winged flight silhouette to stars; *sturnus* is Latin for "a starling," *vulgaris*, "common."

Description

Robin-sized; chunky, short-tailed, dark; large head and long, straight, pointed bill; bill yellow from midwinter to early summer, otherwise brown; adult sexes identical except female eye has yellowish edge around iris; after late summer moult, body feathers are light-tipped, giving a heavily speckled appearance which diminishes by spring as tips wear off.

Behaviour

Social; outside of breeding season gathers in large flocks, especially in migration and wintering; struts about probing ditches, pastures, lawns; aggressive at feeders among themselves and against other species; noisy; voice a series of

R. SAWATZKI ©
1990

whistles, squeaks, gurgles, chirps, and clicks in which it might imitate other birds.

Range

Partially migratory; found throughout Canada wherever human settlements are found, even in the Arctic; a few winter even in northernmost British Columbia, but as you move from north to south, and from inland to coast, winter populations increase to the status of abundant in south coast cities and irrigated farmland where some birds are permanent residents; banding has shown that some of the province's starlings winter in California.

Food

Omnivorous; "gapes" in soft soil and litter for insects and grubs; winter flocks congregate in garbage dumps and feedlots; at feeders takes most seeds, sunflowers last; likes table scraps and suet.

Nest

Cavity nester, including holes in buildings, signs, and light poles; preempts Purple Martin and bluebird houses, if permitted; aggressively evicts flickers and woodpeckers from tree holes; nest a collection of straw, weed stems, and trash with cup of fine plant fibres, feathers.

Comment

This abundant pest vies with the co-immigrant House Sparrow for the title of bird we most love to hate. Pushy and preemptive at feeders, it is particularly hostile to woodpeckers which it seems consistently able to mob and vanquish.

You can make it awkward for them, and still provide for native species at your feeders, by not scattering feed on the ground, by dispensing seeds in hanging feeders, and offering suet in containers accessible only through the bottom.

A bird feeder in Castlegar, Loyd Groutage, dealt with a particularly obnoxious House Sparrow one winter in a way that might have some application if one is plagued with a mob of starlings. Loyd soaked some brown rice in brandy and the sparrow, since he had driven everything else his size away from the feeder, ate his fill, got too tipsy to fly, and was caught by the neighbour's cat.

REF: A(W) - 590; BC - 452; GO - 260; NG 346; P(W) - 280

Sparrows

Family *Emberizinae*

This group includes the Old World buntings and their kin, the New World "sparrows." Employing Godfrey's (*Birds of Canada*) quotation marks acknowledges that our "sparrows" aren't really the same as the Old World birds they were mistakenly named after. Those of us who are slightly adrift about the kinships in this large group of songbirds are in good company; sparrows and "sparrows" have been, and remain, a source of debate among taxonomists. To add to the confusion, our best-known "sparrow," the House Sparrow, is held by some (including Peterson in his most recent guides) to be no sparrow at all, but an Old World weaver finch. However, the American Ornithological Union's latest checklist places the House Sparrow in the Old World sparrow family.

In most of British Columbia there are several species that are commonly seen in winter around yards and farms where there's suitable cover; these are the Dark-eyed Junco, Rufous-sided Towhee, and the American Song Sparrow. Frequent in the southern and coastal areas, less common the further north you get in the interior, are the Fox, White-crowned, and Golden-crowned Sparrow. The White-throated, Harris's, Lincoln's, American Tree, and Savannah Sparrows show up in Christmas Bird Counts in the south and southwest of the province, rarer the further north and west you get.

Compared to the sociable finches, our North American sparrows aren't enthusiastic feeder seekers. In my experience the only real feeder bird amongst this lot is the faithful little junco that comes in flocks to our feeders and may stay the whole winter. The towhee and song sparrow readily come to feeders, but this usually seems to be as an afterthought if they have already settled into the vicinity for the duration. In varying degrees, the same holds for the other wintering sparrows.

A bird synonymous with winter, the Snow Bunting, though regionally abundant, prefers to forage for itself in open fields and only rarely visits feeders unless one has the space, and makes special provisions, to attract it. In areas blessed with snow, where there are open fields, a scattering of chaff and screenings or scratch feed will sometimes hold a flock of these flighty nomads.

In selecting sparrows for discussion as feeder birds the junco, towhee, and song sparrow are easy choices. But as one goes down the Christmas Bird Count summaries, the cut-off point between the species that we have a fair chance of seeing at feeders, and the ones the average bird feeder will never see in winter, gets hazy. In the end, one must simply exercise the author's prerogative. As well as the three above, the Fox, White-crowned, and Golden-crowned made the cut; better luck next time to the White-throated, Harris's, Lincoln's, American Tree, and Savannah.

All in the Family

As anyone with an older field guide can see, both the common and scientific names of birds are constantly being changed. These decisions are the result of deliberations by the American Ornithologist's Union which, among other pronouncements made within my recollection, changed the Canada Jay to the Gray Jay, the Baltimore Oriole to the Northern Oriole, the Sparrow Hawk to the American Kestrel, etc.

At one time the impetus amongst biologists was with the "splitters," those who saw in minor differences in physical form a reason to declare their possessors a separate species, or at least a subspecies. They were opposed by the "lumpers," those who held that many differences claimed by the splitters were superficial and didn't justify setting up a separate species or subspecies.

Juncos are a case in point. Until recently, as detailed in the species account, we had four regional species, five counting the Yellow-eyed of Mexico which retained its species status. The others were reassessed and found to lack sufficient differences to merit status as separate species, so they were lumped into one. The differences between them, the lumpers assure us, are entirely sartorial and don't at all prevent juncos of the various forms from interbreeding where their ranges overlap.

❊ ❊ ❊

Rufous-sided Towhee
Pipilo erythrophthalmus

"Rufous-sided" because of the brick-red sides, "towhee" imitative of the eastern form's call; other names are "chewink," "swamp robin," "ground robin," "jo-ree"; western form previously the "spotted towhee" or "Oregon towhee"; *pipilo* coined from Latin *pipo*, "to chirp"; *erythrophthalmus* from Greek words *erythros*, "red," and *ophthalmos*, "eye," hence "red-eye."

Description

A large, long-tailed sparrow dressed in bright contrasts; head, bib, back, wings, and tail coal-black; white flashes on outer corners of tail and white check marks on back and wings; sides robin-red, belly white; eye a piercing red; female similar but much subdued, the black of the male replaced by sooty brown, very dark in some coastal forms.

Behaviour

Fitfully restless; stands and perches in tilted-forward posture, tail cocked up; generally busy near or on dense shrubbery, drops quickly into it at slightest disturbance; scratches about in ground duff as a hen does, but in a quick forward hop and backward flick with both feet; song a two-note "chip-eeeeeeee," the second a rapid, metallic, one-note trill; call a catlike "meeewwwww."

Range

Breeds across southern Canada from Vancouver Island to eastern Manitoba, and in southern Ontario; in British Columbia breeds across south as far north as Williams Lake in the Cariboo; nonmigratory along the coast, largely migratory in the interior, a few wintering in the southern Okanagan; favours shrubby tangles around edges of clearings, along fences, thickets around yards and parks.

Food

Insects, weed seeds, occasional fruit, berries; at feeders takes sunflower seeds as first choice, millet as second; will go to high feeders placed amongst branches, but prefers ground feeding.

Nest

Usually a cup in ground, rim level with surface, in thick shrubs, often sheltered by plant tuft; rarely above ground in brush tangle, dense bush or vine; thick cup of grasses, bark shreds, rootlets, conifer needles, lined with finer grasses, occasionally hair.

Comment

There are four *Pipilo* genus species, the towhees, in North America, all of them westerners except for the Rufous-sided. Anyone familiar with the "drink-your-teeeee" call of the eastern bird will note, on travelling west through the southern Prairies, that this call changes to "chweeeeeee" as one nears the Alberta border. The two eastern syllables start disappearing in a distinct transition zone beginning in mid-Saskatchewan.

Efforts to imitate, or "syllabize," the calls and songs of birds have resulted in some heroic phonetics. "Chick-a-dee-dee" and "caw" are self-evident and required no imagination. And pub-crawlers immediately recognized a fellow tippler in the Olive-sided Flycatcher with his "quick-three-beers." But more complicated vocalizations weren't so easy. Ernest Thompson Seton had a go at the eastern Rufous-sided Towhee with "chuck-burr-pill-a-will-a-will-a." Taverner thought it sounded like "dick-yoo, chiddle-chiddle-chiddle." The differences could be accounted for by the "ear-of-the-hearer" phenomenon, or by the fact that many species of birds have distinct regional dialects. My own interpretation of the towhees on my turf in Manitoba, where they are neighbours to coyotes, is "keep-yeer-fleeeeeees."

REF: A(W) - 598; BC - 504; GO - 324; NG - 386; P(W) - 330

Fox Sparrow
Passerella iliaca

"Fox" because the eastern type species, and most races east of the Rockies are a bright foxy brown. Choate in *American Bird Names*, (p.143), explains the scientific name thusly: "L. *passer*, 'sparrow'; L. *-ella*, 'little'; hence 'little sparrow' for the genus which has one of our largest sparrows. *P. iliaca* . . .; L. *iliacus*, 'relating to colic,' from L. *ilia*, 'the groin' or 'lower intestine,' the anatomical seat of the Roman bellyache. It is remotely possible that the taxonomist who named the bird had in mind 'flanks,' as this portion of the bird's anatomy is conspicuously streaked."

Description

Larger than House Sparrow; in British Columbia basically a large, dark sparrow with long, slightly notched tail; light underside has rows of heavy spots like upside-down "Vs," clumping together in a ragged spot in the centre of the breast.

Behaviour

Scratches noisily on the ground, usually among trees or under bushes, flipping

leaves and debris into the air behind it; voice strong and clear, song one or more slurred whistles followed by several short, musical "churrrrrrs."

Range

Migratory; breeds in its various forms throughout British Columbia, Yukon, Alaska, Mackenzie District, east through boreal belt to Labrador and Newfoundland; familiar winterer in southwest of province, including southeast Vancouver Island; occasional to rare winterer as one moves from west to east and north to south.

Food

Insects, worms, seeds scratched from beneath woodland ground litter; may occasionally also search through windrows of marine vegetation along beaches.

Nest

On ground; occasionally in thicket or low conifer branch above ground; a thick, deep cup of twigs, bark shreds, grass and weed stems, moss, lined with fine rootlets, hair, feathers.

Comment

The plumage colouration in this bird is quite variable in British Columbia. None of our indigenous races really have the bright, ruddy-brown plumage that gave the eastern bird its name. The darkest form is the sooty-brown race from the extreme southwest, the south coast, and Vancouver Island. A lighter form of the coastal race breeds on the Queen Charlottes. There is a more reddish bird in the southeast and central interior. A form with grey back and head is found in the extreme southeastern corner.

REF: A(W) - 680; BC - 530; GO - 342; NG - 406; P(W) - 324

Song Sparrow

Melospiza melodia

"Song" from bird's obvious talent; *melospiza* from Greek *melos*, "song" and *spiza*, "a finch"; *melodia* from Greek/Latin "a pleasant song."

Description

Same size as House Sparrow; inconspicuously plumaged; relatively long tail rounded at end; rows of heavy brown dashes on white breast and sides come together to form dark, ragged spot on upper breast; top of head brown, with narrow black streaks and midstripe of grey; the rest is a blend of browns, rusts, and tans; various west coast races darker, larger than eastern type form; everywhere its song is the best "field mark."

Behaviour

Not sociable; highly territorial in breeding season; ground feeder; pumps long tail during characteristically short flights; begins singing very early in season, often well before snow is gone where it winters over; sings from elevated perch in "chest-out" posture, feathers puffed out, head thrown back; song starts with three or four clear notes, then a rolling series of sweet warblings ending in a

P.Sauatzki
1991 ©

buzzy trill; no other sparrow sings so well; call note a distinctive "chimp"; easily attracted by a squeaking or "pishing" noise.

Range

Common to abundant over northern three-quarters of continent, excepting high Arctic tundra; found in open bushland, woodland and waterside edges, marshes, and in suburban hedges, gardens, and parks; the most frequent, widespread winterer in British Columbia, from common on coast (where it is a year-round resident) and in extreme southern interior, to scattered and unusual in northern interior.

Food

Weed seeds, insects added during nestling-feeding season; feeder choice is most small seeds, especially thistle and canary, plus sunflower; prefers low table or ground, but will feed high.

Nest

Often builds two or more per season, first one on ground, before leaves are out, second in low bush or tree; ground nest well concealed under tuft, shrub, or fallen branches; base of grass, weed stems, leaves, bark fibres, cup lined with fine grasses, rootlets, hair; tree nest similar, in bush or small tree .4 to 1 m (18 in to 3 ft) up, sometimes up to 4 m (13 ft); high rate of cowbird parasitism.

Comment

This drab little virtuoso is born with its song in its head, and will tenaciously sing the basic Song Sparrow melody even if it's raised with domestic canaries. But it develops best when it absorbs its father's song along with its daily fare of insects and regurgitated seeds. Having done this, it then proceeds in early maturity to invent its own unique song, using variations on many basic themes. The average male has eight to ten separate, extended recitals, but some prodigies have as many as twenty. Thoreau syllabized this bird's basic pattern as: "Maids, maids, maids . . . hang on your tea kettle-ettle-ettle-ettle." Latter-day imitators suggest "sweet" in place of "maids."

In *Birds of Nova Scotia*, Tufts, always interesting, recounts a story of a farmer whose cat, in the summer of 1952, brought in a male Song Sparrow. A check revealed no apparent injury (to the bird), so the farmer released it, expecting that it would fly out of sight in haste. Instead, it flew to a nearby branch, shook itself vigorously, and burst into song. There's a message in there, I think.

REF: A(W) - 681; BC - 531; GO - 342; NG - 392; P(W) - 324

Golden-crowned Sparrow
Zonotrichia atricapilla

"Golden-crowned" from the sulphur-yellow stripe on the top of the head; *zonotrichia* from Greek *zone*, "a band," and *trichias*, "a thrush"; *atricapilla* from Latin *atrus*, "black," and *capilla*, "hair"; we thus have the common name describing one part of the bird's head, the scientific name, another, since the gold band is bordered by black stripes.

Description

House Sparrow-sized; crown of head black with broad, yellow stripe down the middle that changes sharply to grey at back of head; viewed from side, head may appear black; sides of face and throat grey; sexes identical; in winter, head markings are dull, obscure; upper body a pattern of browns, beige; breast and belly uniform light tan-grey.

Behaviour

Moderately social; shows site attachment in winter, either singly or in small flocks; ground feeder, preferring to be in or near dense, broken cover; skims the ground in flight from one patch of shelter to the next; voice a clear, flutelike whistle; cadence of song suggests "Three blind mice" tune, often syllabized as "Oh, dear mee."

Food

In winter seeds, buds, fresh leaves, and shoots; at feeder small seeds, grain, chick scratch on ground.

Range

Migratory; breeds in subalpine timberline, everywhere throughout montane British Columbia except in the extreme southeast; common wintering bird in Victoria and southeast Vancouver Island; fairly common winterer in Vancouver area but rare in southern interior, uncommon and irregular in central interior.

Nest

On the ground at base of low shrub or tussock, or under overhanging plants; thick cup of small twigs, bits of bark, fern leaves, grass stems, dead leaves; lined with fine grasses, hair, feathers.

Comment

When considering, or trying to identify, Song and White-crowned sparrows, particularly in the West, one must deal with at least several different races, or forms. But the Golden-crowned, perhaps because of its relatively limited range, presents the viewer with no such dilemma. Its uniformity may be sustained in part also by its migration pattern. According to Munro and Cowan, and Jewett, referred to in *Birds of the Okanagan Valley*, these birds go south in the fall through the high country of the Coast Ranges and the Cascades, but come back north in spring up the coastal lowlands. Their principal wintering grounds are along the coast from Washington to southern California.

REF: A(W) - 750; BC - 536; GO - 340; NG - 404; P(W) - 316

White-crowned Sparrow
Zonotrichia leucophrys

Zonotrichia from Greek *zone*, "a band," and *trichias*, "a thrush"; *leucophrys* from Greek "white" and *ophrys*, "eyebrow," for the white line over the eye.

Description

"Stripe-crowned" would be more descriptive, since the outstanding field mark of the adult bird is its puffy, black-and-white striped head; there are several forms in British Columbia, including a coastal breeder with somewhat dingy white stripes, and a high Arctic breeder with bolder stripes that is the most common winterer here; chin whitish, underparts plain grey; back and wings brown, bill flesh-coloured; crown distinctly dome-shaped compared to flatter crown of White-throated with which it is most likely to be confused.

Behaviour

Erect posture constitutes a field mark; less a bird of thick brush and woodland than the White-throated; runs rapidly about on the ground, usually perches no higher than eye level; puffs up crown when agitated; many regional dialects to its short song, but basic form is one or more deliberate, plaintive whistles followed by several short trills ending in two or three quick descending notes; call a metallic "chink."

Range

Migratory; nests right across subarctic and Arctic Canada, south in high alpine habitat through British Columbia east of Coastal Ranges, on southern Vancouver Island and lower Fraser Valley; winters along the southwest coast, on southeast Vancouver Island, and sporadically in small numbers in southwest interior, infrequent to rare in central interior.

Food

Weed seeds, gleaned from the ground, buds, berries; at feeder will take ground-scattered sunflower seeds, millet, chicken scratch, other small seed, coming less readily to elevated feeders.

Nest

Cup of grass stems, dead leaves, conifer needles, bark shreds, moss, lined with root fibres, hair, feathers; under grass-tuft, fern, or at base of stunted shrub, rarely in a bush or low tree branch off the ground.

Comment

Migration is gender-linked, the females of any given population tending to migrate further south than the males.

The Birder's Handbook refers to a study done by Gary Fugle at the University of California which demonstrated that brightness of the crown pattern is the key status signal. Adult males with bright stripes are at the top of the heap, with juvenile females, with the dullest striping, at the bottom. By brightening up the headdress of subordinate individuals with a painted stripe job, Fugle found that they immediately rose a notch or two in sparrow hierarchy.

White-crowneds are one of many ground-nesting species in which the females, disturbed at the nest, will scurry away on the ground in a hunched, head-down "mouse run," some giving a distinct mouselike squeak. If the trick works, would-be egg predators are decoyed away from the nest and end up with nothing but a brisk turn of exercise when the scurrying "mouse" flies off.

REF: A(W) - 682; BC - 536; GO - 340; NG - 404; P(W) - 316

Dark-eyed Junco
Junco hyemalis

Also "snowbird," especially by American writers; all except most recent editions of guides list "Slate-colored Junco," "White-winged Junco," "Oregon Junco," "Gray-headed Junco," as separate species, now rated as colour variants (races) of *hyemalis*, the former species name for Slate-colored; Latin *juncus*, "a rush," has no known connection to juncos, but Latin *hyemalis*, "winter," is linked to their appearing only in winter in south-temperate regions.

Description

Sparrow-sized; all juncos have flesh-coloured feet and bill, and outer tail feathers edged in white, visible only when bird flares tail; male of most widespread race, Slate-colored, is unbroken slate-grey on entire upper body; belly, white; Oregon form has coal-black head and cape, rusty back, white belly, all sharply demarcated; rusty-pink flanks blend into white of underparts.

Behaviour

Moderately social ground-foragers; quick to follow other birds to table, shelf, or even hanging, feeders; may dig through light snow cover to reach bare ground; flicks white outer tail feathers from under centrals, especially just before takeoff, flashing them conspicuously in flight; calls variously described as snappy "chip" or "dit"; soft twittering in flight; song a largely one-pitch trill, like Chipping Sparrow but more agreeable to some ears.

Range

Migratory, flying only far enough south to reach adequate forage; breeds throughout the boreal and adjoining mixed-wood forests from coast to coast in

Canada; Slate-colored breeds from central up through northeastern British Columbia; Oregon breeds throughout Coastal Ranges, in interior down through southwest, including Vancouver Island; winterers in the province are predominantly Oregon, abundant in the southwest mainland, eastern Vancouver Island, the Okanagan; common in Kootenays where a few Slate-coloreds join them, fairly common in the central interior, uncommon, replaced by a few Slate-coloreds in the northeast.

Food

Insects during breeding season, seeds in winter; at stations will readily take to sunflower seeds, all small seeds, crumbs, and occasionally suet and peanut butter.

Nest

On ground, in open woodland or forest edge; concealed in tree roots, under debris, a rock, or tussock, occasionally in ferns, or on rubbly slope; rarely in low shrub or conifer; small cup of bark shreds, stems, light twigs, lined with fine grasses, rootlets, hair; prefledged nestlings precociously active and able to scramble away from nest and hide if threatened.

Comment

Where juncos are predominantly migratory and are absent for most of the winter, they partly make up for it by appearing in great numbers during migration. Especially in spring they show up in distinct "waves" that see them around for a month or more before moving on.

As in many species, junco migration is divided along age and gender lines. Females travel further south than males, but juveniles of both sexes remain farther north than adults. It is common for bird feeders, north of the juncos' wintering range, to note that in spring they appear in abundance, usually before the snow has gone, stick around for several weeks, vanish altogether for a week, and then reappear. What has actually happened is migration in two pulses, the males a week or two in advance of the females.

REF: A(W) - 731; BC - 539; GO - 334; NG - 402; P(W) - 332

Cowbirds and Other Blackbirds

Family *Icterinae*

This subfamily is exclusive to the Western Hemisphere and includes the bobolink, orioles, meadowlarks, blackbirds, and cowbirds. *Icterinae* is from Greek *ikteros*, "jaundice." This ailment, named for the yellowing of the skin it causes, was supposed by the ancients to be alleviated if the sufferer were lucky enough to see an oriole, many species of which are also yellow. The Old World orioles belong to the *Oriolidae*, a family not related to our orioles.

The ninety-odd species of our blackbird family are a notably diverse lot, not only in their appearance but in their behaviour. Among its number in British Columbia is the brightly plumaged Northern (formerly "Baltimore") Oriole, a noteworthy singer that weaves a delicate hanging pouch nest. Then there's the drab Brown-headed Cowbird which "sings" in a strangled squeak, and as far as can be determined retains no vestige of an instinct for building a nest of any kind.

Numbers are the "bottom line" indicator of any species' success, although they are certainly no guarantee of survival, as demonstrated by the lamented Passenger Pigeon. Its population at the time Europeans began their assault on the Americas has been credibly estimated at three billion. It could, in such awesome abundance, have been the world's most plentiful land bird, a place now probably occupied by starlings or House Sparrows.

In North America, our "top bird" could now be the Red-winged Blackbird, an avian success story in its ability to cope with habitat alterations inflicted by modern man. If you lump in the plenteous redwing with other blackbirds, and grackles and cowbirds which band together in their wintering grounds to form massive flocks, there is no doubt about which family is the one of greatest apparent abundance.

Some blackbirds, including all grackles, share with starlings the ability to forage by "gaping." They force the bill into rotting wood, clumps of vegetation, flowers, curled leaves, packed ground litter, and moist sod, and then bring into play a special set of jaw muscles enabling them to open the bill forcibly. This makes available to them sources of food such as buried insects, slugs, and worms that surface-foraging birds don't have ready access to.

Adaptability, and the attendant opportunism, have been the ticket to success for species that have become plentiful as an offshoot of human impact. In the early days of bird feeding, blackbirds of any kind were rare visitants; the appearance of a Red-winged Blackbird at a northern Michigan feeder in 1921 was an occasion for publication. Now, often to the dismay of householders in the blackbirds' wintering territory, they are all too ready to come to the banquet board.

Our "Friend"

The versatility of the blackbird family is further demonstrated by the Brown-headed Cowbird. This unassuming bird has evolved to occupy the niche of the nest parasite amongst our Canadian songbirds. It prospers along with the works of agricultural and urban mankind. Where it winters, it benefits from our feeders.

To what degree does our inadvertent benevolence sabotage the well-being of other birds, including migrants under pressure from habitat loss, and our favourites at the feeder? While the cowbird isn't a winter feeder bird in British Columbia to the extent it now is in southern Ontario and the Maritimes, it is a common summer resident in much of the province, a familiar of orchard, pasture, and suburban lawn. Given the direct impact it has on our birds, feeder species included, plus the prospect of its expanding its winter presence here as it has elsewhere, I feel that a general discussion of its natural history is relevant in *any* book on British Columbia birds.

Nest parasites are those that have evolved ways of tricking other birds into raising their young. All the female does is mate and then lay her eggs in somebody else's crib. The success of the scam relies, of course, on the duped birds' (customarily, but somehow inappropriately, called the "hosts,") accepting the foster egg and incubating it along with their own.

Members of widely varying families of birds have independently evolved into nest parasites. Among these the best-known is the cuckoo of Europe, *Cuculus canorus*. Our North American cuckoos build their own nests, albeit fragile affairs. Some honeyguides of Africa are parasitic, and of the cowbirds of the Western Hemisphere, some are parasitic, some are not. There is even a parasitic duck.

Fostering with a Difference

Needless to say, with the variety of species that have taken to parasitism, both their strategies and the effect upon their hosts vary greatly. One of the easiest parasites to foster is the young of the aforementioned duck, the Black-headed of South America. Uninhibited by favouritism, the female dumps her eggs into the nests of any other duck species, as well as those of coots, ibises, spoonbills, herons, storks, and gulls, all of which accept the extra egg. When the duckling hatches all it needs is two days' brooding, then it swims off alone and commences to feed itself.

A changeling of entirely opposite behaviour is inflicted on hosts by two species of African honeyguide. Like its newly hatched nestmates the honeyguide chick is naked and blind, but unlike them has a powerful hooked beak with needle-sharp tips that cross at the ends. It repeatedly bites the host's chicks until they die of multiple lacerations and punctures. Alone, it incessantly imitates the food-begging cries of not one, but two of the hosts' chicks. Halfway through the six-week nestling period, the deadly hooked ends of the beak become blunted. By the time it is ready to leave the nest it weighs twice as much as each of its foster parents.

The Black Sheep of the Family

There is nothing sinister in the appearance of a Brown-headed Cowbird; the sight of it scurrying about the heads and feet of grazing cattle and sitting companionably on their backs is the very stuff of rustic innocence. It looks equally unthreatening amongst the pink flamingos on a suburban lawn, undistinguished in appearance, retiring of manner, reticent as a guest at the feeder. But this unassuming mien is in fact the quintessential cover; the forgettable public *persona* masks a covert life of deception, subversion, and, at times, ghoulish infanticide.

My most memorable confrontation with cowbird parasitism was at our hut in the country. One year, on a rafter under the extended roof that shelters the front step, the resident pair of Eastern Phoebes built their nest of mud and grass. I was pleased with their gesture of trust, their previous sites having been at more removed locations. The attentive parents didn't seem to mind our constant comings and goings during the weekend visit when we discovered the nest.

When I came back the next weekend there were four naked baby phoebes sprawled dead on the landing below the nest. In their place above was an oversized cowbird nestling, already well covered in budding feathers.

Taken with an irrational urge for retribution I reached up and grabbed it by one wing, whereupon it clutched the nest and began squawking loudly. This brought the phoebes, snapping their bills around my ears in such alarm that I let go and left them to finish rearing their murderous fosterling.

Like many other writers, I have indulged my emotional biases, imputing human motives, and the rhetoric of condemnation, to this entirely blameless bird. Much as we might pity the victims of its lethal offspring, much as we might decry its impact on more lovable species, it is simply playing the role that the drama of survival long ago cast it in.

A New Relationship

The Brown-headed Cowbird is known to have laid in the nests of over two hundred species. Some—like waterfowl, killdeer, hawks, and even humming-birds—are manifestly unsuitable foster parents. And its hosts are similarly naive; many of them uncritically accept a cowbird egg even though, from its size and pattern, it's obviously a plant.

One supposes, therefore, that this is a relatively new relationship; neither party has had the time to evolve sophisticated responses to the other's tactics. The cowbird has an incubation period of eleven to twelve days which, while short, is not fast-track development; only in some host nests does it confer a head start. In some cases the cowbird pushes its foster siblings out of the nest. Or, blessed with a loud voice and a huge appetite, it may simply starve them to death. There are, however, plenty of examples of its coexisting with apparently healthy nestmates.

One puzzle worth pondering is how young cowbirds avoid what should be a severe identity crisis. Every cowbird you will ever see has to have been raised by other birds, but it will not have imprinted on them. Once fledged and on its way, it joins its own kind.

Predawn Infiltration

Identity problems or not, come the nesting season a young female cowbird knows exactly what to do. She stakes out a piece of good nesting habitat, but apparently doesn't drive other female cowbirds away from it; they seem able to sort out their spacing without territorial aggression. Males court her, and she mates with one or more of them. Patrolling her territory, she cues onto potential hosts by their nest-building activities and keeps them under surveillance.

Her own egg-laying is apparently triggered by the presence of one or more of the host's eggs in their nest. If she laid an egg in an empty nest, the foster parents would likely desert, or eject the egg. Most songbirds, by the way, lay an egg a day, early in the morning, staying off the nest until they have a full clutch. The cowbird usually removes one of the host's eggs and eats it, sometimes the day before laying her own egg, sometimes the day after. She makes her calls, including the one on which she lays her egg, in early dawn, before the owner returns to lay her own daily egg. The cowbird is a sit-and-run layer, taking from five seconds to several minutes, then she's gone.

The literature cites cases of two or more cowbird eggs or nestlings in one nest. The usual explanation is that more than one cowbird has parasitized it.

A cowbird's first round of egg-laying (one hesitates to call it a "clutch"), in which she usually lays six eggs, all of them in different nests, may be followed by one or two more rounds, depending on the availability of host nests. During a good season she could lay twenty or more; some authors claim forty.

The question then is, why aren't there more cowbirds than there are? Very possibly there are more cowbirds than there *were*, particularly compared to the period after the demise of the bison and before the replacement cow was installed on the plains. Mankind has been good to the cowbird. The *Atlas of the Breeding Birds of Ontario* notes that it was well established there by 1880. It further observes that in otherwise cowbird-free Algonquin Park there is a line of sightings, recorded during the atlasing surveys, running through it. It turns out that this line is Highway 60, showing how little man-made clearing the cowbird needs to move in. One wonders if logging roads in British Columbia open up similar avenues of infiltration.

To get back to the question of the numbers of cowbirds, there are, for the cowbirds, problems. Some birds, such as robins, catbirds, Blue Jays, Eastern Kingbirds, Cedar Waxwings, and Brown Thrashers either puncture or eject cowbird eggs. This rejection is an odd-egg-out reflex; if given several cowbird eggs and one of their own, they eject their own! Some warblers tend to nest in loose association with Red-winged Blackbirds and sustain a lower incidence of parasitism because the aggressive blackbirds drive off trespassing cowbirds. Cowbird chicks in American Goldfinch nests frequently die of malnutrition on the straight diet of seeds their nest mates thrive on.

What with normal predation added to the evasive tactics of their hosts, cowbirds have to lay large numbers of eggs to sustain their numbers. According to *The Birder's Handbook*, a recent study shows that only 3 percent of cowbird eggs result in adults.

❅ ❅ ❅

Red-winged Blackbird

Agelaius phoeniceus

Formerly, and regionally, "swamp blackbird," "red-winged starling," "marsh blackbird," "redwing," "soldier blackbird" and (best description of all) "red-shoul-

dered blackbird"; *agelaius* from Greek *agelaios*, "flocking"; *phoeniceus* is Latin for "red," from crimson or purple dye made in Tyre from shellfish and traded by the Phoenicians.

Description

Smaller than robin; adult male glossy black with bright red shoulder patch partially edged in yellow; adult female sparrowlike, dusky-flecked brown above, pale undersides boldly streaked in dark brown; first-year male dull black overlain with rusty feather edges, shoulder patch dull, flecked with brown.

Behaviour

Very social; community nester; forages in flocks large enough in autumn to be regarded as pest to grain crops; flocks visit feeders, eat hurriedly, then depart; males show stronger tendency than females to form one-sex groups; very agile, quick to adapt to hanging feeders; song a very distinctive, musical "onk-la-reeeee," with strong emphasis on the final trill; call an emphatic "chack"; alarm note a down-slurred "tee-err."

Range

Canadian population largely migratory; breeds throughout the continent from northern margin of boreal forest south to Central America; favours marshes, sloughs, and ditches bordered by thick, low vegetation, but will nest in meadows, field edges, even suburban gardens; breeds through most of British Columbia, including Vancouver Island but not the Charlottes or extreme northwest; common winterer in extreme south and southwest, with resident populations in the Fraser delta; casual winterer along coastal marshes and in central interior, congregating around feedlots, fields, orchards, and farmyards.

Food

Omnivorous; feeds on the ground and at the seed heads of field crops, including small grains, corn, and sunflowers; weed seeds, grubs, and insects; at the feeder, cracked grain, sunflower seeds.

Nest

In cattails, sedges, rushes, near or over shallow water; in willows, weed clumps, grass tussocks in dry areas; base of sedge stems, grass, rootlets bound to surrounding stems with strips of plant fibre (milkweed where available); cup lined with fine grasses; from 7 cm to 4.3 m (3 in to 14 ft) high.

Comment

The noisy, active "redwing" is one of our most easily identified birds; the sleek, handsome males are unmistakable. So is their behaviour. When a visitor nears a nesting group the males announce themselves by fluttering aloft in a peculiar, awkward-looking display flight calculated to show off the bright red "epaulettes" to best effect. If the interloper gets too close, the excitable males will gang up to swoop at him. Many a prying human has been clouted smartly on the head for venturing too near. If blackbirds choose a garden hedge to nest in, their aggressiveness makes them less-than-easy tenants.

REF: A(W) - 456; BC - 548; GO - 298; NG - 420: P(W) - 308

Brewer's Blackbird
Euphagus cyanocephalus

"Brewer's" after American ornithologist Thomas M. Brewer (1814–80); *euphagus* from Greek *eu*, "good," and *phago*, "to eat," unclear whether reference is to the edibility of the bird, or to its own appetite; *cyanocephalus* from Greek *kyanos*, "blue" and *kephale*, "head."

Description

Slightly smaller than robin; male all-black with yellow eye; iridescent, the head purple, the body greenish, brightest in late winter and spring; female brownish-grey with no streaking as in female Red-winged.

Behaviour

Strongly social; feeds by "gaping," a habit it may use even among loose seeds on a feeder shelf; call a harsh "chack," song a wheezing creak, "tuk-tuk-ksheee."

Range

Migratory in most of province, nonmigratory resident on southwest mainland coast; in early settlement times, a bird of the western plains and mountains, now breeding eastward in Canada to southern Ontario; breeds in open, brushy habitat through British Columbia except for the northwest corner and the Charlottes; some winter in southwest and central interior, southern and eastern Vancouver Island.

Food

Insects, spiders, weed seeds, grain; may occasionally wade and dabble in shallow water; at feeder, hen scratch, sunflower seeds.

Nest

From low shrubs to trees as high as 45 m (150 ft) up, often conifers; in tall sedges, or on hummocks of vegetation growing in water; even occasionally in tree cavity

or on broken snag; sturdy base of fine twigs and grasses, cup of grasses, pine needles, plant fibres often mortared with mud or cow manure; lining of fine rootlets, hair.

Comment

Elsewhere on the continent blackbirds have demonstrated their versatility by becoming regular, and in many cases all too plentiful, feeder birds. In John V. Dennis's *A Complete Guide to Bird Feeding* they are dealt with in a chapter titled "Things That Go Wrong" under a subhead "Unruly Guests." They do not, as yet, appear to be a major factor for most British Columbia bird feeders. But the appearance of both the Red-winged and Brewer's Blackbirds in large numbers in the Christmas Bird Counts in the Vancouver area and the Okanagan, and in much smaller but significant numbers in places as far removed as Prince George and Smithers suggests that they have the potential for becoming feeder guests over a large part of the province.

REF: A(W) - 551; BC - 553; GO - 298; NG - 422; P(W) - 306

Finch Family

Family *Fringillidae*,
Subfamily *Carduelinae*

Depending upon which reference one consults, and its date, the family *Fringillidae* totals over five hundred species, the largest in the bird world. The great majority are native to the Old World. Within this group are some one hundred and twenty-five species (again writers differ) comprising the subfamily *Carduelinae*, twelve of these being Canada's familiar native finches.

The contradictions arise because bird classification is a constantly evolving process that renders old references ever more obsolete. It generates debate and jobs within the ornithological establishment, and it's good for the field guide business. But unless you are very sensitive to the scorn you might suffer by appearing afield with a guide that is two or three names out of date, don't rush off to the bookstore.

Eleven cardueline finches occur in winter in British Columbia, more-or-less dependably, although numbers for any of them can vary wildly from season to season. This number includes the Hoary Redpoll. Although the field guides still list it as a separate species, its similarity in all but range to the Common suggest it will soon lose this status.

Finches are regarded, along with the corvids (jays and crows) as the most recently evolved birds, showing great adaptability and success at colonizing new territories and exploiting new habitat. The finches of the Galapagos Islands helped Charles Darwin formulate his monumental theory of evolution. From a single species that somehow reached these remote islands evolved a variety of new species to fill every available niche.

One of the most famous of these is the Woodpecker Finch. Lacking a chiselling beak and long tongue to probe for wood-boring grubs, it uses a twig or thorn held in its bill. If a probe isn't suitable as is, the bird will clip and trim it to the right size and shape, a highly evolved level of tool-making.

Finches are predominantly seed-eaters, with stout bills, heavy skulls, and strong jaw muscles for cracking tough husks and crushing hard seeds. The Eurasian Hawfinch, with a bill even larger than that of our Evening Grosbeak, can exert a force of forty-five kilograms (100 lb), sufficient to crack olive pits.

Most finches have a crop for storing food and a powerful gizzard for grinding it up. Some feed their young exclusively on a milky porridge of regurgitated seeds, others may provide a mix of seeds and insects as a starter formula, switching exclusively to seeds as the nestlings develop.

Compulsive Songsters

A feature common to the carduelines is their singing ability. While most birds sing only in their nesting territories in the breeding season, carduelines sing wherever they happen to be, and at any time of year.

The familiar canary, bred from the wild serin of the Canary Islands, *Serinus canaria*, has been a domesticated cage pet since at least the time of the Ancient

Greeks. The variety that has brightened generations of homes from its wire cage was imported into Italy from the Canary Islands in the sixteenth century. Easy to keep on a simple diet of seeds, it is now bred in an astonishing variety of plumage colours and patterns.

Its singing ability is legendary. In the early years of this century, British fanciers taught a bullfinch to whistle "God Save the King." The bird invariably hesitated at the end of the third line, and if he paused a bit too long, a canary in the next room, that had picked up the melody on its own, would chime in and finish it for him.

The finches of our Canadian winters are famous throughout the continent (and the northern hemisphere for the five that are circumpolar) for their erratic, usually massive, winter migrations, or "eruptions." The degree of eruptive behaviour of these "northern" finches depends on the diet of each species. The American Goldfinch, the least "northern" of the lot, is also the least erratic. It feeds primarily on the seeds of low-growing plants, particularly dandelions and thistles. These either scatter irretrievably upon ripening or are covered by snow in winter. Thus, their northern food supply scattered or buried, goldfinches fly south far enough to avoid the problem, in all winters staying over, in greater or lesser numbers, in southern British Columbia.

By contrast, other wintering finches such as crossbills find their natural food higher up in spruce and pine trees well above the snow, and do not follow a set migratory pattern.

Feeding above the snow level is no guarantee of stability, however. Crossbills are the most eruptive northern finches. Years of superabundant spruce cone crops alternate with years of sparse production over vast expanses of boreal forest. Crossbills have therefore evolved into foraging nomads, migrating east-west as well as south in search of productive tracts of evergreens. Finding them, they not only settle in to feed, but may commence nesting. They are on record as raising broods every month of the year throughout the northern hemisphere where conifer forests happen to have produced abundantly for that particular season.

❄ ❄ ❄

Rosy Finch

Leucosticte arctoa

Leucosticte from Greek *leucos*, "white," *sticte*, "varied"; *arctoa* from Greek *arcto*, "north"; in less recent guides "Gray-crowned" form is a separate species, *L. tephrocotis* from Greek *tephros*, "grey," *kotis*, "back of head."

Description

Sparrow-sized; male rusty-pink on rump, belly; darker wings pink with black, off-white lines; forehead black, back of head light grey; back, throat, and bib light brown; female brown with suggestion of dusky flecking, lighter patch and bar on wings; stubby bill yellowish with dark tip.

Behaviour

Highly social in winter, in close-formation flocks; ground feeder, occasionally

in company with juncos, other finches; prefers open country; "cheew" call similar to House Sparrow, song a rich goldfinch-like warble.

Range

Vertically and latitudinally migratory; breeds above timberline in mountains from Alaska to southern California; breeds through montane interior of British Columbia and hence is absent from northeast quarter of province; absent from Queen Charlottes and Vancouver Island; in winter migrates to lower elevations, northern populations drifting south and west through central and southern interior, west to coastal lowlands.

Foods

Forages in tight flocks for seeds of grasses and weeds in open, windswept slopes, meadows; small and large seeds at feeders.

Nest

On sheltered rock ledges, in crevices, rubble, and holes up to and into snow line in montane tundra habitat; cup of grasses, mosses, with coarser stems, grasses, rootlets toward inside, final lining of feathers, fur, other fine materials.

Comment

These are high-mountain birds, nesting up among the rock slides and alongside the glaciers where Hoary Marmots whistle and lupines wave. When they migrate it tends to be downhill, the most easterly into the foothills and, infrequently, well out onto the Prairies. "Islanded" into separate races by their broken habitat, their semi-isolation reinforced by restricted migration behaviour, they have developed distinctive regional plumage patterns that at one time had them divided into separate species—the Brown-capped, Black, and Gray-crowned. These have now been lumped into a single species with the variants considered to be subspecies or races. It is the Gray-crowned that occurs in British Columbia.

The Birder's Handbook says that males outnumber females by up to six-to-one throughout the year. If true, it poses some very interesting questions about how such an astonishing gender imbalance comes about and what adaptive advantages it confers on the species.

REF: A(W) - 571; BC - 561; G - 318; NG - 438; P(W) - 334

Pine Grosbeak

Pinicola enucleator

Finch family. *Pinicola* from Latin "pine" and *colere*, "inhabit"; *enucleator* Latin for "one who shells (out)," descriptive of the birds' habit of husking cones of various tree species.

Description

Chunky, robin-sized; short, dark, strongly curved bill; adult male dusky-pink, may have patches or flecks of grey, with darkish line through eye; moderately long, dark, slightly forked tail; wings dark with two white bars; noticeably larger than crossbill and Purple Finch; subadult male soft grey with crown and rump rusty-rose; adult female grey with shading of olive to russet on crown and rump; call a gentle, high-pitched "tew-tew-tew"; song a brief, pleasant, unenergetic warble.

P. SAWATZKY ©
1990

Behaviour

Sociable; often segregated by gender and age, females and immatures flocking separately from mature males; placid, sometimes very tame.

Range

Nomadically migratory; circumpolar in distribution; breeds much further north than Evening Grosbeak; nests through interior British Columbia south of Fort St. James, including the Charlottes and Vancouver Island; winters throughout much of its breeding range, occurrence varying widely from season to season.

Food

Shares with waxwings a liking for dried fruit, and for seeds and berries of ornamentals, including lilacs; feeds on spruce seeds, periodic failures of this source accounting for its drift south in some winters; readily accepts sunflower seeds at feeders.

Nest

Loose, bulky platform of twigs, fibres, lichens; midheight in a conifer or birch, or low in a juniper or underbrush.

Comment

"Ridiculously tame" is the phrase used for these easygoing birds in *The Birder's Handbook*. Tufts, in *Birds of Nova Scotia*, recalls days at the turn of the century when boys could hit them with snowballs and kill them with their slingshots. I have never encountered any so foolishly trusting, but around the feeder they are calm and unexcitable, exhibiting none of that busy finch energy typified by the Evening Grosbeaks.

Occasional reference is made to their apparent evolution away from dependence on tree seeds to a diet of buds, fruits, and weed seeds, and to their special fondness for crabapples. *The Birds Around Us* says they relish cranberries, either canned or fresh. For several winters past I have therefore stored a bag of highbush cranberries in the freezer where they await the opportunity to test the postulated change of tastes of these lovely winter birds.

REF: A(W) - 725; BC - 561; GO - 316; NG - 436; P(W) - 342

Purple Finch
Carpodacus purpureus

"Finch" is from Germanic *fink*, and Anglo-Saxon *finc*, but ultimate roots are possibly from Indo-European *pingo*, echoic of birds' calls; *carpodacus* is from Greek *carpos* for "fruit" (i.e. seed), and *dacos* for "biting"; *purpureus* is Latin for "crimson," more descriptive of bird's colour than misleading English "purple."

Description

Peterson's famous, "Like a sparrow dipped in raspberry juice," best describes male; colour brightest on head and rump, lighter on throat, breast, and flanks; dark ear patch on side of head, light eyebrow streak; dark brown wings checked

P.SAWATZKI ©
1990

and lined with subdued pattern; the all-over raspberry wash is the feature most helpful in differentiating it from the House, Rosy, and Cassin's Finches; tail dark, well notched; females and immatures heavily streaked on breast and back in browns and light beige; belly off-white.

Behaviour

Sociable; flocks may be divided by sex and age, all-male or all-female-and-immatures; aggressive behaviour at feeders is intensified by crowding and/or feed shortage; flight fights have been observed in which grappling pair thrash straight up for many metres and fall back to the ground, still struggling desperately; call a musical "churr-lee," and a sharp "tink" in flight; song a rapid, clearly enunciated, rich warble, ending with down-slurred "too-eee," delivered from treetops, occasionally also from on the wing with no loss of exuberant energy.

Range

Variably migratory; breeds from coast to coast in boreal forest and south in mixed woodlands; breeds through British Columbia south from about Fort St. John, not in the Charlottes or on western Vancouver Island; winters in sporadic, casual numbers in the southern interior, more regularly on the southwest coast, Vancouver Island.

Food

Primarily seeds; some tree buds and poplar catkins; insects and fruit in summer;

sunflower seeds favourite feeder fare, but will eat other seeds, and suet, if these run out; will use high shelves; agile enough to use hanging feeders.

Nest

Well up in tall conifer if available, otherwise at variable heights in deciduous trees or shrubs; well-hidden cup of fine twigs, grasses, and rootlets selected to blend into surroundings.

Comment

In his *Joy of Birding,* Chuck Bernstein notes that warblers don't really warble, that Purple Finches and goldfinches do. Among my warmest recollections of bird feeding at our cottage are bright late-winter days when the trees in the yard were thronging with these merry finches. About noon each day they would fill the sheltered valley with song.

Recalling these idyllic interludes brings to mind an incident related by Seton in *The Birds of Manitoba.* On May 14, 1884, he "collected" a male Purple Finch. Shooting birds was then the standard method of verifying sightings, but it seemed a trifle ghoulish of him to go on and note that he blew it away "in full song." We can be thankful that the ready-made technology of modern cameras, binoculars, and field guides has made such "collecting" largely unnecessary.

REF: A(W) - 723; BC - 563; GO - 316; NG - 440; P(W) - 342

House Finch

Carpodacus mexicanus

"House" presumably for association with dwellings; *carpodacus* from Greek *carpos* for "fruit," *dacos* for "biting," half-apt since bird is seed-eater that occasionally bites fruit; *mexicanus* is Latinized "of Mexico" where type specimens were collected in 1776.

Description

Slimmer than slightly larger Purple Finch; male House has brown cap, red "headband" over eyes, red throat, breast and rump; red areas brighter, more clearly demarcated than in male Purple; wings and back brown-patterned without the raspberry wash of the Purple Finch; underbelly more streaked than in Purple; in some males, the coloured areas, especially breast, are yellow or orange; female brown-streaked overall, unlike female Purple has no obvious light eyebrow line.

Behaviour

Sociable; equally at home in cities and suburbs as in the countryside; city habits resemble House Sparrow except it sings pleasantly; comes very readily to feeders, sometimes in noisy, take-charge bunch where it may displace House Sparrows; call notes shrill "wheer" or sharp "pit"; both sexes sing, a cascade of sweet notes and whistles mixed with slurred, harsh "wheer" notes in descending pitch.

Range

Largely nonmigratory; native to southwest United States, Mexico; introduced to American northeast, expanding in both areas; has spread into central British Columbia as far as Prince George, and well north along eastern Vancouver Island; absent from Charlottes.

Food

Very much a seed-eater, consuming very few insects; occasional fruit, berries, nuts, especially from ornamentals in urban areas; at feeders goes for most small seeds and sunflowers.

Nest

In variable sites, including buildings, birdhouses, tree cavities, or old nests of Cliff Swallow, robin, oriole; open nest an untidy collection of twigs, grasses, and debris, lined with same material; 1.5 m (5 ft) or higher in dense foliage in vine, shrub or tree.

Comment

This native finch is an ongoing sensation in the bird world by virtue of its becoming a successful "exotic" in its own country, and in its rapid colonization of new range. The excitement began in 1941 when a Dr. Edward Fleisher was surprised to discover a pet shop in Brooklyn with twenty "Hollywood finches" for sale. Knowing that the capture for sale of native birds was illegal under the Migratory Bird Treaty, Fleisher notified the Audubon Society which was equally surprised to find that of twenty shops it checked, all were selling these finches. Shipment of the birds from the source in California was subsequently banned. To avoid prosecution at least one dealer surreptitiously released his stock.

In April of 1941 a lone male finch was seen at Jones Beach on Long Island, and in 1942, a small flock in nearby Babylon. Once acclimatized to Long Island, they moved out. First recorded in southern Ontario in 1972, they are now well established and expanding their range there.

Whilst all this energetic expansion was going on in the east, the western population was spreading northward and eastward. It seems that this adaptable bird, somewhat belatedly, had found a great ally in man and was taking full advantage of the alliance in both its established and its introduced populations.

According to *Birds of the Okanagan Valley* it was first recorded there in the mid-1930s. It appeared in Victoria in 1937, and shortly after, in Vancouver. Their colonization pattern is interesting; the first pioneering birds are migratory, but as subsequent generations acclimatize themselves they become sedentary, redirecting their travelling urge to scouting out, and settling, new territory.

Given the westerly push of the transplanted eastern population, and the eastward shift of the original western population, the two will soon reunite, if they haven't already met and melded somewhere in East Texas or Oklahoma.

REF: A(W) - 588; BC - 564; GO - 316; NG - 440; P(W) - 342

Crossbills

Genus *Loxia*

Worldwide there are only three species of crossbills; our Red and White-winged range throughout the northern hemisphere and are joined in Eurasia by the Parrot Crossbill, *Loxia pytyopsittacus*. All of them closely resemble each other, and all are specialized to harvest the seeds of cone-bearing evergreens. Such differences as there are arise from further specialization according to which particular conifers each species is most closely associated with. In spite of the obvious, vast abundance of cone-bearing trees in the subarctic reaches of the Northern Hemisphere, there are difficulties connected to a conifer-dependent existence. Conifers are erratic sources of very small seeds, housing them under tough scales in cones that open when it is in the trees' interests to release seeds to the wind. Cracking ripe but unopened cones is hard work, demanding special skills. Some cone-feeders have even developed special tools.

The twisted beak of the crossbill is such a tool. As a fledgling it has a normal bill. But at four weeks the ends of the bill begin to twist sideways, one to the right, the other to the left. Which does which is varied, some birds being left-crossed, some right. The jawbones themselves are straight; it is only the horny outer sheaths that are crooked.

A Red Crossbill attacks a cone by gripping it solidly with its powerful, oversized feet, perhaps first clipping the cone off for more convenient handling on the nearest steady perch. It inserts the tip of the upper mandible under a cone scale, bracing the lower mandible against the outside of the scale at the bottom. With special muscles it moves the jaws sideways in a lateral shearing action to pry the scale out, aiding this move with a twist of the head. This cracks the cone scale vertically. Holding it open, the bird inserts its large, muscular tongue equipped at the tip with a cartilaginous cutting edge and shears off the enclosed seed.

This shucking process is carried on with rapid, assembly-line efficiency. A horde of crossbills working through a grove of evergreens create a sound like falling rain, what with the noise of the snapping scales and the shower of debris hitting the ground.

Among conifers, pines generally bear the hardest cones. The most extreme case is found in Lodgepole Pines; anyone who has tried to force apart the hard, thick scales of an unopened cone discovers that it is built to stay resolutely clenched until time, or the heat of a forest fire, melts the cementing resin and it opens to release its imprisoned seeds. Spruce cones are midsized, but the scales can be pried open, while the larch bears the smallest and least-armoured cones.

The Parrot Crossbill of Eurasia is associated with pines and has the largest and heaviest bill, the larch-loving White-winged the lightest, with the Red, reflecting its affinity for spruce, in between.

Feast-and-Famine

Another problem for conifer-dependent seed-eaters is the trees' irregular fruiting cycle. With no obvious, consistent connection to environmental causes such as weather, they alternate a year of abundant cone production with several years of meagre production. The only consistencies seem to be that all the trees of a given species over great expanses of northland do it in rhythm, and the years of greatest plenty are followed by those of greatest impoverishment.

Nut-bearing trees follow a similar cycle. Even cultivated ones retain their own agenda, frustrating orchardists' best efforts to optimize growing conditions and otherwise beguile them into "forgetting" their imprinted capriciousness.

It has been postulated that the trees use this mechanism to control the populations of animals that feed on their seeds but offer no trade-off benefits like pollination or seed dispersal. Many cone-seed-eaters can thus be described as seed predators. Locked into a contest of evolutionary one-upmanship, each side has developed its own strategies. The trees alternately swamp the predators with so many seeds they can't possibly eat them all, and then cut production almost entirely to starve them out. Given the vast expanses over which this supposedly managed famine is wrought, it is for the numberless, unwitting seed-eaters a calamity of awesome proportions and incalculable misery.

Red Squirrels hedge against this feast-and-famine regime by storing two winters' worth of feast-year spruce cones—as many as fifteen thousand.

Crossbills don't have this option. What they do have is the ability to fly vast distances, and to nest whenever and wherever they find abundant food. For, while conifers over great areas might synchronize their seeding schedule, it is not continent-wide, nor is it coordinated between species. Thus, when the White Spruce of Labrador/Quebec abruptly fail, the regional Black Spruce or tamaracks might partially fill in. If they don't, perhaps the spruce of montane British Columbia might have produced a bumper crop.

In response to this fly-or-die imperative the birds erupt in huge numbers from their breeding grounds in an urgent search for food. Whether salvation is a matter of luck, or whether there are subtle clues that tell them where to look, is not known. Whichever is the case, they sometimes swarm into places far removed from their normal haunts. Cameron B. Kepler, in *The Encyclopedia of Birds*, reports that from a batch of migrant crossbills banded in Switzerland, some were recorded the following autumn and winter in southwest Europe, while others appeared in later years in northern Russia (Siberia), some four thousand kilometres from the banding site. The suggestion is that, however widely crossbills rove, they retain fidelity to a home range and may return there if they survive long enough.

Historic Invasions

If they find a land of plenty, and it also happens to be a year in which several conifer species are producing bountifully, with cones ripening in sequential seasons, the opportunistic birds will keep on nesting as long as the food holds out, irrespective of the weather. Their ability to raise young in the bitterest of conditions was discussed in Chapter 6, "Midwinter Nests."

Irruptions of crossbills have been so massive they have been written into history. In 1251, Matthew Paris wrote about the unusual birds that invaded England and devastated the apple crop. Chroniclers in Europe, Japan, and North America have noted the mysterious and sometimes destructive invasions of strange birds that abruptly appeared and then vanished, not to be seen again for generations.

When they show up at our feeders, they might demonstrate that, while they are highly specialized foragers, they haven't lost the adaptability that typifies the finch family. They can turn their bent bills to sunflower seeds, and even suet. And in keeping with their exotic appearance, they often betray a quirky taste for highly unusual foods. Mystified observers have watched them eating ashes, frozen dishwater, tea leaves, charcoal, bits of mortar, spots of frozen dog urine in the snow, and salt—especially salt. They frequently suffer heavy mortality on highways when they go after road salt. Perhaps these unpalatable substances help to counteract the sticky resin they constantly encounter in their normal feeding.

❅ ❅ ❅

Red Crossbill

Loxia curvirostra

Finch family. "Crossbill" descriptive of the seemingly misshapen beak; *loxia* from Greek *loxos*, "crooked"; *curvirostra* is Latin for "curved bill."

Description

House Sparrow-sized; ends of large bill crossed; tail short, notched; adult male dull red with sooty brown wings and tail; abdomen and undertail coverts grey; female olive-buff on back and head, with close pattern of brown check marks; belly, undertail, and rump olive-yellow; wings and tail dark.

Behaviour

Social, usually in flocks, chattering in flight; swarm through conifers like miniature parrots, climbing with bills and feet; grip cones with oversized feet and busily and expertly pry open the scales; at close quarters, as at a window

feeder, further parrotlike behaviour in obvious use of the large tongue to work kernels out of sunflower seeds; often very tame and easily approached; call a repeated sharp "jit-jit-jit," song a melody of vigorous canarylike warbles punctuated with clear "too-tee too-tee too-tee-tee" whistles.

Range

Circumpolar; wanders widely and sporadically far from boreal and mountain coniferous forests where it usually breeds; in British Columbia breeds through most of the interior and in west coast rain and montane forest, including the Charlottes and Vancouver Island; less common in northern interior; may winter anywhere in or out of breeding range, depending on available food.

Food

Seeds of spruce, larch, and especially Douglas-fir; will eat fruit, including orchard apples; nestlings fed a porridge of regurgitated seeds and fluid; at feeder takes sunflowers, nutmeats, cracked cereal grains.

Nest

In conifer at edge of woodland; usually high up, well concealed among twigs at end of branch; bulky base of twigs, built up with grasses, lichen, bark shreds; lining of fine grass, hair, fur, feathers; punky wood worked in as filler in winter nests; eggs pale bluish-white with purplish-brown specks and scrawls near the large end; only female broods, fed by male.

Comment

One of the real delights of winter feeding is to have a flock of these unique northerners share space with you. Even if you live far from the coniferous forests they call home, you may still make their acquaintance if nearby shade trees include the prerequisite spruce, pine, or fir. If they have borne a good crop of cones, the crossbills might decide to settle in and raise a brood, as a pair did in a recent winter at my station in Winnipeg. From late January through to early March the male and female regularly fed on sunflower seeds at my office window shelf, an arm's length from my word processor. Whether they succeeded in raising young I don't know, for none came to the feeder. They shared the nearby spruce and pines with Blue Jays, and the neighbourhood was prowled by the inevitable skulk of cats. I also wonder if sunflowers were an adequate substitute for the nestlings' natural diet of conifer seeds.

REF: A(W) - 721; BC - 565; GO - 322; NG - 436; P(W) - 340

White-winged Crossbill

Loxia leucoptera

Finch family. Wings are actually black, with two white bars, making the common British name "Two-barred" more descriptive; *loxia* from Greek *loxos*, "crooked," *leucoptera* from Greek *leucos*, "white," and *pteran*, "wing."

Description

House Sparrow-sized; ends of bill crossed; short tail notched; adult male dusky rose, eye darkly shadowed; wings black, with white tips on tertials and two bold

white bars; female yellowish-olive under lines of brown spots, with white bars on dark wings.

Behaviour

Social, flocks chattering in flight; often very tame and trusting; parrotlike in climbing about conifer cones and twigs with bills and feet as they forage, and in use of large tongue husking sunflower seeds at feeders; call a single, clear "peet" or a rapid, raspy "jeet-jeet-jeet" in flight; song a sustained series of canarylike warbles and trills punctuated by harsh rattles.

Range

Circumpolar, in boreal and mountain evergreen forests in northern hemisphere; somewhat more northerly in Canadian breeding range than Red Crossbill; found widely scattered through interior British Columbia, rare on the coast, with a few records for Vancouver Island and the Charlottes; erratic winter visits determined by abundance of conifer cone crop.

Food

Seeds of conifers, especially larch and spruce; at feeder takes sunflower seeds, peanuts, cracked grains, and, occasionally, suet.

Nest

Indistinguishable from that of Red Crossbill; eggs pale bluish or greenish-white, spotted or splotched lightly with dark purple at large end; male feeds female during incubation and for first few days of brooding, his calling and hovering flight song a clue to nest location; like Red, may nest at any time of year.

Comment

Both the Red and White-winged Crossbill are food specialists, their breeding governed by the abundance of conifer seeds, their eruptive dispersals by scarcity of this wild crop. The White-winged favours larch seeds, borne in a small cone of relatively flimsy construction, and some spruce, also lighter compared to the much heavier pine cones favoured by the Red. Tools matching task, the White-winged's bill is noticeably less rugged than the Red's.

REF: A(W) - 722; BC - 567; GO - 322; NG - 436; P(W) - 340

Redpolls

Genus *Carduelis*

This genus includes goldfinches and siskins; *Carduelis* is Latin for "goldfinch."

Redpolls are circumpolar, and in both Eurasia and North America have the same scientific names. In English field guides our Common Redpoll is simply the Redpoll, and our Hoary is the Arctic. Whether they should continue to be two species is a question that birders and taxonomists on both sides of Bering Strait continue to debate. Peterson, in the most recent edition of his field guide to western birds, treats them as one species, stating that the Hoary is ". . . now regarded as a northern population of the 'Common' Redpoll." The Audubon field guide to western birds, however, says that in areas where their ranges overlap, they do not interbreed, ". . . although some experts consider them two forms of a single species."

The problem for bird watchers and taxonomists is that between the extremes of the darkest Commons and the lightest Hoaries the distinguishing field marks gradually blend from one to the other. In this continuum there is no point where one can say "Up to here they're all Commons, beyond here, all Hoaries." This suggests to me that they do in fact interbreed, and that they will be reclassified as one species.

During migratory rambles Hoaries mingle indiscriminately with Commons. Therefore, bird feeders will continue to squint through their binoculars and field guides, hanging on the pickets of indecision. Is it a genuine Hoary or just a pallid Common? Like the other "northern" finches, redpolls are erratic migrants, appearing in huge flocks one winter, virtually absent the next. I recall that several winters ago a farmer near our cottage left part of a small field of sunflowers unharvested. By late winter redpolls swarmed like locusts over the ranks of frozen stalks. In the last two winters, however, we have been lucky to have one or two of these birds at our feeder all winter.

Whatever their winter abundance, they vanish in spring from all of British Columbia except, according to Godfrey, where the Common nests in the extreme northwest corner. As an adaptive adjustment to the harsh conditions of their high Arctic and mountain summit breeding grounds, redpolls have been found better able to withstand cold temperatures than any other songbird yet studied. Their short incubation period of ten days is a further survival advantage in the hurry-up summer of the high Arctic.

In common with many other northern birds, redpolls often show remarkable tameness. There is at least one record of a bird-bander able to pick them off her window feeder, and there are many accounts by captivated people of these bold little birds fluttering around them, landing on their heads and shoulders as they reload their feeders. This tameness is often attributed to the birds' northern origins where they have no contact with humans and have therefore not learned to fear them. Another theory is that they are conditioned by the uncertain productivity of their environment to suspend normal caution and go for food whenever the chance presents itself.

They are very fond of birch seeds, which they harvest in three stages. They first flutter and climb about in the trees, swallowing some seeds, but knocking most of them out of the tiny cones onto the snow below. They then pick the seeds off the snow, gulping them hurriedly and storing them in the diverticulum, a bilobed pouch similar to a chicken's crop, about halfway down the gullet. This done, they fly to a sheltered spot, or to their nighttime roost, where they can regurgitate the seeds at leisure, shell them out, and swallow them. This minimizes the time spent on food-collecting, and consequent exposure to predators and harsh winds. It also gives the bird a bedtime store of food for snacking on during the long night.

❄ ❄ ❄

Common and Hoary Redpolls

Carduelis flammea and *C. hornemanni*

Finch family. "Redpoll" from colour of cap or "poll," from Middle English *pol(le)*, "top of the head"; *carduelis* is Latin for "goldfinch," *flammea* "flame-coloured" from pink wash on some parts of male plumage; *hornemanni* named after J. W. Hornemann, Danish scientist; "hoary" refers to frosty appearance of plumage.

Description

Chickadee-sized; both sexes have satiny red forehead patch and black chin; back, rump, and flank heavily streaked with brown; two pale bars on brown wing; stubby, sharp, conical bill; tail sharply forked; males have pink wash on breast, and often on rump; Hoary is like a Common veiled in hoarfrost, through which the underlying markings show very faintly or not at all; best clue is all-white rump; bill shorter.

Behaviour

Social; often in large twittering flocks; feeds on ground, weed heads, or trees; may hang about livestock feedlots; very tame and trusting; agile at hanging feeders; feisty with own or other species; flight very undulating, with rattling "chit-chit"; perch call a protracted "swee-eee-t"; song a series of trills and twitters.

Range

Circumpolar; erratically migratory; breeds throughout northern boreal forest and tundra, the Hoary on tundra above tree line and on highest Arctic islands; in British Columbia the Common nests only in extreme northwest; may show up in winter anywhere in the province, but rarely, if ever, on Vancouver Island and the Charlottes.

Food

Weed, birch, alder, larch seeds, insects when abundant; small seeds at feeding stations, but handles black sunflower seeds with no trouble; a ground forager but quickly adapts to shelves and hanging feeders.

Nest

Small cup of fine twigs, grass, plant stems, lined with plant down, feathers, hair; in tree, low shrub, or on ground; often close together since birds are not territorial nesters; in high Arctic, old nests might be relined and used again; nest surroundings messy with droppings.

Comment

Whether it eventually becomes a race of the Common or not, an indisputably hoary Hoary at one's feeder should be rated as an occasion for calling one's birding friends. An even more exciting event would be the appearance of an obviously oversized Common, especially here in British Columbia; the "giant" subspecies breeds in Greenland and Baffin Island.

REF: A(W) - 769/70; BC - 568/9; GO - 318; NG - 438; P(W) - 342

Pine Siskin

Carduelis pinus

Finch family. "Siskin" from same echoic root as Dutch *sidskin*, "a chirper," or Russian *chizh*, "siskin" or "small bird"; Latin *carduelis*, "a goldfinch" from *carduus*, "thistle"; Latin *pinus*, "pine."

Description

Much smaller than House Sparrow; body and head buff with darker brown stripes; darker wings and tail; yellowish wash at base of tail; yellow on inner third of flight feathers not obvious except when in flight or when wings raised in threat display; sexes indistinguishable (to us); bill smaller and more pointed than other finches.

Behaviour

Often in large flocks that swoop and swirl in swift synchrony, alternately bunching up and flaring apart; in spite of small size, able to displace House Sparrows at feeder, using impressive raised-wing threat display; call a raspy, rising "zweeee," a subdued "tit-a-tit" or a loud "clee-it" chirp; song a harsher version of goldfinch's melody.

Range

Migratory, nomadic winter wanderer; nests throughout Canadian mixed and boreal forest coast to coast, including through most of British Columbia except for the Charlottes; erratic winterer throughout British Columbia, often in abundance, less frequent in northeast.

Food

In the wild, seeds of small cones such as alder, birch, larch; shares goldfinch's liking for dandelion and thistle; in season, insects and buds; at feeder takes most small seeds, but quickly shows preference for black sunflower seeds.

Nest

Adaptable, preferring conifer but will use shrubs and trees of any species, from 1 to 15 m (3 to 50 ft) high; large cup of twigs, fibres, fine grass; lining of feathers, hair, rootlets; often messy since adults stop disposing of faeces after about nine days.

Comment

Like many northern finches these erratic wanderers shift about on a continent-wide scale, super-abundant some winters, scarce or totally absent the next. Almost always in a bunch, they tend to take over feeding stations when they appear, squaring off at much larger birds at the tray and pursuing them in the air. Although unable to bully Evening Grosbeaks, they feed with them by dodging in and out, often picking up bits dropped by the larger birds.

REF: A(W) - 752; BC - 570; GO - 320; NG - 434; P(W) - 344

American Goldfinch
Carduelis tristis

Also "wild canary," since colour and singing ability match those of the cage canary; less commonly "thistle bird" due to liking for thistle seeds; *carduelis* is Latin for "goldfinch," from root *carduus*, "thistle"; Latin *tristis*, "sad," a singularly inappropriate label for this embodiment of cheerfulness; older guides give generic name *spinus*, from Greek *spinos*, "a linnet," British name of the European cousin of our goldfinches.

Description

Smaller than House Sparrow; stubby tail and bill; winter males and females uniform brownish olive, sometimes with yellowish wash on head and neck; one or two light bars on dark wings; in early spring males acquire patches of yellow that spread as feather wear reveals summer body plumage of bright yellow with natty black cap, wings, and tail.

P. SAWATZKY
1991 ©

Behaviour

Roves in flocks in winter and early summer; "bouncing" flight, wings flicked quickly for upward swoop, folded for downward, with rapid "per-chic-o-ree" or "potato chip" call with each "bounce"; song a bubbly succession of sweet trills punctuated frequently by a rising "swee?" whistle.

Range

Migratory; breeds through woodlands and agricultural areas from coast to coast in Canada, including southern British Columbia up to Prince George in the interior, increasingly rare north of that point; winters irregularly in southern parts of breeding range in province.

Food

Young fed on porridge of regurgitated seeds, with no "starter ration" of insects as provided by most other seed-eaters; heavily reliant on thistle and dandelion seeds; black sunflower and smaller seeds at the feeder.

Nest

Latest regular nester of all our songbirds, commonly in June and even July;

small, deep cup in shrubbery, tall weeds or low tree, usually near water or swampy area, in open setting, including orchards; body of plant fibres, lined with plant down, including cattail and thistle, rim bound with spider and/or insect webbing; often woven tightly enough to hold water; nest and supports messy with droppings.

Comment

Our "wild canary's" talent for mimicry is apparently essential to his love life, for he bonds to his mate by learning the notes of her song and "playing them back" to her, the couple thus developing a shared, unique vocabulary.

The goldfinch's late, extended breeding season is timed in part, if not altogether, to coincide with the seed-bearing schedule of thistles and other late-blossoming weeds. The seeds are essential food, the downy fibres equally important for nest-building. These birds are frequent victims of the cowbird, but the foster nestlings do very poorly on the finch diet of straight seeds and often succumb to malnutrition.

REF: A(W) - 578; BC - 571; GO - 320; NG - 434; P(W) - 344

A Word About "Grosbeaks"

The name "grosbeak" has been applied as a handy descriptive name to several birds in different subfamilies, all of whom bear similarly heavy-duty bills. The result has been slightly confusing; Evening and Pine Grosbeaks aren't really grosbeaks, taxonomically, but are members of the Cardueline Finch subfamily. Cardinals, Rose-breasted and Black-headed Grosbeaks, and Lazuli Buntings are true grosbeaks, members of the *Emberezidae* family. This is why, in properly ordered reference books and field guides, Evening and Pine Grosbeaks are illustrated amongst the goldfinches and Purple Finches, not among the true grosbeaks.

❄ ❄ ❄

Evening Grosbeak
Coccothraustes vespertinus

Finch family. "Evening" assigned in 1823 by American ornithologist W.C. Cooper who first recorded it, one evening, northwest of Lake Superior; "grosbeak" from French *gros*, "large" and *bec*, "beak"; *coccothraustes* from Greek *kokkos*, "kernel" and *thrauo*, "shatter," nicely describes feeding method; *vespertinus* is Latin for "evening."

Description

Chunky, robin-sized with thick, heavy bill; males in bold pattern of black, white, and yellow that can't be mistaken for any other winter bird; females shaded grey-buff on head (darkest), back, breast, belly, and rump; wings and tail black with white marks; chalky white bill of both sexes peels in late winter to uncover light lime-green breeding colour.

Behaviour

Sociable, in noisy flocks of a

half-dozen and up, often many more; crowds onto feeders with considerable jostling and threatening; tame when habituated to presence of feeder attendant; undulating flight; call a loud, clear chirp; song a robust, rambly warble.

Range

Erratically migratory; breeds in northern mixed woods and southern boreal forest coast to coast in Canada, down through mountains of western United States and in Mexico; winters in breeding range but frequently wanders far south and east; in British Columbia breeds from central interior southward; winters on Vancouver Island, but not recorded as nesting there, nor on the Charlottes; rare in northern interior.

Food

Tree seeds, nuts, juniper berries, fruits; insects during nestling-feeding; large appetite for both black and striped sunflower seeds at feeders; seeks salt from treated roadways or livestock licks.

Nest

Shambly cup of twigs thinly interwoven with lichens and plant fibres; usually well up in tree, preferably conifer, close to trunk in crotch or well out on limb concealed in twigs.

Comment

Used to be called the Sociable Grosbeak; this or "wandering" or "western" would be more descriptive than the meaningless "Evening." The ornithologist (Cooper) who named it is the same fellow after whom the hawk is named.

The Evening Grosbeak has been noted from the early 1800s as an irregular winter visitant throughout the East, sometimes appearing in great numbers in the Maritimes and down the east coast of the United States. Once breeding strictly in the West, it has rapidly shifted eastward. Its spread has been attributed to a combination of winter bird feeding, the widespread planting of Manitoba Maples (box elder) with their abundant winter-fast seeds which the birds favour, plus habitat changes accompanying settlement.

What seem to be irregular, aimless wanderings may in fact be a flexible itinerary of alternative paths that the birds follow in search of winter feed. Certainly they range far; birds banded at Seven Sisters in eastern Manitoba have been recovered in Tennessee, Washington (state) and Winterburn (Alberta). The fact that they have the longest wings in proportion to their size of any of the other North American finches suggests they evolved in response to the benefits of long-distance flight.

REF: A(W) - 717; BC - 572; GO - 310; NG - 442; P(W) - 344

Old World Sparrows

Family *Passeridae*

Passeridae is derived from Latin *passer*, "sparrow." The same root gives us "*Passeriformes*" the name of the huge Order of songbirds that includes, among many others, that most unsparrowlike, unmusical bird, the raven.

The *Passeridae* are Old World sparrows, numbering 141 species native to Eurasia and North Africa. Two species were introduced to this continent, the House Sparrow and the very similar-looking Eurasian Tree Sparrow. The Tree Sparrow has not spread much beyond the environs of St. Louis, Missouri, where it was originally released in 1870. The House Sparrow is another story altogether.

Unlike many exotic plants, insects, fish, birds, and mammals that have become uncontrollable scourges, the House Sparrow was not set free by accident. Eight pairs were released in Brooklyn, New York, in 1852. These didn't take. Later the same year one hundred more were brought in and fifty were released. These also vanished. The fifty others held in captivity over the winter were set free in 1853 in Brooklyn's Greenwood Cemetery. They took, and the bird world's most successful introduction of a foreign species was unleashed.

Many reintroductions followed, some for the sentimental ties with homeland England that they represented, some due to the misguided assumption that inspired the initial release, which was to control the accidentally introduced canker worm. Two major potato growers in Nova Scotia imported a number from either New York or Massachusetts in 1856 or 1857, intending cheap elimination of potato beetles, another introduced pest. In 1870 they were imported into Ottawa. Their effect on the worms and beetles was negligible, but their unanticipated impact on many native species of songbirds was incalculably harmful.

To their credit, not all our predecessors were motivated by self-interest or sentiment. Eminent bird biologist Elliot Coues vehemently opposed the House Sparrow, labelling it "public enemy number one." But his, and others', protests came too late. Settlers questing westward on the newly built rail lines had already carried along cagefuls of sparrows to be released at their destinations.

Sparrows were often inadvertently carted hundreds of miles when they were shut into rail cars loading at elevators and stockyards. And the tracks, strewn with spilled grain, linked sparrow-friendly farms and villages easy flights apart along corridors through otherwise hostile wilderness. Whether in grain cars or by stages along the right-of-way, they appeared in Churchill, Manitoba, by 1930. Of twelve counted in 1931, all froze to death that winter, but later arrivals fared better and they are long established at this northern grain terminal.

With or without help, sparrows moved quickly across Canada. In 1870 at least one was spotted in Toronto. In 1894 the first one turned up in Winnipeg; they are recorded as "abundant" in Regina from 1907. They arrived in the Okanagan, probably moving up from Washington State, in 1909. And since they were recorded in Seattle by 1897, their arrival in Victoria and Vancouver in time for the turn of the century was assured.

The Perfect Partnership

During its peak in the second decade of this century the House Sparrow was reckoned to be America's most abundant bird. In many areas it doubled the number of all other species combined. It flourished on the grains fed to domestic animals on countless small farms, and in villages where thrifty householders kept a cow and a small flock of chickens. But the draft horse was the sparrows' chief ally. Until after World War I it was the mainstay of public and private transportation in cities, the principal source of farm power, and an important adjunct to the logging business. Its droppings and spilled feed provided abundant and nutritious food, its barns nest sites and shelter from winter's cold.

North America has not been the only victim of the whirlwind takeover by the House Sparrow. It was taken to Australia in 1863-1864 (for "aesthetic reasons"!); to New Zealand in a number of transplants from 1859 to 1871; to South Africa from 1890 to 1897. Other introductions saw it loosed on South America, the Falkland Islands, Mauritius, and Mozambique, all coincidental with the arrival of European colonizers. In all of these locations it spread rapidly, in all it became a permanent resident at the expense of indigenous species. It now occupies two-thirds of the land surface of the earth.

In spite of the success of the sparrow and starling here, it would be wrong to assume that North America has been an ecological pushover for every exotic bird to hit its shores. By 1900 up to one hundred and fifty species of birds had been released on this continent, and countless captives had escaped. But only six besides the House Sparrow have been successful: Starling, Rock Dove, Mute Swan, Ring-necked Pheasant, Chukar, and Gray Partridge. A few others have been able to establish themselves in restricted local habitats. The others vanished, victims of bad judgement by those who thoughtlessly dumped birds, pink flamingos among these, into environments they had no chance of coping with.

In environments it shares with humans, the House Sparrow has proven to be a master of adaptability, a talent that has not always been appreciated. Among the uncomplimentary names attached to it are "feathered rat," "avian cockroach," and "Woolco warbler." Shrilling at its world from an inner-city dumpster, it may be demonstrating that a strident voice is an advantage in an environment filled with traffic noise. It has learned to hunt insects at night under street lights.

The ultimate in adaptability was demonstrated by three that got into the Frickly Coal Mine in Yorkshire, England in the summer of 1975 and stayed down at the 640-metre (2100 ft) level until the spring of 1978. Two of them nested and hatched three young but they died.

"I'm With Him"

Away from people the bird has been notably unadaptable. It is rarely found far away from human habitation, and seems unable to hang on for long after farm homesteads are abandoned. A nest in a site more than several hundred metres from occupied buildings is unusual. Perhaps, in addition to food, it may well need the protection from predators that the close company of humankind affords. The one exception seems to be a shift to another protector. In a personal communication C. Stuart Houston of Saskatoon observed that it often builds a nest at the base of a hawk's nest, sometimes miles from the nearest farm. It gains the same kind of "I'm with him" protection from the hawk that it gets from humans.

Bird lovers might be grateful that the House Sparrow's impact on native species has at least been limited to those that can tolerate closeness to us. Thus, the cheery House Wren, Eastern and Mountain Bluebird, Cliff, Barn, and Tree Swallows, and other desirables, have been seen as the most-mourned losers to the quarrelsome import.

A moment's reflection on human history suggests that the sparrow is more a symptom of a greater problem than a prime cause. The arrival of this brash exotic coincided with the beginning of the railroad age in North America and the consequent burgeoning of settlement. The wholesale habitat destruction that ensued guaranteed the dislocation of most wildlife. Given time, more native birds might have weathered the change and adapted to street and backyard life. But that niche was taken, even as the human immigrants arrived, by their avian tag-along, and the native birds were put to a double disadvantage. In the self-forgiving way we have of shifting blame, the House Sparrow takes the rap for what was very much a human offence.

The only type of habitat that is not decreasing is man-altered habitat. This should have continued to favour House Sparrows in Canada. But they suffered a marked decline after World War I, a loss that paralleled the drop in horse populations. The downturn levelled out, but in many areas sparrow numbers continue a gradual fall. Farms are disappearing, and much livestock is concentrated in intensive-feeding animal factories. Most people now live in cities. The sprawling new suburbs, with their tightly built houses, are not as compatible to the tough little sparrow as were the leafy backyards, gardens, ramshackle cow-sheds, and garages of yesteryear.

❊ ❊ ❊

House Sparrow
Passer domesticus

Old World Sparrow family. Also "English" Sparrow; *passer* is Latin for "sparrow," *domesticus* for "house."

Description

Chunky, dingy, short-legged; back and wings brown-streaked, breast plain dust-grey; male has black chin and bib; cap and rump grey; grey-buff ear patch, band of brown from eye widening around back of neck; markings of winter male much subdued, clearest in spring breeding season.

Behaviour

Social; forages in small flocks, may congregate at night roosts in large numbers; prefers to feed on ground; rather heavy flier; noisy, squabbling occupant of streets, vacant lots, shopping malls, and barnyards; aggressive hang-about at

feeders; voice a loud "chir-rup," often repeated monotonously; flocks may gather in bush or tree at certain times of day where, for an extended time, all seem intent on out-shrilling each other.

Range

Nonmigratory; universally, and exclusively, where human settlement has extended; breeds everywhere in British Columbia, absent only in farthest north and the Charlottes.

Food

Grain, weed seeds, edible human refuse, insects; at feeders favours small seeds, breadcrumbs, and cracked grain, but with a bit of time soon learns to handle sunflower seeds.

Nest

Hatful of dusty trash, straw, and feathers jammed into holes in eaves of buildings, in light standards, large signs, or birdhouses; often appropriates nests of Cliff Swallows; on rare instances builds a large, domed ball of grass with side entrance, high in tree.

Comment

A feeder heavily streaked with droppings is the sign of a clientele of House Sparrows, although native finches can also be messy. Opportunism is this scrappy little bird's middle name. I have watched them on hot summer days diligently working service stations and campground parking lots, pulling insects out of the radiators and bug screens on newly arrived vehicles.

No exception to the rule that undesirables must be prolific, the males begin competing for nest sites the autumn before the next breeding season, and pairs can be seen in March, or February in milder parts of British Columbia, hauling nesting material about the eaves and into Purple Martin and any other birdhouses they can get into. This head start, abetted by an incubation period as short as ten days, allows double-, often triple-brooding.

REF: A(W) - 592; BC - 574; GO - 296; NG - 432; P(W) - 346

CHAPTER EIGHT

The Walk-In Trade

I have already referred frequently to some animals other than birds that routinely answer the call of your hospitality, for better or worse. In the annals of bird feeding in Canada some quite unusual beasts have joined the regulars at the table. These have included deer, elk, and moose; black bears and raccoons; porcupines, woodchucks, and all the ground squirrels; mice, voles, and shrews; foxes, weasels, and mink, for suet and for the rodents the seeds attracted; snakes, probably also for the mice; and oftener than one might suspect, coyotes which, it turns out, can develop quite a liking for sunflower seeds! I haven't heard, but wouldn't be at all surprised to hear, that stations in the far north have been visited by polar bears, caribou, and muskoxen.

The two animals that attract the most attention and comment, however, are cats and squirrels. A close runner-up in some locations is the raccoon, well established urbanite that it has latterly become.

Because these mammals are so much a part of the feeder scene, it is essential in my view to deal with them other than solely as nuisances to be discouraged or dispatched. They do, after all, have their own natural history, even though cats play theirs out as indoor pets, outdoor predators.

As with the birds, I felt it would be useful to provide a reference source. My choices are A.W. Banfield's *The Mammals of Canada* (1974), and Adrian Forsyth's *Mammals Of The Canadian Wild* (1985). The code letters are, respectively, "B:" and "F:".

Squirrels

Family *Sciuridae*

Sciuridae is Latinized "shade-tail," from Greek *skia*, "a shadow" and *oura*, "tail," from tree squirrels' summertime habit of stretching out on limbs with their tails over their backs, supposedly to shade themselves from the sun.

To begin, why at all should squirrels be treated seriously, even sympathetically, in a book about winter birds? Firstly, for most of us they are an unavoidable fact of life. Secondly, squirrels are card-carrying native species toughing out our relentless winters in ways that merit our sympathetic attention. Whether we choose to "fight 'em or feed 'em," they can be worthy foes or fascinating guests.

Arguably, rodents are the most successful order of mammals, and the squirrel family stands near the head of it. Squirrels are present in all the habitable continents except Australia, and fill widely varying niches wherever they occur. In British Columbia the blocky, stolid woodchuck and marmot, the soft-eyed Flying Squirrel and the skittering wee chipmunk are all squirrels. Some are among the world's most profound hibernators; others, like Red Squirrels, go all winter in high gear.

The Teeth Have It

Other admirable attributes notwithstanding, teeth are the rodents' key to success. Most prominent is a set of cutting chisels mounted at the front of the muzzle, giving most rodents a "buck-toothed" look, especially if, as in the case of beavers and porcupines, these teeth are deep orange.

The roots of these four incisors curve an astonishing distance into sockets in the jaws. Hollow-rooted and open at the bottom, they grow constantly throughout the life of the owner at a rate that compensates for normal wear and keeps them chisel-sharp. These features permit rodents to cut through extremely hard and abrasive material and not wear out their tools. Rats can bore holes in concrete and cut through metal sheathing around wires, and Red Squirrels can chisel apart rock-hard Lodgepole Pine cones.

Behind the incisors is a long, arched, toothless gap—the diastema—that permits the rodent to pull its lips shut behind its front teeth. Thus, it can chisel away without biting its lip, and the seal keeps concrete dust, metal filings, and cone debris out of the mouth. Behind the diastema are the grinding molars which, like our teeth, grow only so far and then stop.

Everything is mounted in a set of jaws hinged so that the lower can be switched instantly from cutting to grinding, with special sets of muscles to accomplish this change of gears. In the cutting mode the lower jaw is shifted forward to engage the incisors, in which position the molars are disengaged. When the lower jaw is pulled back, the incisors are out of gear and the molars mesh into action.

Squirrels often exhibit an almost fiendish talent for choosing irreplaceable valuables for random gnawing. It's not vandalism, if that helps. Rather, the gnawing simply compensates for the soft diet of seeds which requires nowhere near the amount of toothwork that shucking the hereditary diet of cones or nuts demands. If the squirrel didn't keep its front teeth ground down they would grow to unmanageable lengths. Indeed, if accident or disease destroys one incisor, its opposite in the other jaw keeps growing, longer and longer until the animal cannot feed at all and dies of starvation.

I have noticed that many rodents, squirrels included, seem to love gnawing on old deer antlers, possibly gaining minerals as they hone down their teeth. Perhaps if you left a chunk of discarded antler, or a large bone, out where it could be chewed on by squirrels they'd be less likely to vandalize your trim.

Compulsive Hoarding

There are a number of accessories and behaviours that various rodents have evolved to augment their teeth. Chipmunks hibernate in a nest built either right on, or very close to, their stash. At intervals of up to two weeks they begin to shiver violently to warm up. Awake, they take a drowsy bathroom break, eat a big snack out of stores, and then curl up again. Their horde is often huge. Banfield's *The Mammals of Canada* records a Least Chipmunk's cache of 478 acorns and 2,734 cherry pits.

The compulsive hoarding instinct and the great energy of the diminutive chipmunk are augmented by handy carrying pouches on each cheek, opening to the inside of the mouth. Their capacity is amazing. Banfield records a Least stuffed with thirteen prune stones at one time; Woods in *The Squirrels of Canada* records an Eastern with six chestnuts aboard.

Conceited as we humans are about our own intelligence, it is a matter of particular interest that squirrels have the largest relative brain weight of any small mammal. Bird lovers, all too familiar with the feeling of defeat that follows every attempt to keep squirrels out of their feeders, have suspected it all along.

The "Squirreliest" Squirrel

The tree squirrel familiar to the greatest number of Canadians is the tough little Red. This noisy busybody is the most strident personality in the wild, the "squirreliest" of the squirrels. Except for rare moments of tranquillity its moods vary from mildly agitated to wildly frenzied. In a human personality its pugnacious hysteria would be intolerable, and accordingly it is judged harshly, and unfairly.

To better understand the behaviour of Red Squirrels it helps to know that, familiar as they are in suburb and park, they evolved in the vast forests of the north. There they feed in summer on a great variety of buds, shoots, seeds, insects, mushrooms, eggs, and nestlings, and whatever else can be harvested or caught. But in winter the menu shrinks mainly to one item, the seeds of spruce.

The key to winter survival where the Red Squirrel evolved is therefore to be the sole, no-nonsense proprietor of a grove of spruce, the seeds of which can be harvested and stored for the winter. The competition is fierce; in city, farmyard, or boreal wilderness it's a "no vacancy" world until a property-holder dies. A new claimant is invariably on hand to move in, establishing boundaries, patrolling them diligently and giving its territorial cry. This is the loud, scratchy, rolling "cheek-eek-eek-eek-eek-eek" that greets the squirrel's human neighbours at dawn and keeps them entertained until dusk.

Established home ownership doesn't mean peace and quiet, of course. A Red

Squirrel's life is a constant round of frantic skirmishing with neighbours as each repeatedly tests the boundary lines of the others. Homeless wanderers are invariably sent fleeing; in a fight the psychological and tactical advantages overwhelmingly favour the owner on home ground. The end of each conflict calls for a fresh burst of defiant territorial cries. There's never a dull moment in the life of a Red Squirrel, nor for those of us willing to be involved observers of its high-tempo existence.

About the end of August, a squirrel with a grove of cone-bearing spruce in its territory goes to work as if possessed, cutting bunches of cones from the tips of the twigs, letting them drop, and then scurrying below to store them. In two weeks it will cache as many as fifteen thousand, an impressive mound if, as some squirrels do, it piles them in a heap before burying them. It may "scatter hoard" the singles, burying them in ground litter. The bunches may go into a labyrinth of tunnels, preferably under a big tree in the centre of its territory. Burial keeps the under-ripened cones moist; otherwise they'd dry out and open, spilling the precious seeds. It also keeps them out of view and in a more defendable stronghold against pilfering neighbours. Near such hoards will be piles of rust-coloured "cone flakes" at stumps and logs where the squirrel perches in winter to shell out its meals.

A full cone hoard is enough to last a Red Squirrel for two winters. It instinctively "knows" that its life supporting trees are capricious. As pointed out in the discussion on crossbills, Chapter 7, a bountiful seed crop is almost invariably followed by a "crop failure," and a winter of privation for squirrels.

Baby "Boom and Bust"

Red Squirrel family life is a trade-off between conflicting imperatives. Mating is brief and tempestuous, after which the male is driven off and returns to his own territory. The young are given all that solicitous single motherhood can offer. But in a foretaste of things to come, before weaning them the female will often shift her pups to a den near the edge of her territory. After weaning, she becomes less and less tolerant of them until her own territoriality reasserts itself and they are all sent off—and kept off, violently.

In the relative abundance of parks and suburbs, new squirrels have more options than their boreal cousins. But for those reliant mainly on the single-resource spruce economy, the options are few. Should they be the progeny of the "baby boom" that follows a winter of cone abundance, they are a luckless lot. Driven into an overcrowded world, they face the winter of famine that invariably follows a year of plenty.

Most are foredoomed to perish, undernourished, easy pickings for predators as they flee distracted from one territorial defender to another. Even for the lucky minority that finds a place, the future is bleak; a store of dried mushrooms and rock-hard Lodgepole Pine cones is a poor substitute for a larder full of spruce cones.

The dispersal of surplus squirrels on the eve of a winter of privation is, ironically, a long-term benefit to their species. A few, a very few, will reach uninhabited pockets of plenty and beget new populations. They will thus play a small part in a grand plan, the dispersal of their species—a trade-off for the sacrifice of the many refugees that won't make it.

If the survivors could only talk, theirs would be tales of perilous runs over open ground, death-defying risks, hairbreadth escapes, and desperate battles. They would be among the rare ones, survivors, thanks to a combination of luck, speed, and dauntless spirit. It is small wonder that their descendants are scrappy and strong, that they will defend their home with the last spark of energy in their tough little bodies.

REF: B - 96; F - 184

❈ ❈ ❈

Red and Douglas's Squirrel
Tamiasciurus hudsonicus and T. douglasii

"Squirrel" from Greek *skiourus*, compounded from *skia*, "a shadow" plus *oura*, "tail," descriptive of animal's using its tail as a shade from the sun; *tamias* from Latin "steward" or "one who stores," plus *sciurus*, "shade tail"; *hudsonicus*, "of Hudson" (Bay) where first type specimen described; *douglasii* from David Douglas, Scottish plant collector who explored British Columbia in the 1820s and 1830s.

Description

Trim, muscular body about 15 cm (6 in) long, fluffy tail about same length, with dark subterminal band; light eye-ring prominent in all seasons in both species. **Red:** in winter, coat paprika-rufous, especially bright in tail and along back; belly, throat, and chin silvery grey; in summer, body olive-brown, underparts white, with black line on side separating them; rain forest forms much darker, slightly smaller than interior forms. **Douglas's:** dark ear-tufts; grizzled on upper body and tail; in winter, indistinct back band and tail reddish-brown, sides greyish-olive; belly pale yellowish-grey; flank stripe indistinct; in summer olive-brown above, distinct black flank line, tail reddish-brown; belly and feet bright orange; overall, Douglas's is slightly smaller and darker than the Red.

Behaviour

Hyperactive, excitable, inquisitive; when alarmed runs and climbs with explosive speed; at rest on haunches coils tail closely over back and neck; noisy; territorial call a scratchy, rattling "chrrrrrr" usually delivered from elevated point; alarm call a sharp, strident "k'cheek!-k'cheek!", often accompanied by agitated drumming of hind feet; drives other squirrels off territory in wild pursuits; often chases birds from feeder and vicinity.

Range

Red: Truly northern, right across Canada throughout boreal forest to tree limit, southward wherever there are woodlands; most of British Columbia, including Vancouver Island; introduced on Graham Island in the Charlottes; absent from southwest coast, adjacent Coastal Ranges and lower Fraser Valley. **Douglas's:** Along west coast to California, and adjacent Coastal Ranges; in British Columbia, the southwest coast, lower Fraser Valley; absent from Vancouver Island.

Food

Both species: In summer, buds, shoots, fruit, seeds, insects, nuts, mushrooms, and occasional eggs and nestlings; in winter, relies on stored acorns, maple samaras in deciduous forests, and spruce, pine, fir, and hemlock cones in coniferous forests; at feeder eats anything, but prefers sunflower seeds, baked scraps, peanuts.

Nest

Favours tree holes, but will accumulate bulky ball of shredded grass and bark in buildings, rock piles, burrows, or in open branches where it is called a "drey."

Comment

In the hyperkinetic world of the Red and Douglas's Squirrels, territorialism can generate nerve-wracking standoffs in the presence of a feeder. The unlimited supply of rich food escalates trespass beyond the resident's ability to drive away the interlopers, unless he or she is overwhelmingly dominant. Everyone edges in on the goodies, tension mounting, adrenalin pumping. They fume, shriek, and growl, cramming frantically for a few seconds until another scuffle explodes in which there might well be significant bloodshed. I wouldn't be at all surprised to learn that Red Squirrels suffer from ulcers and hypertension.

Total peace is impossible, but with management the tension can be eased somewhat and the birds, at least, will benefit. If the main station is the focus of constant mayhem, several other, preferably hanging, feeders, can be deployed nearby. These will give the smaller birds, and perhaps even the beleaguered resident squirrel, a place to feed—out of the crossfire as it were.

REF: B - 138; F - 208

Grey Squirrel

Sciurus carolinensis

Also "black" squirrel; "squirrel" from Greek *skiourus*, from *skia*, "a shadow" plus *oura*, "tail," from animal's resting with tail over back as sunshade; *sciurus*, Latin for "shade tail"; *carolinensis*, "of Carolina," where first type specimen described.

Description

Twice size of Red Squirrel; body 20 to 30 cm (8 to 12 in) long, tail same or longer; in Vancouver and Victoria, a jet black variant dominates; grey phase, when present, has grizzled grey coat with rusty shading on head and flanks; short white tuft behind each ear, light buff eye-ring; tail very full, longest hair tips frosty; belly silver-white; in some local populations a grizzled buff-ochre colour dominates; in all phases coat sleek and smooth in young, roughening with age.

Behaviour

Much calmer, quieter and slower-moving than Red Squirrel; in sitting position curls tail against back and neck in graceful "question-mark"; when moving floats it out behind; when agitated thrashes tail in circular, spasmodic jerks; sometimes tolerates other Greys at feeder; alarm call a grating, protracted, nasal "raaaa-aaak," repeated monotonously; also a short, muted "whuck!"

Range

Originally southeastern United States, expanding northwestward; introduced to western cities like Winnipeg and Saskatoon; abundant in Vancouver's Stanley Park and vicinity, doing well after introduction to Victoria and other locations on southern Vancouver Island.

Food

Buds, shoots, bark, seeds, flowers, nuts, fruit, fungi; occasionally eggs and nestlings; buries nuts singly, accurately unearths them from under deep snow; omnivorous at feeder, but prefers sunflower seeds, peanuts, baked goods.

Nest

In tree hole or building; nest (drey) in branches high in tree, a round, untidy clump of leaves and grass with entrance in side.

Comment

This introduced squirrel is limited in British Columbia to the Vancouver area, and to southern Vancouver Island, principally Victoria and environs. Although its range is restricted, the human distribution here makes it a potential familiar to half the province's population. Well-fed, and having left behind most of its predators when it was turned loose in town, it prospers to the point of being a major nuisance to householders and gardeners, a source of exercise and the thrill of the chase for their dogs. Interestingly, the squirrels working the tourists in Stanley Park are predominantly black, like their fellows in Toronto. Something in urban living favours black over grey.

Despite their more pacific dispositions, Greys can be more demanding guests around feeders than Douglas's or Reds. They eat more, and in spite of their slower gait, can jump higher and farther. When confronting barriers intended to foil them they are much more persistent and can pull off astonishing acrobatics to get where they want to go. For bird feeders who can't accept squirrels, and for whom armed intervention is distasteful and/or unlawful, there are ways of assuaging the humiliation of being outsmarted by a "dumb" animal; some of these are outlined in Chapter 3, "Feeders and Shelters," and Chapter 5, "The Down-Side."

REF: B - 132; F - 205

Northern Flying Squirrel

Glaucomys sabrinus

Occasionally "Canadian" Flying Squirrel or "fairydiddle"; "Northern" as distinct from "Southern" (*G. volans*); "flying" from ability to glide short distances; "squirrel" from Greek *skiourus*, "shade-tail"; *glaucomys* Greek for "grey mouse," Latin *sabrinus*, "river nymph," refers to Severn River west of Hudson Bay where first type specimen described.

Description

Smaller than Red Squirrel; body 13 to 18 cm (5 to 7.5 in), tail slightly shorter; large, dark eyes; very soft, grey-buff fur, cinnamon along back, shaded to light buff underparts; glide membrane dark-bordered; tail noticeably flat, especially on bottom surface.

Behaviour

Strictly nocturnal, from hour or more after dusk to before dawn; swoops rapidly from high in tree to lower landing point, occasionally to ground; scampers up tree when alarmed and immediately turns to head-down launch posture; agile, but not as fast on ground as Red or Grey; may share feeder with others; quiet, voice a soft chatter.

Range

Throughout boreal forest as far north as there are sizeable trees, south in mature mixed woodlands; throughout British Columbia except Vancouver Island and the Charlottes, including well-treed cities and river valleys.

Food

Prefers seeds and nuts; buds, flowers, lichens, fungi, berries, insects, and sweet sap; occasionally eggs and nestlings; caches winter food in den or nearby hollow trees; very fond of sunflower seeds, peanuts at feeder.

Nest

Bed of finely shredded grass, bark in tree holes, occasionally buildings or birdhouses; outside drey a ball of moss, grasses and lichen, sometimes in disused bird nest or drey of Red Squirrel.

Comment

Many years before I ever saw a live Northern Flying Squirrel I would occasionally find their light, fluffy, uniquely flattened tails, testimony to the previous owners' vulnerability to cats and owls. People living in well-forested regions often have no idea that they are kept company, well after dark, by these shy little gliders. The mystery of midnight scurryings on my cottage roof was solved when I placed a small light bulb, with an inside switch, over the window feeder. Turning it on when the squirrels were munching away didn't seem to bother them in the least, and neither did my obvious presence a few inches on the other side of the glass. A friend reports that in a similar situation he was able to reach through the opened window and pat a squirrel without alarming it.

REF: B - 145; F - 210

Least and Yellow Pine Chipmunk
Eutamius (formerly Tamias) minimus and E. amoenus

"Least" from small size compared to other chipmunks; "Yellow Pine" from close association with that tree; "chipmunk" from Algonquian name; *eutamias*, Greek/Latin for "true steward," referring to zeal for storing food; *minimus*, Latin for "least"; *amoenus* Latin for "pleasing."

Description

Both very similar in appearance, Yellow Pine slightly larger, and colours and patterns brighter; both much smaller than Red Squirrel; long, slender tails not as full as tree squirrels'; body 10 to 13 cm (4 to 5 in) long, tail 10 to 11.5 cm (4 to 4.5 in); three prominent dark stripes on face separated by two buff stripes; pointy nose, prominent, light-ringed eyes, large ears; five dark stripes full length of back, outer two on each side separated by light buff; while the Least has an overall greyish cast, the Yellow Pine is more reddish, its flanks noticeably cinnamon coloured.

Behaviour

Quick-moving, darting about on ground; dainty and beady-eyed; usually run with long tail held straight up; readily climb trees, low bushes, and feeder poles, but seek refuge in ground-level hideaways; diligent hoarders of food, especially seeds, fruit pits; hibernate, but are early spring risers and venture out briefly during extended mild spells in winter; voice a clear, high "chip-chip" and low, steady "wok," both with ventriloquistic quality making them hard to pinpoint; in alarm, a slightly rasping "churrrr" followed by a trill issued in flight.

Range

Least: Across boreal and parkland Canada from central Yukon to northwestern Ontario; in British Columbia, north and northwest from Peace River, and in extreme southeast along west flank of Rockies. **Yellow Pine:** In open, dry, Douglas-fir/Yellow Pine zone in the western mountains of the continent from northern California to north-central British Columbia, including the southwest Coast Range, but not including Vancouver Island. NOTE: The ranges of these two overlap only in a narrow strip west of the Continental Divide in extreme southeast of the province.

Food

Seeds, nuts, greens, insects; at feeders fond of sunflower seeds, grains, baked scraps, dried fruit.

Nest

A ball of shredded grass and fibres, deep in a neat, hidden burrow in a rock, trash, or brush pile, or under root tangle or building; nest often built near or on the main underground food cache.

Comment

Chipmunks are the picnic ground, four-legged equivalent of chickadees. Bold, pretty, and pert, they quickly turn their cute ways to good use in training humans to feed them on demand. Their eagerness for handouts is limitless; what they don't sit up and nibble on the spot, they jam into their bulging cheek pouches and scamper off with, a process their benefactors find endlessly comical. Good climbers, but not arboreal, at feeders they usually content themselves with gleaning fallout off the ground.

Unfortunately, these endearing little skedaddlers often vanish just about the time you become thoroughly captivated by them. Cats know a lot more than they let on about such disappearances, chipmunks seeming to be particularly vulnerable to them.

REF: Least—B - 99; F - 214; Yellow Pine—B - 101; F - 217

Raccoon Family

"Some people think of raccoons as wonderfully intelligent creatures, affectionate, playful and downright adorable. To others they are vicious, devious and downright destructive vermin." Thus Des Kennedy, writing of his life amongst the creatures of British Columbia's Denman Island in his book *Living Things We Love To Hate*, sums up the diverse emotions generated by the masked bandit the Algonkian-speaking peoples called "arakun."

It should be noted that Denman Island, which is just off the east side of Vancouver Island in the Strait of Georgia, hasn't been blessed, or cursed, with raccoons just yet, and a determined group of residents has banded together to keep it that way. A bad example exists on neighbouring Hornby Island where opossums were liberated, presumably by hunters brain-damaged on "houn'-dawg" shooting adventures from the American southland. A similar lame-brained effort to manage wildlife for the benefit of trappers saw coons stocked on the Queen Charlottes. There they have no natural predators, and most of their pathogens have been left far behind. The inevitable population boom sees them inflicting massive damage on nesting sea bird populations.

The adaptable, omnivorous coon has turned mankind into an aid, making itself at home in farmyards and suburban developments. Here it dines well on garbage, pet food, and other back-step freebies, and on succulent garden produce. It quickly becomes a night raider of any bird feeders it can reach. For accommodation it settles into fireplace chimneys, culverts, ventilation ducts, garden sheds, attics, and crawl spaces, most of which are superior to the traditional den tree. My personal experience includes being awakened one night in my suburban home, then in Winnipeg, by the sound of a large coon purposefully ripping the shingles off my roof to get into the attic. I interrupted his work with a well-aimed billet of firewood.

Altogether, for the upwardly mobile coon, life in the city is much superior to what it was back in the old swamp. It follows that the urban coon is bigger, healthier, and raises more young than its country cousin.

Although originally and exclusively North American, the raccoon has been introduced—either deliberately or in the form of escapees from fur farms—into France, Germany, Ukraine, and a number of places in Siberia.

As well as their value as bearers of thick fur on a good-sized, durable hide, raccoons have found favour as pets. While very young a coon is the most engaging of companions—cute, inquisitive to a degree, intelligent, cuddly, and full of endearing sounds and mannerisms. However, while it may be as tame as you please, it is not domesticated. Any young coon will, if given the liberty of the house, become a thorough nuisance, climbing, prying, poking and pilfering into places no dog, cat, or small child could ever get at.

At about twelve weeks of age this cute little bandit becomes assertive; restrained or chastised it may explode into a clawing, biting, shrieking bundle of highly intense aggression, exactly as it would in dominance battles with its littermates.

The fury subsides as abruptly as it erupted, but the vicious outburst lurks just below the veneer of tameness and trust. Anyone who has raised a raccoon or two almost invariably has the scars to prove it. Sterling North, author of the best-selling book *Rascal* had to return his raccoon to the wild after it turned on him.

Emergency wards and clinics in suburbs across the country get raccoon-bite victims every summer. These are often men who unwisely attempted to get physical with a coon in a shed, loft, flue, or some other disputed turf. The assisting family dog might at the same time be whisked off to the vet for repairs. But at least as often the victims are children who were approached by coons or who enticed them close. The incentive is always food; what the children mistook for friendliness was simply a bold approach by a wild animal in search of an easy meal. If the kids try to grab or pick up the coon it defends itself, sometimes with very bloody results.

To the pain and shock of attack and physical hurt is added the possibility that the animal was rabid or afflicted with encephalitis. The etiology of rabies is well known; encephalitis can be transmitted from raccoons to dogs, but not to humans, for whatever comfort there is in that.

Northward-bound

Coons are members of the family that includes coatimundis, ringtails, and kinkajous, all of them subtropical to tropical animals. It may be that the resemblance between the goggled faces of the raccoon and the Giant Panda isn't coincidental; there is evidence that indeed they are related.

In the south of its range the raccoon stays up and about all year round. But as a southern animal moving ever northward, the vanguard has had to adapt to survive the long famine that northern winters impose. Like other food generalists—badgers, skunks, and bears—it simply sleeps through its problem.

Raccoons have an enormous capacity for food, tucking away two kilograms or more a day where supplies permit it. Under the right conditions they'll be rolling fat by fall. Although they grow torporous in their winter dens, they don't hibernate. Their heart rate if anything speeds up during cold weather, driving a metabolism that costs about twenty-one grams (three-quarters of an ounce) of body weight per day. A mild spell may bring them out to shuffle about for awhile before turning in again.

In the northern parts of their range snow depth is critical: anything deeper than fifteen centimetres (six inches) is too difficult to get around in, and they are virtually compelled to retire. During a long, cold winter a coon may lose up to 50 percent of its autumn weight. If a coon's supply of fat runs out before the snows of spring recede below the crucial fifteen centimetres, it dies. A high percentage of young coons don't make it through our northern winters.

It is interesting to note that the arrival of raccoons in the suburbs has drawn in another furtive visitor, the cougar. British Columbia supports a sizeable population of these big cats which now and then show up in town. These appearances trigger alarm, headlines, and usually the death of the cougar. Rarely, however, there are confrontations that end with people getting hurt or even killed. These out-of-place cougars may be roving youngsters, seeking territory, or they may be adults that have learned to hunt the acreages. Here the aforementioned coons, and often deer, are both plentiful and unwary, and there are domestic cats and small dogs for the taking. In several western American cities, Denver among them, cougars are several generations into suburban living, breeding well within the sprawling semirural developments wherever patches of sufficient cover or rough terrain provide denning refuge.

❈ ❈ ❈

Raccoon

Procyon lotor

Also "coon"; "raccoon" from Algonkian *arakun* or *arathune*, variously interpreted as "scratcher" or "scratches-with-hands"; *procyon* from Latin *pro*, "before," and *cyon*, Greek for "dog," supposedly linked to the group of stars that rises in the summer sky just before the dog star, Sirius; *lotor* from Latin "to wash," from animal's perceived habit of "washing" its food.

Description

Low-slung, heavy-furred, with a thick, black-ringed tail; black facial "mask" made very prominent by light muzzle and broad, very light brow lines over mask; erect, light-edged ears; stands with arched back higher than shoulders; coat a grizzled grey, brown or tan, sometimes with a ruddy cast to it; likened in motion by some to a very fat cat; average weights for males 7 to 8 kg (15 to 18 lb), for females 5.5 to 7 kg (12 to 15 lb), heavier in fall than in spring; young-of-year appreciably lighter, occasional adult males much heavier.

Behaviour

Males solitary, females and young-of-year social; runs with a rolling, hump-backed gait; readily climbs, and relaxes in, large trees; can descend trees head-first; frequently sits on haunches, especially when feeding or grooming; individuals conditioned to feeding by humans can become very bold, aggressive scroungers; a slow runner, when pursued takes refuge in a tree, burrow, hedge, culvert; when cornered, by dog or human, a very tough, determined fighter; produces great variety of sounds, including a coughing growl, buzzy snarl, hiss, musical churring call, soft chattering, high squeaks, purring; front paws handlike in dexterity; famous for habit of captive animals' "washing" their food.

Range

Throughout temperate North America except for driest parts of southwest United States, south through Central America; through most of agricultural Canada from coast to coast, up into southern boreal zone; in British Columbia in extreme southern interior, on southwest coast, and Vancouver Island; introduced to the Queen Charlotte islands; favours woodlands and farmlands adjacent to water; has adapted well to city existence.

Food

Omnivorous; in the wild reptiles, insects, small mammals, birds and eggs, fish, snails, clams, crayfish, fruit, nuts, roots, bulbs; forages in shallow water by rapidly dabbling about with both front paws; in cities feeds on garbage, garden produce (especially sweet corn in the "milk" stage), and whatever wild food (baby rabbits, mice, grubs, eggs, etc.) may be available; at feeders prefers sunflower seeds and suet.

Nest

Hollow tree or log, disused woodchuck or fox den, rock pile, cave; around dwellings, in attics, lofts, barns, sheds, disused machinery, culverts, chimneys; females bear litters of three to five in a nest of grass, leaves, wood chips, or paper, cloth, and other discarded materials.

Comment

As a feeder of birds in several very different locations, all of which have raccoons in varying levels of evidence, I make a point of keeping my distance. I take pains to keep garbage, stored bird seed, and suet out of reach, and maintain my buildings in a raccoon-proof state of upkeep. If a coon broke into one of my buildings I would, depending on where the incident occurred, live-trap and/or shoot it.

The place where the raccoons in my life have been most numerous is rural Manitoba where, thanks to the cold winters, they are strictly mild-weather visitors. To sustain an arms-length truce I keep feeders as coon-proof as possible. Thus far I have never had to destroy one, but from time to time, in a live trap intended for a stray cat, I find a very dejected-looking raccoon. Following the indignity of being inspected (through the wires) and weighed (in the cage), it is liberated with, I hope, the trauma of capture painful enough to make it avoid my yard thereafter.

The question of whether coons "wash" their food or not has been discussed at length in popular literature and lore. It is noted that captive animals habitually dunk food into water and manipulate it about in a motion that looks much like purposeful scrubbing. Thus, millions of zoo visitors will swear that coons won't eat unless they can wash their food first, even if it's something like a soaking-wet frog just out of the pond. Others, privy to the habits of wild coons, say the habit is much less pronounced in them. They also observe that wild coons rub dry food between their paws, and captive ones without access to water do the same thing. Wild coons also rub their front paws together in a kind of compulsive reflex even when there is no food involved.

For an animal that evolved to make a living feeling about for prey in the shallow margins of rivers, ponds, and swamps, crayfish must have become, early on, a major staple of diet. Raccoons have slim, sensitive front toes much more heavily stocked with nerve receptors than our own fingers. Crayfish have horny pincers and a powerful grip, as anyone who has been caught by one can attest.

Dabbling about, poking your delicate fingers into crayfish lairs under muddied water where you can't see what you're doing is a sure way of getting repeatedly pinched. To avoid the nasty pincers but keep in contact with the crayfish, a rapid, hand-to-hand buffeting would keep it disoriented until the claws could be pinned down prior to a quick disabling bite. This rapid, double-handed batting motion, repeated out of context as an evolved reflex, in or out of water, is at the root of the "washing" myth.

REF: B-313; F-142

Domestic Cat

Felis catus

The sunny, wintry scene at my study window is cheery and heart-warming. On the feeding tray at the sill, chickadees and nuthatches come and go in the manner of their kind, grabbing sunflower seeds and darting away with them.

Abruptly there is a heavy thump, a shower of seeds, and an instant of frantic scrambling. On the feeder is a neighbour's tomcat with a chickadee jammed in its jaws. He fixes me with a momentary stare and is gone. He leaves behind some drifting feathers and two converging downstrokes smeared on the glass where his flailing paws trapped the bird.

Had my chickadee fallen prey to a full-time, wild predator I would have viewed the little casualty at my window with fascinated excitement quite untinged by resentment. But the cat is a subsidized predator that does not live by the ecological rules of the game. He does not need what he kills. His depredations diminish the prey base of real predators that do, such as small owls and hawks. Turned loose to fend for himself he could not survive a prairie winter on his own.

Having licked his chops and smoothed his fur, this on-again, off-again predator would have meowed for readmission to his keeper's cosy house and its unlimited supply of kitty-dins. Another mild day and the urge for some excitement, and he would be back, as would my resentment at seeing my birds turned into cat treats.

Tooth-and-claw Genetics

The cat's nonprofessional status as a predator is no reflection at all on his efficiency as a killer. Cats, at least the "brand X" variety that constitute the overwhelming majority, have retained their physical and behavioural integrity despite generations of dependency on humans. They have done so because house, or "alley" cats, unlike their pedigreed counterparts, and almost all dogs, are not the products of arranged matings. However pampered a suburban tom might be, he must still win his reproductive rights in tooth-and-claw brawls out behind the garage. He is thus prevented from passing on to his descendants anything but physical prowess of the winning kind.

This heritage includes dazzling athletic ability. The chickadee-hunter beneath my window pinpointed the location of his unseen victim by the sound of its feet on the wooden tray. He sprang five feet up, blasted over the edge of the platform and retained sufficient balance and control to make an accurate, lightning-fast grab in whichever direction the bird's own split-second reflexes launched it.

At one time, the keeping of cats was judged to be a matter of good household and barnyard management, to prevent the premises from being overrun with mice and rats. Mice, yes, and birds. But the average cat's reputation as a ratter is largely baseless. Cats, having once tackled a rat, will rarely take on another, having learned they are tough, frenzied fighters if attacked. A study of feral cats in Sweden disclosed that they ate weasels more frequently than they did rats! Alley cats and rats in New York City have been photographed rummaging through garbage virtually nose-to-nose, ignoring each other.

But today's pet cats need claim no practical justification to be cherished; sentiment and affection rule the day. Good citizens, concerned about the impact of Amazonian forest burning on our migrant birds, automatically open the door every time the cat wants out, unaware of the impact of this action on those same birds. If it tucks away an occasional warbler, that's "just nature's way." Puss returns from its forays, soft-furred and purring, its adventures cloaked in inscrutable mystery.

Inscrutability doesn't mystify scientists in search of truth. A couple of them in Britain—Peter Churcher and John Lawford—turned an analytical eye on just what impact pet cats have on the animal life they prey on. In a study begun in 1981 they monitored cat predation in a small Bedfordshire village by having owners tally all prey their pets brought home or were seen eating.

Their discoveries included some interesting insights into cat behaviour. It appears to make no difference if a pet cat is well fed; hunger is not the main motivator. There is indeed a credible argument that feeding a cat merely enhances its hunting success by keeping it in top form. Amongst wild predators, hunger beyond a certain point actually diminishes their efficiency. Beyond kittenhood, the younger the cat, the more animals it catches, whether it's male or female. Most cats grow indifferent to hunting as they age; neutering hastens this process. Cats are fair-weather hunters, disinclined to go afield on cold, wet, or windy days.

Town and suburban cat owners might note that cats living in the centre of the village caught less prey in total, but the percentage of birds, relative to mice and other small mammals, increased. The heaviest months were June and July, due to the large proportion of easily caught baby birds, followed by September, the month of migration.

Massive Impact

From figures tallied at the close of the study, the total impact of pet cats on small animals is enormous. The village cats averaged four birds each per year. Churcher and Lawford note that this figure is a minimum, since it is based only on actual tallied kills. An American study showed that cats bring home only half of what they catch, either eating the rest on the spot or leaving them behind. This raises the annual average to a credible eight birds per cat.

I believe this estimate to be low, a view supported by personal observation. For example, while house-sitting for friends on vacation from their rural farmstead in Manitoba I saw one of the family cats eating a fledgling junco on the lawn. It evaded my effort to intervene and, before the evening was out, caught and ate four more.

If one makes a simple proportional estimate of the toll by cats in North America, the figures are appalling. Creditable estimates put the number of cats in the United States at close to sixty million. If their average annual kill is eight birds, they destroy 480 million a year.

An estimate based on cat-owning statistics from other North American cities gives greater Vancouver a cat population of over 800,000. With a mild climate that allows year-round hunting, cats could kill as many as 6,400,000 Vancouver birds per year. In parts of Vancouver Island and the southwest mainland, feral cats, many generations born in the wild, heavily impact songbirds, nests, and other small game, and can be serious nuisances around domestic poultry.

Most of us have heard people brag that their cat (usually a female, usually with kittens) is a "good hunter" and brings home a steady succession of prey. In a suburb, such cats, far from performing a service, simply ensure the needless death of untold songbirds. The only conscionable course of action is to do what conscientious owners, and all breeders of show cats do, and keep them in.

For those insistent on giving cats their liberty, but still concerned about birds, declawing certainly has some effect on their ability to catch birds. But clawless adult males on the prowl would suffer a great handicap in the violence that goes with sex in the cat world. In good conscience, if one has a tom declawed it should also be neutered and retired gracefully from the mating game.

There is room for serious consideration by bird lovers about whether owning a cat and turning it outdoors at all is an environmentally justifiable luxury.

CHAPTER NINE

Census-taking

One doesn't have to join a club to learn about bird feeding or to enjoy what is essentially a rather solitary pleasure. However, trading ideas with a group of experienced bird feeders speeds up the learning process. New relationships and warm friendships develop around common interests.

As well as these benefits and pleasures, nature clubbing keeps one in touch with environmental issues. While most people share concerns over the environment, very few have the time, the resources, or the nerve to speak out individually. Joining forces with a group of like-minded folks can give direction and impact to those concerns when they are voiced in concert.

The Appendix lists the names and addresses of most of the naturalist clubs in British Columbia, most of which are affiliates of the Federation of British Columbia Naturalists.

An opportunity to share your interests and participate on a national basis in local bird-oriented projects is provided by two well-established activities: the Christmas Bird Count and Project FeederWatch.

Christmas Bird Count

It was an issue dealing with environmental abuse that led to the organization, in 1900, of the Christmas Bird Count. Among naturalists of the day there was considerable anger over a barbarous custom among sport hunters, the Christmas "side hunt." The sportsmen would assemble on Christmas Day, choose sides, then fan out over the countryside. According to Frank Chapman, The American Museum of Natural History's ornithologist, they shot ". . . practically everything in fur or feathers that crossed their path." The team that killed the most, including piles of songbirds and other nongame species, was the winner and given the hero's treatment in the sporting press.

To give positive vent to the outrage and frustration over this bloodthirsty ritual, Chapman organized a humane alternative. He summoned members of the Audubon Society to spend a portion of their Christmas Day "with the birds." The objective, which acknowledged a certain competitive bent in human nature, was to correctly identify, and count, as many species as possible. The time spent, the weather conditions, locality searched, and names of participants were recorded and handed in. In February of 1901 the results were published in *Bird Lore*, the then journal of the Audubon Society, which was edited by Chapman.

In the "CBC" of 1900, twenty-seven counters censused twenty-six localities. It was a small beginning, but the canny Chapman had started something that was to have lasting appeal and enduring value. Today's CBC draws around forty thousand counters and covers all of the United States, most of Canada, and localities in Central and South America and the Caribbean. Some guidelines for the count have changed: area boundaries are more specific, and the counts are no longer limited to Christmas Day but can be done on any day within a two-week period around Christmas. But the methods remain essentially those laid down by Chapman, and this element of consistency means that there is a continuum of comparable statistics going back to 1900.

The CBC is still run by the Audubon Society, and the results, with the names of all the counters, are published in a substantial book distributed to all counters. Each counter pays a small fee ($5.00 as of 1992) which covers part of the cost of printing and distributing the results.

Today's CBCs are usually coordinated by local naturalists groups. To find out how to join or organize one contact your nearest naturalist club (see the Appendix), the nature columnist in your local paper, a museum, or the biology teachers in your local school. You should, by the way, begin your planning around the time school starts in September; *don't* leave it until a few weeks before Christmas.

One of the most interesting results of CBCs is the variety of species that turn up, particularly after the counters have a few seasons under their belts and gain experience. Songbirds, hawks, owls, and various waterfowl, some far north of their usual winter range, are tallied, along with hordes of House Sparrows and Rock Doves (pigeons).

Important Statistics

At first acquaintance, a local CBC may seem a rather scattered and insignificant effort. How, after all, can the birds counted over eight hours (the required time period) in one day, by a half-dozen people, have any value? They can't possible count *all* the birds!

Of course they can't. The value of what they find lies in that it is only a small part of a much grander effort that has been going on for decades. Every counter's findings, rated for each species on a birds-per-person-hour-scale, can be compared with results everywhere else, for that species, that year. There is a rule of statistics that says the longer you accumulate data, and the more you gather, the less effect small errors will have if your methods remain consistent.

For example, records compiled in the CBCs in the 1940s and early 1950s revealed long-term, inexplicable declines in raptor populations. The resulting investigations led to the discovery of the lethal effects of pesticide residues on the eggs of hawks and falcons.

Project FeederWatch

Project FeederWatch was set up by Dr. Erica H. (Ricky) Dunn and the Long Point Bird Observatory at Port Rowan, Ontario, on Lake Erie. As the name suggests its purpose is to gather the observations of people who feed birds. It was run for ten years as the Ontario Bird Feeder Survey, proving so successful that the Cornell Laboratory of Ornithology in Ithaca, New York, agreed to join in and make it continent-wide. The Canadian section is still managed by the Long Point Bird Observatory, and there is an extra newsletter (*FeederWatch North*) for Canadian participants, who also receive the biannual Project newsletter, *FeederWatch News*.

All that is required is the ability to identify the species that visit your feeders, and the time to record your observations on computer-readable forms. This means filling in little circles with a soft-lead pencil, a relatively simple routine once you get the hang of it.

The survey lasts from November to April, with observations spaced two weeks apart during that period. On any two consecutive days in each fortnight you take note of weather and snow accumulation, and of the greatest numbers of each species you see at one time at your feeder(s) during the two days of observation.

I like the idea of Project FeederWatch, not only for the bird data it is accumulating, but for the fact that it involves thousands of ordinary folks in the business of recording their observations in the interests of a greater scientific purpose. By encouraging people to participate in an organized way, Project FeederWatch will very likely get many people into the habit of taking notes, which not only gives them a record of what they observe, but sharpens up their powers of observation.

The fee for joining Project FeederWatch for one season is $12.00. For the address in Canada look under National Organizations in the Appendix.

Appendix

The Non-KISS Gourmet

The following recipes call for rendered beef fat, either suet or trimmings. Remember to save the cracklings; they are excellent broken up and scattered on your feeder shelf along with the seeds. For buying and handling suet, see Chapter 2, "Suet."

This is a mere sampling of bird recipes—entire books have been published on the subject. See References for these sources.

East Kootenay Bird Pudding

2 cups whole rolled oats
1 cup rendered suet
1 or 2 tbsp sugar (or honey)
Half cup peanut butter

Cook the oats thick; remelt fat (don't overheat) and pour it into the hot oats; add sugar and peanut butter; stir to even consistency, let cool. Hang out of reach of squirrels, since the scent of the peanut butter will attract them more than pure suet. This versatile mixture can be put in a net bag, plugged into holes in a suet log or between the scales of a big pine cone. Thanks to a good friend in Nelson for this recipe.

Protein Pemmican

3 parts rendered suet
1 part meat—lean burger, moist cat or dog food, unspiced bologna, etc.
Raisins, chopped fruit, dried wild berries

Remelt fat, mash up the meat and stir it in. Add fruit and stir mixture as it cools to get a consistent blend. Experiment with fruit to determine how much of any given kind you can add; too much, and the cooled block won't hold together. This mix adds a sweet energy kick from the fruit, and the protein could help a robin, Varied Thrush or other partially insectivorous bird make it through the winter.

Bread Pudding Block

Rendered suet
Stale bread, doughnuts, crackers, etc, and/or corn meal

Remelt fat, crush or grind up baked goods and stir them in. Stir again as it begins to cool to get uniform mix. Pour into moulds and let set. Experience will dictate just how much of any given baked product can be used and still have the block hold its shape.

Baron von Berlepsch's "Bird-stone"

I can find no biographical reference to von Berlepsch, evidently a European gentleman of the early twentieth century who achieved recognition as an authority on birds.

This is just the ticket for the bird feeder who likes to be one-up on the neighbours. It is also a humbling reminder to us that ours isn't the first generation to care for the birds. "Bird-stone" is a term coined by old-time bird feeders for rendered, hard suet. This recipe was printed in a booklet written in 1923 by R. Owen Merriman, of Hamilton, Ontario, published by the National Parks of Canada.

White bread, dried and ground	4.5 oz
Meat, dried and ground	3 oz
Hemp (the *seeds*, of course)	6 oz
Crushed hemp	3 oz
Maw*	3 oz
Poppy flour	1.5 oz
Millet, white	3 oz
Oats	1.5 oz
Dried elderberries	1.5 oz
Sunflower seeds	1.5 oz
Ants' eggs	1.5 oz
Chopped nuts (various)	3 oz
Chopped green (unroasted) peanuts	3 oz
Ground bone**	2 oz
Sharp sand (for grit) ***	2 oz

To the total quantity of dry food add about one and one-half times as much melted beef or mutton suet. Mr. Merriman helpfully points out: "It will be found convenient to dry the bread before grinding it, but to grind the meat before drying it."

* "Maw" is the seed of the opium poppy, commonly used as food for cage birds. It is mentioned in some books on cage bird care.
** Bone meal, or perhaps cuttlebone, would do nicely here.
*** I would serve the sand as a side dish. I know birds don't have teeth, but the mere thought of that sand in the mixture puts my fillings on edge.

Price List

The prices of seeds and feeds change from year to year and from place to place, depending partly on supply, partly on the competitive situation at any given outlet, partly on whether you buy in quantity.

The following list is to be taken as a rough guideline only. The first column lists prices at one reasonably competitive feed and garden supply outlet on Vancouver Island in the spring of 1992. The second is from a wholesaler whose prices are quoted on the basis of a 22.7 kg (50 lb) bag, which does not include freight costs if the seeds are to be shipped.

	Feed Store		Wholesale	
Barley, crushed, whole	.49/kg	.22/lb	.22/kg	.10/lb
Canary seed	.99/kg	.45/lb	.40/kg	.18/lb
Canola	1.39/kg	.63/lb	.80/kg	.36/lb
Chick scratch	.49/kg	.22/lb		
Corn, cracked	.49/kg	.22/lb	.66/kg	.30/lb
Corn, whole			.66/kg	.30/lb
Corn, popping, whole	.69/kg	.31/lb		
Grit (sifted gravel)	.26/kg	.12/lb		
Hemp seed			3.41/kg	1.55/lb
Hen scratch	.49/kg	.22/lb		
Inga	(see niger)			
Millet, red & white	.79/kg	.36/lb	.40/kg	.18/lb
Millet, gold German			.88/kg	.40/lb
Milo	.69/kg	.31/lb	.40/kg	.18/lb
Mix (wild bird)	.89/kg	.40/lb	.66/kg	.30/lb
Niger	4.99/kg	2.27/lb	3.63/kg	1.65/lb
Oats, crushed	.49/kg	.22/lb		
Oats, groats, recleaned			.72/kg	.33/lb
Peanut hearts & bits	1.49/kg	.68/lb		
Peanuts in shell, raw			3.74/kg	1.70/lb
Peanuts shelled, raw			3.74/kg	1.70/lb
Pumpkin seed			3.30/kg	1.50/lb
Rape	(see canola)		(see canola)	
Safflower	1.59/kg	.72/lb	.66/kg	.30/lb
Scratch	(see chick & hen)			
Sunflower, black oil	1.69/kg	.77/lb	.66/kg	.30/lb
Sunflower (shelled)	3.00/kg	1.36/lb		
Sunflower, striped	1.89/kg	.86/lb	.66/kg	.30/lb
Wheat, whole, cracked	.49/kg	.22/lb	.33/kg	.15/lb
Wild bird mix	(see mix)		(see mix)	

Feeders and Shelters

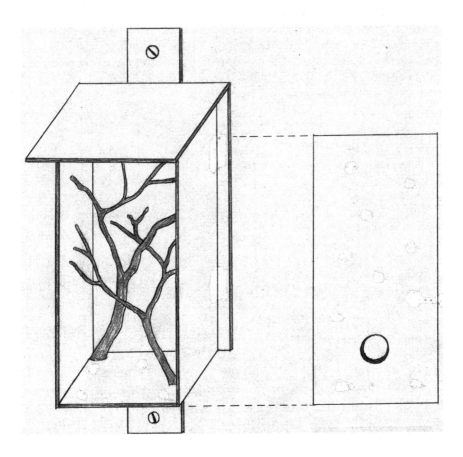

Roosting Box. *Big isn't necessarily better, since it's also less snug. This is about bluebird-nestbox size—12 x 12 x 20 cm (5 x 5 x 8 in). Tuck in a small forked branch or two for perches, and add a couple of centimetres of sawdust to the floor. Note that the hole is best located low down in the box.*

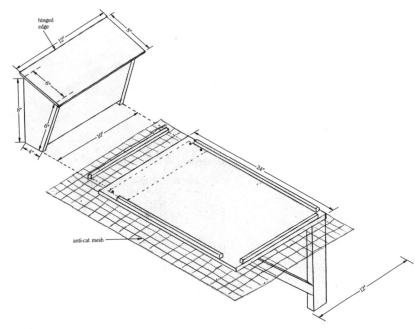

Window Shelf and Hopper. *These dimensions are approximate only: actual size depends in part on the width of the window. In mild climates a roof should be added to prevent rain or melting snow from pooling on the shelf and soaking up into the hopper.*

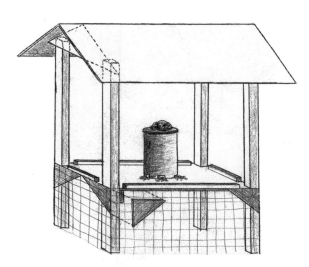

Roofed Table. *This can be any size; this is about 60 x 100 cm (2 x 3 ft). The deck, roof, and corner braces on the legs are 8 mm (quarter inch) plywood, the gable pieces 12 mm (half inch) ply. The edges around the deck can be either 20 x 20 mm (1 x 1 in) or 20 x 44 mm (1 x 1 in). The deck supports are 20 x 44 mm, the legs 44 x 44 mm (2 x 2 in).*

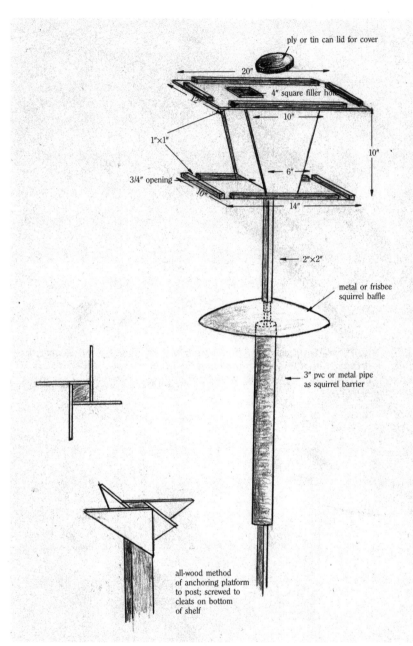

ply or tin can lid for cover

20"

4" square filler hole

10"

1"×1"

10"

3/4" opening

6"

10"

14"

2"×2"

metal or frisbee
squirrel baffle

3" pvc or metal pipe
as squirrel barrier

all-wood method
of anchoring platform
to post; screwed to
cleats on bottom
of shelf

Flat-topped Double-decker. *The suggested dimensions provide hopper-supplied lower decks, protected from rain by the larger, flat upper deck which also doubles as a fair-weather feeder shelf. Make sure the edge around the filler hole is waterproof; a generous bead of caulking compound under the edge pieces and at the corners will do this, plus a double coat of good paint. The filler hole cover can be part of a tin can, or a piece of ply with a screw through one corner, adjusted just tight enough to hold the lid in place but permitting it to be slid aside for filling.*

Naturalist Clubs & Agencies

National

Canadian Nature Federation
453 Sussex Drive
Ottawa, ON KlN 6Z4
(613) 238-6154

Project FeederWatch
Long Point Bird Observatory
P.O. Box 160
Port Rowan, ON N0E 1M0
(519) 586-3531

Canadian Wildlife Service Offices:
P.O. Box 340
5421 Robertson Road
Delta, B.C. V4K 3Y3
(604) 946-8546

2392 Ospika Blvd.
Prince George, B.C. V2N 3N5
(604) 561-5525

3567 Island Highway West
Qualicum Beach, B.C. V9K 2B7
(604) 952-9611

Institute Ocean Services
P.O. Box 6000, 9860 W. Saanich Rd.
Sidney, B.C. V8L 4B2
(604) 356-6537

P.O. Box 6010
Whitehorse, Y.T. Y1A 5L7
(403) 668-2285

Provincial/Regional Agencies

Okanagan College (courses in birding)

Keremeos Centre - 499-5952
Oliver/Osoyoos Centre - 498-6264
Penticton Centre - 492-4305
Princeton Centre - 295-3111
Summerland Centre - 494-1300

Nature/Interpretive Centres

Creston Valley Wildlife Management Area
Wildlife Interpretation Coordinator
Box 640, Creston, B.C. V0B 1G0
(604) 428-3259

Provincial Nature/Environmental Groups

The Federation of B.C. Naturalists
321-1367 West Broadway
Vancouver, B.C. V6H 4A9
737-3057

Local Naturalist Clubs

Lower Mainland

Affiliates of the B.C. Federation of Naturalists

* Alouette Field Naturalists
12554 Grace St.
Maple Ridge, B.C. V2X 5N2

* Bowen Nature Club
Box 20, Site G, RR#1
Bowen Island, B.C. V0N 1G0

* Burke Mountain Naturalists
Box 52540, 1102-2929 Barnet Hwy
Coquitlam, B.C. V3B 7J4

* Chilliwack Field Naturalists
Box 268, Chilliwack, B.C. V2P 6J1

* Delta Naturalists
4992 Stephens Lane
Delta, B.C. V4M 1P1

* Langley Field Naturalists
Box 3243, Langley, B.C. V3A 4R6

* Pender Harbour & District Wildlife Society
Box 220, Madiera Park, B.C.
V0N 2H0

* Royal City Field Naturalists
c/o 125 Bonson St.
New Westminster, B.C. V3L 2J9

* Sechelt Marsh Protective Society
Box 543, Sechelt, B.C. V0N 3A0

* Squamish Estuary Conservation Society
Box 1274, Squamish, B.C. V0N 3G0

* Vancouver Natural History Society
Box 3021, Vancouver, B.C. V6B 3X5

* White Rock & Surrey Naturalists
Box 75044, White Rock, B.C. V4A 9M4

Vancouver Island

* Arrowsmith Naturalists
Box 1542, Parksville, B.C. V0R 2S0

* Comox-Strathcona Natural History Society
Box 3222, Courtenay, B.C. V9N 5N4

* Cowichan Valley Naturalists
Box 361, Duncan, B.C. V9L 3X5

* Mitlenatch Field Naturalists
Box 413, Hariot Bay, B.C. V0P 1H0

* Nanaimo Field Naturalists
Box 125, Nanaimo, B.C. V9R 5K4

* Salt Spring Trail & Nature Club
Box 998, Ganges, B.C. V0S 1E0

* Victoria Natural History Society
Box 5220, Stn. B, Victoria V8R 6N4

Thompson - Okanagan

* Central Okanagan Naturalists Club
Box 396, Kelowna, B.C. V1Y 7N8

* Kamloops Naturalists
Box 625, Kamloops, B.C. V2C 5L7

* North Okanagan Naturalists Club
Box 473, Vernon, B.C. V1T 6M4

* North Shuswap Naturalists
General Delivery, Celista, B.C. V0E 1L0

* Oliver-Osoyoos Naturalists
Box 1181, Osoyoos, B.C. V0H 1V0

* Shuswap Naturalists
Box 1076, Salmon Arm, B.C. V0E 2T0

* South Okanagan Naturalists Club
Box 375, Penticton, B.C. V2A 6K6

Vermillion Forks Field Naturalists Society
Site 19, Compartment 12
RR1, Princeton, B.C. V0X 1W0

Cariboo

* Bella Coola Trail & Nature Club
Box 280, Bella Coola, B.C. V70 1C0

* Quesnel Naturalists
RR#3, Box 12, Milburn Lake Rd.
Quesnel, B.C. V2J 3H7

* Williams Lake Field Naturalists
Box 4575, Williams Lake, B.C. V2G 2V6

North Central

* Bulkley Valley Naturalists
Box 3089, Smithers, B.C. V0J 2N0

* Prince George Naturalists
Box 1092, Stn. A
Prince George, B.C. V2L 4V2

* Skeena Valley Naturalists Club
c/o 2711 Skeena St.
Terrace, B.C. V8G 3K3

Peace

* Timberline Trail & Nature Club
Box 779, Dawson Creek, B.C. V1G 4H8

Kootenay

* Arrow Lakes Naturalists Club
Box 294, Nakusp, B.C. V0G 1R0

* Boundary Naturalists Association
Box 2194, Grand Forks, B.C. V0H 1H0

East Kootenay Environmental Society
(address not available at time of publication)

* Rocky Mountain Naturalists
Box 161, Kimberley, B.C. V1A 2Y6

* West Kootenay Naturalists Association
Box 3121, Castlegar, B.C. V1A 2Y6

References

Birds

Field Guides

Harrison, Colin. *A Field Guide to the Nests, Eggs and Nestlings of North American Birds*. New York: Collins, 1978.

Harrison, Hal H. *A Field Guide To Birds' Nests* (east of the Mississippi River), Peterson Field Guide Series. Boston:Houghton Mifflin Company, 1975.

Peterson, Roger Tory. *A Field Guide to Western Birds*. Boston: Houghton Mifflin Company; 3rd Edition, 1990.

Robbins, Chandler S. et al. *Birds of North America*, Golden Guide Series. New York: Golden Press, 1983.

Scott, Shirley L., editor. *National Geographic Society Field Guide to the Birds of North America*. Washington, D.C.: National Geographic Society, 1987.

Udvardy, Miklos D.F. *Audubon Society Field Guide to North American Birds* (Western Region). New York: Alfred A. Knopf, 1977.

General References

Bent, Arthur Cleveland. *Life Histories of North American Birds*. New York; Dover Publications, Inc., Dover Edition, 1964.

Boswall, Jeffery. *Birds for all Seasons*. London: BBC Publications, 1986.

Burton, Robert. *Bird Behaviour*. New York: Alfred A. Knopf, 1985.

Choate, Ernest A. *The Dictionary of American Bird Names*. Boston: Harvard, Common Press, 1985.

Corral, Michael. *The World of Birds*. Chester: Globe Pequot Press, 1989.

Ehrlich, Paul et al. *The Birder's Handbook*. New York: Simon & Schuster, 1988.

Forsyth, Adrian. *The Nature of Birds*. Camden East, Ontario: Camden House Publishing, 1988.

Godfrey, W. Earl. *The Birds of Canada*. Ottawa: National Museums of Canada, 1986.

Kilham, Lawrence. *On Watching Birds*. Chelsea (Vermont): Chelsea Green Publishing Company, 1988.

Mace, Alice E., editor. *The Birds Around Us*. San Francisco: Ortho Books, Chevron Chemical Company, 1986.

Martin, Brian. *World Birds*. Enfield: Guinness Superlatives Ltd., 1987.

Miller, Millie, and Cyndi Nelson. *Early Bird-Western Backyard Birds*. Boulder, CO: Johnson Books, 1991.

Page, Jake, and Eugene S. Morton. *Lords of the Air*. Washington, D.C.: Smithsonian Books, 1989.

Pasquier, Roger. *Watching Birds*. Boston: Houghton Mifflin Company, 1980.

Perrins, C., and A. Middleton, editors. *The Encyclopedia of Birds*. New York: Facts On File Publications, 1985.

Proctor, Noble. *Song Birds* (with cassette). London: Quarto Publishing, 1988.

Root, Terry. *Atlas of Wintering North American Birds*. Chicago: University of Chicago Press, 1988.

Savage, Candace. *The Wonder of Canadian Birds*. Saskatoon: Western Producer Prairie Books, 1985.

Weidensahl, Scott. *The Birder's Miscellany*. New York: Simon & Schuster, Inc., 1991.

Regional References

Bovey, Robin, and Wayne Campbell. *Birds of Vancouver*. Edmonton: Lone Pine Publishing, 1989.

Campbell, Eileen C. et al. *Waterbirds of the Strait of Georgia*. B.C. Waterfowl Society, and MacMillan Bloedel Limited, 1990.

Campbell, R. Wayne et al. *Birds of British Columbia*. Victoria: Royal British Columbia Museum & Canadian Wildlife Service. Vols. I and II, 1990; Vols. III and IV, 1993/94.

Cannings, Robert A. et al. *Birds of the Okanagan Valley, British Columbia*. Royal British Columbia Museum, 1987.

Haras, Willie. *Wings Across Georgia Strait*. Comox: Lindsay Press Limited (undated).

Holroyd, Geoffrey, and Howard Coneybeare. *Compact Guide to Birds of the Rockies*. Edmonton: Lone Pine Publishing, 1990.

Lewis, Mark G., and Fred A. Sharpe. *Birding in the San Juan Islands*. Seattle: The Mountaineers, 1987.

Mark, David M. *Where to Find Birds in British Columbia*. New Westminster: Kestrel Press, 1984.

Nehls, Harry B. *Familiar Birds of the Northwest* (U.S). Portland: Audubon Society of Portland; 3rd Edition, 1989.

Taylor, K. *A Birders Guide to Vancouver Island*. Victoria: Top Drawer Infosystems, 1990.

Wareham, Bill. *British Columbia Wildlife Viewing Guide*. Edmonton: Lone Pine Publishing, 1991.

Bird Feeding/Attracting

*Of special interest to B.C. readers

Burton, Robert. *National Audubon Society North American Birdfeeder Handbook*. New York: Dorling Kindersley, 1992.

Butler, Elaine. *Attracting Birds*. Edmonton: Lone Pine Publishing, 1991.

Campbell, Scott D. *Easy-to-make Bird Feeders for Woodworkers*. New York: Dover Publications, 1989.

Dawe, Neil and Karen. *The Bird Book.* New York: Workman Publishing, 1988. (Packaged in small, clear, plastic window feeder.)

DeGraaf, R., and M. Witman. *Trees, Shrubs & Vines for Attracting Birds.* Amherst: University of Massachusetts Press, 1979.

Dennis, John. *A Complete Guide To Bird Feeding.* New York: Alfred A. Knopf, 1978.

Dennis, John. *Summer Bird Feeding.* Northbrook, ILL: Audubon Workshop, Inc., 1990.

Dobson, Clive. *Feeding Wild Birds in Winter.* Scarborough: Firefly Books, 1981.

Harrison, Kit and George. *The Birds of Winter.* New York: Random House, 1990.

Kress, Stephen. *The Audubon Society Guide to Attracting Birds.* New York: Charles Scribner's Sons, 1985.

Levesque, Joseph, and Michell Prevost. *Getting To Know Birds At Your Feeder.* Scarborough: McGraw-Hill Ryerson Limited, 1989.

Mahnken, Jan. *Feeding the Birds.* Pownal: Storey Communications, 1983.

Merilees, Bill. *Attracting Backyard Wildlife.* Vancouver: Whitecap Books, 1989.

Schutz, W. *How to Attract, House and Feed Birds.* New York: Collier Books, 1974.

Vriends, Matthew M. *Feeding and Sheltering Backyard Birds.* Hauppauge, NY: Barron's Educational Series, Inc., 1990.

Warton, Susan, editor. *An Illustrated Guide to Attracting Birds.*

Witty, Helen, and Dick Witty. *Feed the Birds.* New York: Workman Publishing, 1991 (mesh suet bag included).

Mammals

Banfield, A.W. *The Mammals of Canada.* Toronto: University of Toronto Press, 1974.

Forsyth, Adrian. *Mammals of the Canadian Wild.* Camden East, ON: Camden House Publishing Ltd., 1985.

Savage, Candace. *Wild Mammals of Western Canada.* Saskatoon: Western Producer Prairie Books, 1981.

Index

Brown Creeper, 147
Brown-headed Cowbird, 183-186
Brown-headed Nuthatch, 140
Buckets, as hoppers, 40
Bullfinch, 191
Bunting, Rustic, 2
Burrows. *See* Cavities, snow
Burton, Robert, 164
"Bush partridge." *See* Ruffed Grouse
Bushtit, 129, 137
Bushtits, 136
"Butcher bird." *See* Northern Shrike

C
Cage traps. *See* Trap
California Quail, 76, 85
Callipepla californica. See California
Quail
Calypte anna. See Anna's Hummingbird
Campbell, Wayne, 123, 157
"Camp robber." *See* Gray Jay
Canada Jay. *See* Gray Jay
Canary, 190, 191. *See also* American
Goldfinch
Canary seed, 15
Cannings, Robert, Richard, Sydney, 45
Canola, 11, 16
Cape Penduline Tit, 136
"Cardinal bait." *See* Safflower
Cardinals, 210
Carduelis flammea. See Common Redpoll
Carduelis hornemanni. See Hoary Redpoll
Carduelis pinus. See Pine Siskin
Carduelis tristis. See American Goldfinch
Carl Zeiss Optics, 46
Carpodacus mexicanus. See House Finch
Carpodacus purpureus. See Purple Finch
Carrion, as feed. *See* Meat
Carthamus tinctorius. See Safflower
Cat: ambush points, 21, 28, 61; eating
seeds, 11; populations, 234; wire deter-
rent, 33. *See also* Cats
Cats, 42, 51, 59, 233; bell, 61; feral, 235;
ownership obligation, 60; stray, 59;
trapping, 59; predation study, 234
Cavities, 42; artificial, 43; nests, 100,
139, 167, 169; roosts, 42, 66; as trap,
100, 129
CBC. *See* Christmas Bird Count
Cedar Waxwing, 158, 161
Certhia americana. See Brown Creeper
Certhiidae. See Creepers
Chapman, Frank, 159, 236
Checklists, bird, 3
Chestnut-backed Chickadee, 134

Chickadees, 35, 43, 64, 233; accurate re-
call, 66; fat deposit, 67; torpor, 66. *See
also* Black-capped, Boreal, Chestnut-
backed, Mountain Chickadee
Chicken, domestic, 64, 66, 74
Chick scratch, 15
Chipmunks, 219, 226. *See also* Least &
Yellow Pine Chipmunk
Choate, Ernest A., 72, 175
Christmas Bird Count, 5, 236
Chukar, 76, 78
Churcher, Peter, 234
Clark, L., 169
Clark's Nutcracker, 120
Clay, J.O., 98
Coccothraustes vespertinus. See Evening
Grosbeak
"Cod" fat, 21
Colaptes auratus. See Northern Flicker
Cold tolerance, 64, 65, 204
"Collecting," 67, 196
Collisions. *See* Window collisions
Columba fasciata. See Band-tailed Pigeon
Columba livia. See Rock Dove
Combat, 153, 167, 195
Common Grackle, 12
Common Raven, 113, 115, 126
Common & Hoary Redpoll, 205. *See also*
Redpolls
Computer software, 45
Cones. *See* Conifers
Conflict with animals, 51
Conifers, 199; seeds, 200, 202, 203, 220
Cooking grease. *See* Fat
Coon. *See* Raccoon
Cooper, W.C., 210
Corn, 16
Cornell Laboratory of Ornithology. *See*
Project FeederWatch
Corvids, 113-115; as prey, 114. *See also*
Crows
Corvus brachyrhynchos. See American
Crow
Corvus caurinus. See Northwestern Crow
Corvus corax. See Common Raven
Coues, Elliot, 212
Cougar, 229
Cowbirds, 9, 183-186
Cracked grains. *See* Grains
Creepers, 146
Crested Myna, 167
Crop, 67, 190, 205. *See also* Pigeon
"milk"
Crossbills, 191, 199-201; eating salt, 25;
food preferences, 201; nesting, 68,

200. *See also* Red and White-winged Crossbills.

Crow. *See* American Crow, Northwestern Crow

Crows, 113; diet, 114; hoarding, 66

Cuckoos, 184

Cuddling up, 66

Cyanocitta cristata. See Blue Jay

Cyanocitta stelleri. See Steller's Jay

D

Dancing ground. *See* Lek

"Dark" meat. *See* Muscles

Dark-eyed Junco, 181

Darwin, Charles, 190

Dead birds. *See* Specimens

"Decadent." *See* Trees, aged

Deer, 16

Den tree. *See* Cavities, Shelters

Denman Island, 228

Dennis, John V., 130, 149, 189

Dendrocopos. See Hairy Woodpecker

Diastema. *See* Teeth

Digging, in snow, 41, 75

Diseases: prevention, 41

Disinfecting feeders, 41

Diverticulum. *See* Crop

Domestic cat, 233-235. *See also* Cat

Douglas, David, 221

Douglas's Squirrel, 221. *See also* Red Squirrel

Dove. *See* Mourning Dove

Down-Side, 51

Downy Woodpecker, 43, 54, 55, 102

Drilling. *See* Woodpeckers

Drumming. *See* Ruffed Grouse, Woodpeckers

Dryocopus pileatus. See Pileated Woodpecker

Dunn, Erica H., 237

E

Ether. *See* Squirrels, destroying

Eagle feeder, 23

Eagles. *See* Bald, Golden

Eastern Phoebe, 185

Eggs, 74; in nest parasitism, 184-186

Emberizinae. See Sparrows

Energy conservation, 66

Eruptions, 191. *See also* Irruptions

Ethics: of feeding, 6-8; of cat ownership, 60

Euphagus cyanocephalus. See Brewer's Blackbird

Eurasian Tree Sparrow, 212

European Starling, 167

Eutamius amoenus. See Yellow Pine Chipmunk

Eutamias minimus. See Least Chipmunk

Evening Grosbeak, 210

Exile. *See* Relocation

Exotic species. *See* Introduced

F

Family accounts, 71

Fan. *See* Window management

Fat (as feed): "cod," 21; cooking grease, 22; slab fat, 21. *See also* Suet

Fat, body. *See* Body fat

Feather wear, 170, 208

Feathers, 64; in hats. *See* Plume trade; Loss of. *See* Suet, Peanut Butter

Feeds, 19 -24; preferences, 11; storage, 6; spoilage, 17, 21, 41

"Feeder," definition of, 2

FeederWatch North, 238. *See also* Project FeederWatch

Feeders, 26-42; beer-box, 30; cleaning, 27, 33, 42; colour, 33; filling, 31, 36, 40; glass-mounted, 32; ground, 27; hanging, 34-37; height, 30; in-window box, 32; Javex jug, 34; maintenance, 42; mounted on glass, 32; placement, 26; pole, 28-31; pop bottle, 36; shelf, 31-34; suet, 37-39; table, 27, 28; thistle, 35-37; tube, 35 - 37; window, 31-34; windshield washer jug, 34. *See also* Bottles, Buckets, Hoppers

Feeding: discontinuing, 7; diversionary, 16, 222; ethics, 6; getting started, 5; importance of, 7; power, 19; principles, 1. *See also* Foraging, "Gaping"

Feeds, 19-25; breadcrumbs, 10; manipulation, 11, 16, 222

Feet: heat loss, 65; toe combs, 75; of predators, 163

Felis catus. See Cat, Domestic cats

Field glasses, 45. *See also* Binoculars

Field guides, 44, 73

Fighting. *See* Combat

Film. *See* Solar films

Finch mix. *See* Seed, mixed

Finches, 190; Galapagos, 190; Hawaiian, 99

Fir. *See* Conifers

Fleisher, Edward, 197

Flicker. *See* Northern Flicker

Flight, 63; in foraging, 64; of grouse, 74; of hummingbird, 95; muscles, 63, 74, 75, 88; speed, 89; weight limits of, 63

Flying Squirrel. *See* Northern Flying
  Squirrel
"Fool hen." *See* Spruce Grouse
Foraging: chickadees, 64; gender-divided,
  103, 153, 169; "guilds," 130; mixed
  flocks, 10, 130, 149, 168; natural, 11,
  19; redpolls, 205. *See also* "Gaping"
Forsyth, Adrian, 217
Fox Sparrow, 175
Franklin's grouse. *See* Spruce Grouse
Fringillidae. See Finches
Fruit, 23, 24; robins as pests of, 153; diet
  of, 159
Fruiting cycle, of conifers, 199, 200, 220
Fugle, Gary, 180
Fumigants. *See* Nest fumigants
Funnels, 36, 40

G
Galapagos Islands, 190
Galliformes, 74-76
"Gaping," 168, 183, 188
Garbage, as problem, 8; dump, 23
Geis, Dr. Aelred D., 12. *See also* Feeds,
  preferences
Gibbard, L. & V., 115
Gilded Flicker. *See* Northern Flicker
Glass-mounted feeders, 32
Glaucomys sabrinus. See Northern Flying
  Squirrel
Godfrey, W. Earl, 44, 71, 124, 136, 151,
  172, 204
Golden-crowned Kinglet, 149, 150
Golden-crowned Sparrow, 178
Golden Eagle, 23
Golden Pheasant, 66
Goldfinch, 208; cold tolerance, 65. *See
  also* American Goldfinch
"Gopher," 67
Grains, 15
Grant, James, 115
Gray Jay, 115; eating moose ticks, 69;
  nesting, 68
Gray Partridge, 74, 76
Gray-headed Junco. *See* Dark-eyed Junco
Grease, cooking, 22; damage to feathers,
  22. *See also* Fat
Great Grey Shrike, 163
Greek names. *See* Scientific names
Green Pheasant, 81
Grey Squirrel, 30, 223
Grit, 25
Grosbeaks, 210. *See also* Evening, Pine
  Grosbeak
Ground feeding, 27

Grouse, 74-76; *See also* Ruffed, Sharp-
  tailed Grouse
Groutage, Loyd, 153, 171
Gruson, Edward S., 71, 72
"Guilds," 130, 132
Guizotia abyssinica. See Thistle seed
Gum (resin), as repellent, 139

H
Habitat assessment. *See* Assessment
Hairy Woodpecker, 66, 103
Hanging feeders. *See* Feeders
Hardware cloth, 38. *See also* Wire
"Harts." *See* Sunflower and Peanut
Hatching time. *See* Incubation time
Hawfinch, 190
Hazards to birds: frozen metal, 20; irregu-
  lar feeding, 7; musty grain, 17; net
  bags, 37; peanut butter, 19; rancid
  suet, 21; water, 25. *See also* Cats, Win-
  dows
Heart, 64; rate, 64, 96
"Hearts." *See* Sunflower, Peanut
Helianthus annuus. See Sunflower
Helleiner, Fred, 153
Hen. *See* Chicken, domestic
Hen scratch, 15
Hibernation, 219
Hill Myna, 167
Hoarding, 66, 68, 116, 120, 140; shrikes,
  163; squirrels, 219, 200, 220
Hoary Redpoll, 204, 205
Holdovers, 7. *See also* Migration
Honeyguide, 184. *See also* Nest parasite
Hoppers, 39-41. *See also* Buckets, Bottles
Hornemann, J.W., 205
House Finch, 24, 196
House Sparrow, 37, 212-216; fat deposit,
  67
Houston, C. Stuart, 68, 214
Hummingbird feeders, 96; disinfecting, 42
Hummingbirds, 95. *See also* Sweets
"Hun." *See* Gray Partridge
Hungarian Partridge. *See* Gray Partridge
Hunting, 74, 75, 86, 94, 236; cripples, 22.
  See also Plume trade

I
Icterinae. See Blackbirds
Imports. *See* Introduced species
Incubation time, 100, 185, 204, 216
Ingenuity. *See* Intelligence
Injured birds, 53. *See also* Windows (col-
  lisions)
Insects, as pests, 6

Intelligence, 113; Blue Jay, 120; crow, 113; finch, 190; raven, 113; squirrel, 219; starling, 167, 169
Introduced species, 76, 78, 81, 167, 212, 228
Irruptions, 200. *See also* Eruptions
Ixoreus naevius. See Varied Thrush

J

Jack pine. *See* Lodgepole pine
Javex bottle feeder. *See* Feeders
Jay. *See* Blue Jay, Gray Jay, Steller's Jay
Junco hyemalis. See Dark-eyed Junco
Juncos, 172, 181. *See also* Dark-eyed Junco
Jungle fowl. *See* Red Jungle Fowl

K

Kennedy, Des, 228
Kepler, Cameron B., 200
Kilham, Lawrence, 54
King, Joan, Harold, 98
Kinglets, 149. *See also* Golden-crowned, Ruby-crowned
KISS principle, 10

L

Ladder, low-rise, 31
Laniidae. See Shrikes
Lanius excubitor. See Northern Shrike
Latex, liquid, 20, 39
Latin names. *See* Scientific names
Lawford, John, 234
Least Chipmunk, 219, 226
Legs: heat loss, 65; leggings, 75
Lek, 85
Leopold, Starker, 86
Leucosticte arctoa. See Rosy Finch
Lewis's Woodpecker, 101
Linnaeus. *See* Linne
Linne, Karl von, 71
Listers, 5
Live traps. *See* Traps
Lodgepole pines, 199, 218, 220
Loggerhead Shrike, 164. *See also* Northern Shrike
Long-lived, 115
Long Point Bird Observatory. *See* Project FeederWatch
Loxia curvirostra. See Red Crossbill
Loxia leucoptera. See White-winged Crossbill
"Lumpers," 173. *See also* Species differentiation
Lungs, 64

M

Macleod, R.D., 72
Magpies, 38, 114. *See also* Black-billed Magpie
Maintenance kit, 42
Mammals, 55, 217. *See also* Walk-In Trade
Manitoba Maple, 211
Maui Parrotbill,99
Meat, as feed, 22
Melanerpes carolinus. See Red-bellied Woodpecker
Melospiza melodia. See Song Sparrow
Memory. *See* Recall
Merilees, Bill, 60, 137
Merriman, R. Owen, 240
Mice, 3, 55, 64
Migration: and feeding, 6; holdovers, 7, 65; juncos, 182; waxwings, 158
"Milk." *See* Pigeons
Millet, 15
Milo, 17
Mimicry, 120, 209
Mixed seed. *See* Seed, mixed
Mixed species foraging. *See* "Guilds"
Molothrus ater. See Brown-headed Cowbird
Moose ticks, 69
Mothballs, 55, 58
Moult. *See* Feather wear
Mountain Chickadee, 132
Mountain Quail, 76
Mourning Dove, 92
"Mouse run," 181
Muscicapidae. See Kinglets, Thrushes
Muscles, 74, 88
Mylar. *See* Solar films

N

Names, "book," and "common," 72. *See also* Scientific names
Nest collecting, 67
Nest fumigants, 169
Nest hole. *See* Cavities, nests
Nest parasite, 9, 183-186
Nest pathogens, 169
Nest predation, 8
Nests, 67, 72, 136, 169. *See also* Cavities, Shelters
Net bag, as hazard, 37. *See also* Suet dispensers
Netting, for windows, 53
Niger seed, 18, 35. *See also* Seeds
Non-KISS Gourmet, 239
North, Sterling, 229

About the Author

Bob Waldon brings to his calling as an author a lifelong fascination with nature and the outdoors, an interest he maintained during a twenty-five-year career in newspaper and magazine publishing in Winnipeg. In their spare time he and his wife Carole took to Manitoba's wilderness—canoeing, sailing, and cross-country skiing. These interests led to involvement with the environmental movement; Bob is a former president of the Manitoba Naturalists' Society and of the Canadian Nature Federation.

At a time of life when most people contemplate retirement, Bob quit the publishing business and launched a new career. For five years he worked summers as an interpretive naturalist at Riding Mountain National Park in Manitoba. Winters, while continuing his hobby of bird feeding, he became a nature columnist and book reviewer. The two interests combined, in time, to produce a series of regional books on feeding winter birds. This book is the fourth of that series.

Bob and Carole now divide their time between a quarter section of excellent chickadee habitat in Manitoba, and Vancouver Island.

About the Illustrator

Photo by Jim Erickson

Peter Sawatzky's career developed from a blending of his fascination with wildlife and his profession as a painter and commercial artist. In 1973 he was first introduced to woodcarving and saw in this medium both a creative challenge and a means of earning a livelihood as a full time artist.

As a carver Peter has won international recognition and a growing list of awards and exhibitions. He works mainly with American Basswood, using traditional hand tools almost exclusively and working as much as possible from a single block of wood. He recently branched out into bronze castings and, characteristically, mastered every step of the process, including the actual casting with a furnace of his own.

Never having set aside his interest in the graphic arts, Peter was pleased to accept the offer from his long time friend Bob Waldon to do the illustrations for this series of books on winter birds.

Peter lives in Glenboro, Manitoba, with his wife Karen and their teenage children Jeremy and Erin.